CRIMINAL LAW AND PRIOR FAULT

This book offers fresh perspectives on the role of addiction in prior fault culpability by integrating legal, psychological, neuroscientific and philosophical dimensions.

Are intoxicated defendants responsible for harms they cause to persons and property when intoxicated? Should they be criminally liable for those harms, even if they act without intention or control? What if their intoxicated state is associated with addiction?

Analysing the complex interactions between addiction, intoxication and law, prior fault is addressed from various jurisdictions including predominantly England and Wales, Scotland, and the Netherlands, while also incorporating multiple disciplines, thereby discussing prior fault structures from overarching, non-jurisdictional perspectives. These different disciplines and legal systems are not merely described but closely integrated through co-authored chapters, involving academics from different disciplinary fields and legal traditions.

This collection is a thorough resource for students, academics, researchers, and practising lawyers who aim to deepen their understanding of the law's approach towards addiction and intoxication. Moreover, it illustrates the importance of a collaborative approach between different legal traditions and interdisciplinary scientific understanding, thereby laying the groundwork for future legal reforms, informed legal practice and research.

Criminal Law and Prior Fault

Comparative Perspectives on Addiction and Intoxication

Edited by
Anna Goldberg
and
Paloma Manguele

•HART•
OXFORD • LONDON • NEW YORK • NEW DELHI • SYDNEY

HART PUBLISHING

Bloomsbury Publishing Plc

Kemp House, Chawley Park, Cumnor Hill, Oxford, OX2 9PH, UK

1385 Broadway, New York, NY 10018, USA

Bloomsbury Publishing Ireland Limited, 29 Earlsfort Terrace, Dublin 2, D02 AY28, Ireland

HART PUBLISHING, the Hart/Stag logo, BLOOMSBURY and the Diana logo are trademarks of Bloomsbury Publishing Plc

First published in Great Britain 2025

A catalogue record for this book is available from the British Library.

A catalogue record for this book is available from the Library of Congress.

Library of Congress Control Number: 2025945741

ISBN: HB: 978-1-50998-128-1
ePDF: 978-1-50998-130-4
ePub: 978-1-50998-129-8

Typeset by Compuscript Ltd, Shannon

For product safety related questions contact productsafety@bloomsbury.com

To find out more about our authors and books visit www.hartpublishing.co.uk. Here you will find extracts, author information, details of forthcoming events and the option to sign up for our newsletters.

ACKNOWLEDGEMENTS

The idea for this collection emerged from a symposium on prior fault in June 2022, organised in Maastricht. We, the editors, first met at this event and were inspired by the interdisciplinary range of presentations. After some encouragement from John Child, we embarked on this edited collection project, and we are thrilled to present the manifestation of this collaboration. Because so many people contributed to its contents, we would like to use this opportunity to express our gratitude.

Of course, this collection would not exist without its authors. We want to thank James Browning, John Child, Hans Crombag, Gavin Dingwall, Claire Hogg, Kyriaki Nikolaou, Nicholas Sinclair-House, Reinout Wiers, Michiel van der Wolf and Gideon Yaffe for their time and efforts in writing such interesting chapters, as well as for their pleasant collaboration. You have all brought such relevant expertise along, and we are happy to have worked with you. We also want to thank Susan Dimock and David Roef for their interest and input during earlier stages of this collection.

We also want to thank and acknowledge the work of the reviewers. The feedback provided by James Browning, Dominik Buchmueller, John Child, Hans Crombag, Alwin van Dijk, Adrian Hunt, Doug Husak, Findlay Stark, Wouter Wegkamp, and Gideon Yaffe, on one – or sometimes even more – chapters of this collection has been invaluable. We appreciate you taking the time.

A special word of thanks to Birmingham Law School for hosting the 'Reforming Prior Fault Criminalisation' conference on 15–16 September 2023, where most authors were able to meet for the first time and share their preliminary thoughts on their respective chapters. Additionally, we thank Hart Publishing for their interest and confidence in this collection and their support in the production thereof.

Last but not least, we want to separately acknowledge all the effort, time and assistance that John Child has devoted to this collection. From the beginning, he has encouraged and guided us, both in the content of the collection as well as in editorial and publishing activities. Thank you, you have been an incredible support. To all authors: we are excited for this collection to be the first materialisation of our collaboration, and we certainly hope it won't be our last.

With gratitude,
Anna Goldberg and Paloma Manguele, editors

CONTENTS

LIST OF CONTRIBUTORS

James Browning is a PhD candidate and supervisor in criminal law at the University of Cambridge. His research focuses on responsibility for criminal conduct in the context of drug- and alcohol-addicted defendants. James previously taught at the London School of Economics, and before taking up doctoral research, he was a journalist and columnist at *The Lawyer* in London. He holds an LLM from the University of Birmingham and an LLB from the London School of Economics.

John J Child is a Professor of Criminal Law at the University of Birmingham, Co-Director of the Birmingham Centre for Crime, Justice and Policing, and co-Director of the Criminal Law Reform Now Network. John's research interests centre on criminal law theory and doctrine, and the relationship between criminal law and neuroscience, where he has published widely. John is the co-author of leading textbooks *Simester and Sullivan's Criminal Law* and Smith, *Hogan and Ormerod's Essentials of Criminal Law*.

Hans S Crombag is Professor of Behavioural Neuroscience in the School of Psychology and Sussex Neuroscience at the University of Sussex UK. His research explores the neurobiological and psychological foundations of motivated action, the role of associative learning in motivation, the mechanisms underlying substance use and addiction, and broader mental health issues. Additionally, he examines how these insights can be applied to criminal law and justice.

Gavin Dingwall is a Professor in Law at Northumbria University, UK. He is the author of five books on criminal law and justice. As well as work on the theory of criminal defences, he writes widely on penal theory, law and policy adopting philosophical, doctrinal, qualitative and comparative methodologies.

Anna Goldberg is an Assistant Professor of Criminal Law at the University of Groningen. During her PhD research at Maastricht University, she addressed addiction and the role of neuroscience in criminal law. Her research on mental disorders and the law is highly interdisciplinary and characterised by the use of different research methods, including legal comparative designs, normative research, as well as qualitative and quantitative empirical research.

Claire Hogg is a lecturer in law at the University of Surrey, UK. Her research looks at mental disorder as a factor relevant to culpability within the criminal law, with a focus on doctrines of insanity and automatism. She completed her PhD in law in 2021 at King's College London, followed by an ERC-funded post-doc at UCL.

Claire also holds an MA in Medical Law and Ethics from King's College London and a BPhil in philosophy from Oxford University.

Paloma Manguele is a postdoctoral cognitive neuroscience researcher at the University of Sussex and the University of Birmingham. Her work primarily focuses on the effects of alcohol intoxication on cognition, metacognition and behaviour. In her PhD, she investigated neural correlates of inattention and mind wandering, and the use of neuroimaging for decoding the contents of spontaneous thoughts. She is a lecturer in the Department of Psychology at Eduardo Mondlane University (UEM), in Mozambique.

Kyriaki Nikolaou is a lecturer at the University of Sussex. Her research has explored the brain processes involved in biases to alcohol-related stimuli in binge drinkers and in individuals with an Alcohol Use Disorder (AUD). She has investigated the effects of genetic variations, acute alcohol and acute stress on these biases. Kyriaki's work aims to advance understanding of executive control, learning, and cognitive biases in individuals with AUD and binge drinkers. Kyriaki completed her PhD at Goldsmiths University of London.

Nicholas Sinclair-House is an Assistant Professor of Criminology at the University of Sussex. His PhD employed a multidisciplinary approach to examine Magistrates' decision-making processes in the sentencing of addicted, intoxicated and mentally-disordered offenders, highlighting inconsistencies in the prior fault reasoning on which those decisions are based. He is the co-director of the Sussex Crime Research Centre (CRC).

Reinout W Wiers is Professor of developmental psychopathology at the University of Amsterdam (UvA), leading the Addiction, Development and Psychopathology (ADAPT)-lab, and as co-Director of the UvA centre for Urban Mental Health. Wiers is widely known and cited for his work on assessing and changing implicit or relatively automatic processes in addictions and related disorders, for which he received the VIDI and VICI grants from the Netherlands National Science Foundation. Weirs is also a licensed cognitive behavioural therapist.

Michiel JF van der Wolf is a Professor of Forensic Psychiatry at the Institute of Criminal Law and Criminology at Leiden University and an associate professor in Criminal Law at the University of Groningen, in the Netherlands. Trained in two disciplines, in practice he worked as a psychologist in a high-security forensic mental (TBS) hospital and is now a deputy judge at the criminal court of Amsterdam and the court of appeal in Leeuwarden.

Gideon Yaffe is the Wesley Newcomb Hohfeld Professor of Jurisprudence and Professor of Philosophy and Psychology at Yale Law School. He writes books and articles about criminal responsibility and has published several papers about the responsibility of addicts for wrongful behaviour.

1

Prior Fault, Intoxication and Addiction: An Introduction

ANNA GOLDBERG AND PALOMA MANGUELE

I. Prior Fault: What this is All About

This collection is devoted to the study of prior fault. Although nuances exist across jurisdictions, prior fault can generally be defined as culpable prior conduct by the defendant before the commission of an offence, which results in an exception to the traditional approach towards criminal liability by allowing such previous conduct outside of an offence or defence definition to affect liability directly. Thus, prior fault rules operate as a unique mechanism of inculpation in circumstances where conventional analysis of a defendant's conduct might otherwise result in non-responsibility.[1]

A classic example of where a prior fault mechanism is typically employed arises where a defendant (D) voluntarily consumes substances, causing acute intoxication, or – in slightly more complicated cases – substance-induced psychosis. The intoxication or resulting mental disorder likely impairs the defendant's mental capacities, possibly to the extent that either *mens rea* elements cannot be satisfied or the insanity defence or diminished responsibility defences may apply (the specific doctrinal implications will, of course, vary between jurisdictions). Yet, despite apparent grounds for offence denial and/or exculpation and/or mitigation, D remains culpable *because of* their prior voluntary choice to consume the intoxicant.[2] Hence, in cases where defendants a priori seem to lack the legal elements necessary to be held responsible, prior fault rules can negate

[1] AE Goldberg and others, 'Prior-fault blame in England and Wales, Germany and the Netherlands' (2021) 8 *Journal of International and Comparative Law* 53. Note that the general term 'non-responsibility' is used here on purpose: depending on the jurisdiction and the conceptualisation of prior fault rules, prior fault can prevent various outcomes such as acquittal but also dismissal of (criminal) proceedings. As such, the umbrella term 'non-responsibility' is used.

[2] AE Goldberg, *Blaming the Addicted Brain: Building Bridges Between Criminal Law and Neuroscientific Perspectives on Addiction* (The Hague, Eleven International Publishing, 2022) 119–120.

exculpation because the defendant's prior conduct culpably created these exculpatory conditions.

The exact mechanism of prior fault depends on specific jurisdictional approaches and the circumstances of each case. We can distinguish between two main approaches towards prior fault, however: that of prior fault as a means to construct an offence versus prior fault as a mechanism to block a defence.[3] Constructing an offence refers to situations in which D lacks the required mens rea and is perhaps involuntary at the time of the offence (Time 2; T2), where that absent culpability is essentially substituted using evidence of prior fault choices at the earlier time (at Time 1; T1). Here, D's prior culpable conduct at T1 can be used to replace his missing mental state at T2, thereby using prior fault as a means to *construct* the necessary elements of the offence. Using prior fault to block a defence, on the other hand, refers to situations in which the defendant might otherwise rely on a justification or excuse at T2, but due to his prior culpable conduct at T1, the application of this defence is *blocked*. The scenario in which prior fault blocks a defence is common in cases of self-defence and, of particular interest in this collection, may also apply (in certain jurisdictions at least) to the defence of insanity.[4]

The context of the current volume's discussion relates to the use of prior fault in situations where the defendant has committed an offence whilst intoxicated, and pays specific attention to the situations where an underlying addiction causes that intoxication. The consequences of substance use can be discussed as a lack of *mens rea* during the offence, in light of insanity criteria, or even at sentencing, but in most situations exculpation or mitigation is commonly prevented by appealing to prior fault rules.[5] This volume delves into the causes and consequences of intoxication, specifically when related to substance addiction, and critically examines why and how prior fault is applied in such cases.

Although prior fault rules are common to most criminal law jurisdictions, the construction and application thereof vary between them.[6] They are also – as we will see – some of the most contested rules within the law, where different jurisdictions are actively looking for reform alternatives and/or incremental improvements. Doctrinal variations between jurisdictions are relevant and important, as international legal comparison can serve as a means to further improve

[3] JJ Child, 'Prior fault: Blocking Defences or Constructing Crimes' in A Reed and M Bohlander (eds), *General Defences in Criminal Law* (Milton Park, Routledge, 2014). There are large differences between common law and civil law jurisdictions when it comes to the structure in which prior fault plays a role. Section II of this chapter briefly elaborates on this difference.

[4] HS Crombag, JJ Child and GR Sullivan, 'Drunk, Dangerous and Celusional: How Legal Concept-creep Risks Overcriminalization' (2020) 115 *Addiction* 2200. Ch 2 of this collection is devoted to prior fault in situations of insanity and diminished responsibility.

[5] HS Crombag, JJ Child and R Fortson, 'Understanding the 'Fault' in Prior-fault Intoxication: Insights from Behavioural Neuroscience' in A Reed and others (eds), *Fault in Criminal Law* (Milton Park, Routledge, 2022).

[6] For an overview of prior fault rules in England and Wales, Germany, and the Netherlands, see: Goldberg and others (n 1).

national approaches. Differences between jurisdictions are also relevant on a more conceptual level by identifying theoretical constructs that underlie prior fault, allowing for the comparison of conceptual framing, and thereby giving context to the potential for learning between states. More broadly still, the exploration of prior fault allows us to better understand the nature of voluntary and culpable conduct, as well as the justification for exempting from conventional methods in establishing criminal liability.

Within this context, the treatment of addiction as a complex example of intoxication *should* prompt particular concern and scrutiny of prior fault rules, and yet, as we will see, part of the motivation for this collection is the apparent absence of disagreement between states regarding the treatment of addiction. Although the different jurisdictions have different mechanisms towards prior fault, they all seem to apply prior fault rules in cases of addiction-related intoxication in an apparently similar fashion as regular intoxication cases.[7] In other words, the presence of an underlying addiction in cases of intoxication does not seem to significantly change the application of prior fault rules. Prior fault mechanisms strongly rely on the assumption that almost all intoxication is brought about voluntarily, and therefore, the defendant ought to take responsibility for the consequences thereof.[8] Yet this collection aims to identify those situations in which addiction and the ensuing intoxication are not straightforwardly voluntary, to ultimately address the fairness of the current prior fault rules in cases of addiction and intoxication.

The scope of this collection covers perspectives from various disciplines in order to provide a coherent overview of the problems associated with prior fault rules in cases of intoxication and addiction. In terms of legal scope, the primary jurisdictions covered are England and Wales, Scotland, and the Netherlands, engaging both common and civil law traditions. Because this collection presents insights from non-legal disciplines as well, including criminology, psychology, neuroscience and philosophy, prior fault structures are also discussed from overarching, non-jurisdictional perspectives. In terms of the scope of addiction, the focus is solely on substance addiction and intoxication, despite the term also covering other conditions, such as behavioural addictions (eg, gambling or sex addictions). Because of the strong relationship between substance intoxication and crime,[9] and due to the direct effect of substances on the brain and behaviour,[10] this

[7] Goldberg and others (n 1). For a thorough discussion in the Dutch context on prior fault in cases of intoxication, see AE Goldberg and others, 'Verslaafd en Verantwoordelijk? Complexe Culpa in Causa Kwesties in Rapportage Pro Justitia en Jurisprudentie' (2024) 10 *Delikt & Delinkwent* 833.

[8] Goldberg (n 2); J Bijlsma, 'Drank, Drugs en Culpa. Zelfintoxicatie en Culpa in Causa: Pleidooi voor een Voorzienbaarheidseis' (2011) 6 *Delikt & Delinkwent* 654.

[9] T Bennett, K Holloway and D Farrington, 'The Statistical Association between Drug Misuse and Crime: A Meta-analysis' (2008) 13 *Aggression and Violent Behviour* 107; C Jorgensen, NE Anderson and JC Barnes, 'Bad Brains: Crime and Drug Abuse from a Neurocriminological Perspective' (2016) 41 *American Journal of Criminal Justice* 47.

[10] C Regan, *Intoxicating Minds: How Drugs Work* (New York, Columbia University Press, 2001).

collection is predominantly concerned with substance addictions. Importantly, substances here do not only include illicit drugs, but also alcohol as well as the use of prescription drugs.

The content of this collection can be summarised as follows. In chapter two, the insanity defence (England and Wales) and the Dutch insanity equivalent (non-accountability: *ontoerekenbaarheid*) are discussed, as well as prior fault in the context of diminished responsibility.[11] In chapter three, the role of prior fault in sentencing is explored. Afterwards, in chapters four to nine, the problems that arise within the legal frameworks in situations of addiction and intoxication are explored from various legal and non-legal disciplines. Chapter four serves as a bridging chapter by outlining in what ways other disciplines could interact with the law. This sets the stage for the later chapters by helping the reader understand the relevance of non-legal disciplines in a prior fault discussion. Chapter five provides a thorough overview of addiction from psychological and neuroscientific perspectives, aiming to familiarise the reader with the complexity of substance use disorders and the legally relevant consequences of addiction on capacities and behaviour. Chapter six uses these insights on addiction by opening a discussion on whether addiction can be considered a blameworthy condition to which criminal responsibility can be ascribed, based on an analysis of theories of responsibility. Chapter seven explores psychological and neuroscientific insights into the pre-drinking decision-making and initiation to drink, as well as the effects of alcohol intoxication on the capacities of the individual, and the legal relevance of such effects. A more philosophical-legal perspective is offered in chapter eight, whereby the author examines the relationship and possible interconnectedness of addiction, voluntary intoxication, automatism, and culpability. This collection ends with chapter nine, questioning whether individuals are at fault for being addicted by addressing a well-known economic theory of addiction by Herrnstein and Prelec.

In what follows in this chapter, we provide introductory comments on some of the major themes explored across the other chapters of the collection: intoxicated offending and the challenges of addiction on rules of prior fault; the need for interdisciplinary research; understanding the effects of addiction on the brain and behaviour; and the novelty of the collection. Before doing so, we briefly outline a general legal framework for understanding prior fault in intoxicated offending.

[11] It has to be noted that there are fundamental differences between the common law insanity defence and the Dutch equivalents thereof, which is reflected in the differences between the terms. Non-accountability reflects the normative nature of accounting for an offence by the defendant rather than focusing on the pathology per se. Nonetheless, the term 'insanity (defence)' is used consistently to encompass all national law equivalents of this defence, even though the term insanity is unfitting in the context of civil law. Yet unless specifically addressing Dutch legal doctrine, this volume employs the term 'insanity' for readability purposes.

II. An Introduction to Prior Fault Frameworks in the Law

Much has been written about specific jurisdictional approaches in dealing with prior fault and the legal challenges that arise therein.[12] Neither this introduction nor this collection as a whole is intended to repeat such a discussion. Nonetheless, in this section, we provide a brief and general outline of prior fault frameworks in civil and common law jurisdictions for paradigm cases of intoxicated offending, in order to fully understand the more complicated situations concerning the addicted defendant in the chapters to come.

A. Civil Law Approaches: Germany and the Netherlands

Whilst acknowledging the nuances in each respective jurisdiction when it comes to prior fault rules, there are overarching similarities in civil law countries. Looking at Germany and the Netherlands, we see that prior fault rules function as a mechanism to block otherwise exculpatory or mitigatory defences. In cases of intoxication, this means that possible insanity defences or pleas of diminished responsibility – based on impaired capacities as a result of voluntary intoxication – are generally unsuccessful.[13] Thus, to emphasise, prior fault rules operate on the level of defences (excuses and justifications), thereby concerning the unlawfulness of the offence (in case of blocking a justification) or the blameworthiness of the actor (in case of blocking an excuse). Prior fault cannot generally negate the *mens rea* (ie, intent or negligence). This approach can easily be understood through the tripartite structure towards criminal liability in both countries.[14] As opposed to a bipartite structure, as common law systems employ, Germany and the Netherlands create clear distinctions between three aspects that together constitute criminal liability. First is the fulfilment of the offence definition (concerning both the criminal act, *actus reus*, as well as the criminal mind, *mens rea*). Only once the offence has been established and proven beyond reasonable doubt does the judge continue to address whether there are any applicable justifications and, if not, whether there are applicable excuses.[15] Here, prior fault may play a role and may negate the applicability of one of these defences.

Although the overarching structure towards criminal liability (and thus prior fault rules) is largely identical, Germany and the Netherlands have markedly different approaches towards the exact manifestation of prior fault criteria. Germany is well-known for its structured approach towards intoxicated offending. It consists

[12] *cf* Goldberg and others (n 1); Child (n 3); Crombag and others (n 4); Crombag and others (n 5).

[13] The Netherlands, see Bijlsma (n 8). Germany, see B Fischer and J Rehm, 'Alcohol Consumption and the Liability of Offenders in the German Criminal System' [1996] *Contemporary Drug Problems* 707.

[14] J Keiler, 'Actus Reus and Mens Rea' in J Keiler and D Roef (eds), *Comparative Concepts of Criminal Law* (Cambridge, Intersentia, 2019) 115.

[15] ibid.

of a two-way mechanism of *actio libera in causa* (*alic*) and the *Vollrausch* offence of §323a German Criminal Code (GCC): a bespoke intoxication offence.[16] The difference between these two pathways towards prior fault is the normative link between the substance use, intoxication, and the offence at hand.[17] Consider a defendant who used substances and became so intoxicated that he could not understand the wrongfulness of his acts. Based on his impaired capacities alone, the German equivalent to an insanity defence may apply: §20 GCC (*Schuldunfähigkeit wegen seelischer Störungen*). In such cases, the two pathways of the German prior fault doctrine differ as follows. If the defendant voluntarily used substances and could have foreseen (or even intended) that it would lead to harmful behaviour, *alic* can be used to prevent exculpation. Even though the offender may have impaired or absent capacities during the commission of the offence, the defendant is considered to have prior fault, as he could have foreseen such consequences and thus ought to have acted differently. Raising the insanity defence will not be successful, and the defendant may be considered responsible for the original harms caused. On the other hand, when no such culpable link is present, for instance, because the defendant could not have foreseen the severe impairments in capacities that arose from the substance use, the defendant is excused for the primary offence based on §20. After all, it would be unfair if: (1) he did not have the capacities to be held responsible; and (2) he did not foresee/could not reasonably have foreseen that his substance use would cause such risky and harmful consequences. Yet the German system also does not allow voluntary intoxication to lead to complete exculpation. Instead, he is then prosecuted for a separate intoxication offence (§323a GCC: *Vollrausch*).[18]

Consequently, the German system does not excuse voluntary intoxication, but prosecutes based on what the defendant can be blamed for: foreseeing or intending criminal behaviour through intoxication, or simply being recklessly intoxicated, but without a specific normative connection to the specific harm caused. With this intoxication offence, Germany achieves doctrinal consistency in acknowledging that a (severely) intoxicated individual does not have the required mental capacity to be held liable for his harmful conduct, whilst at the same time accommodating societal disapproval by preventing voluntary substance use from becoming a method of exculpation.[19]

[16] Fischer and Rehm (n 13).

[17] ibid.

[18] The provision reads as follows: '(1) He who intentionally or negligently puts himself into a state of intoxication by consuming alcoholic beverages or by other intoxicating means is punished with imprisonment of no more than five years if he commits an unlawful act while in this state and may not be punished for it because he was not legally responsible due to the intoxication or because this cannot be excluded. (2) The penalty must not be more severe than the penalty prescribed for the offence committed while in a state of intoxication.' Translation from the German provision copied from S Hardt and N Kornet, *The Maastricht Collection, Volume II: Comparative Public Law* (Amsterdam, Europa Law Publishing, 2019) 245.

[19] See also the more detailed discussion in Goldberg and others (n 1).

In the Netherlands, there is no specific intoxication offence. Historically, foreseeability was presented as a criterion for prior fault, ie, the defendant must (be able to) foresee some form of risky or harmful consequences in order to be blamed for using substances.[20] Yet current case law suggests that foreseeability does not have any differentiating value. This means that whether D foresaw, or reasonably could have foreseen, that the intoxication could result in harm or whether they did not foresee such effects, the outcome is the same: prior fault applies and liability can be established.[21] What remains is the voluntariness of the substance use, here defined negatively as meaning any substance use that was not forced or taken unknowingly. Consequently, voluntariness seems to remain the only criterion for prior fault.[22] When looking at the two situations Germany distinguishes, whereby the normative link between the intoxication and the offence is crucial, we can conclude that the Netherlands does not employ such a distinction. In both situations, the voluntary intoxication of the defendant is sufficient to claim that there was prior fault. Although this system cannot be applauded for doctrinal sophistication, it is a pragmatic and quick solution. Of course, as we explore throughout this collection, it may also lead to over-criminalisation in more complex cases, such as those involving long-term and severe addictions.

B. Common Law Approaches: England & Wales

England & Wales (hereafter: England) address prior fault through other means. As common law jurisdictions are based on a bipartite structure – differentiating between *offences and defences* only[23] – the role of prior fault can operate on different levels than in civil law jurisdictions. Briefly mentioned in the introductory section, English law employs prior fault arguments to either construct the offence or block an applicable defence. Constructing an offence means that the defendant lacks the prerequisite *mens rea* at the time of the offence (T2), but has acted in a blameworthy manner at a moment in time prior to the offence (T1). The culpable mental state at T1, thus, is used to replace the lack of a *mens rea* at T2.[24]

Specifically, in cases of intoxicated offending, these prior fault rules are more commonly addressed as intoxication rules. Intoxication *sec* is not a defence.[25]

[20] Bijlsma (n 8).

[21] Goldberg and others (n 7).

[22] AE Goldberg, 'Foreseeability and Prior Fault: Examining the Assessment Framework for Intoxication, Blame and Criminal Responsibility' (2024) 29 *Bialystok Legal Studies* 69.

[23] For a comparative discussion on how elements of a bipartite and tripartite structure relate to each other, see Keiler (n 14) ch IV.

[24] The fact that the German and Dutch systems do not recognise this distinction between constructing and blocking applications of prior fault, is largely explainable given the objective nature of the intent and the voluntary act requirement. As these are hardly negated by mental states, there is no need to use prior fault doctrines to construct these elements.

[25] The defendant cannot use as an excuse the argument that if he had been sober, he would not have acted this way; he may also not raise an automatism plea based on voluntary intoxication.

Consequently, for purely intoxicated offending, the main approach in English law is that of discussing and potentially negating *mens rea*.[26] Once reasonable doubt as to mens rea is established, prior fault rules become relevant as a potential route to inculpation (ie, substituting for the missing mens rea elements as a route to liability). To establish intoxicated prior fault, it is necessary to demonstrate a *blameworthy choice* at T1: the intoxicant must be recognised legally as a 'dangerous drug' (ie, blameworthy), and D must have taken it voluntarily at T1 (ie, through choice). Voluntariness of intoxication is, as with Dutch law, an inversely defined premise. Intoxication stemming from coerced consumption, spiked drinks or adverse side effects of prescribed (and properly taken) medication can be considered involuntary.[27]

Once intoxicated prior fault is established at T1, such fault is not sufficient to substitute for any/all missing mens rea at T2. Rather, it becomes necessary to distinguish between offences of so-called basic intent (where substitution is possible) and offences of specific intent (where it is not).[28] Within the caselaw, this is more typically described in negative terms: voluntary intoxication can be raised as an argument to deny the presence of specific intent, but not basic intent. For offences of basic intent, intoxication can 'replace' the missing *mens rea* elements.[29] In cases of strict liability or negligent offences, intoxication is irrelevant.[30]

This approach has been met with criticism. One may wonder, for instance, whether voluntary intoxication can indeed be considered equivalent to missing subjective *mens rea* elements:[31]

> […] any claim of equivalence between prior-fault intoxication (ie objective foresight of nonspecific future risks from T1) and missing states of recklessness (ie subjective foresight of specific risks in action at T2) ignores fundamental differences between the two.

It is clear that voluntary intoxication gives rise to some blame on the defendant's behalf, which the law may need to consider, but this does not automatically render simple substitution appropriate. Moreover, if cases of 'simple' intoxication are already riddled with concerns of equivalence, one can only imagine that cases of intoxicated offending with more complicated backgrounds, such as

See: *DPP* v *Majewski* [1977] AC 443, 482 and *R v Lipman* [1970] 1 QB 152 (CA). In this collection, chs 2 and 8 discuss the frameworks of insanity and automatism, respectively, for more complex cases of intoxicated offending in more detail.

[26] MJ Allen and I Edwards, *Criminal Law* (Oxford, Oxford University Press, 2019) 173. See also: AP Simester 'Intoxication is Never a Defence' (2009) 1 *Crim LR* 3, 4.

[27] The Law Commission, 'Intoxication and Criminal Liability' (2009) Law Com No. 314 paras 2.76, 2.88.

[28] Simester (n 26) 7. The author also discusses the differences between specific and basic intent in more detail: see Simester (n 26) s IV.

[29] 'If the drunken man is so drunk that he does not know what he is doing, he has a defence to any charge, such as murder or wounding with intent, in which a specific intent is essential, but he is still liable to be convicted of manslaughter or unlawful wounding for which no specific intent is necessary …': *Bratty v Attorney-General* (Northern Ireland) [1963] AC 386 HL, 410.

[30] Allen and Edwards (n 26) 173.

[31] Goldberg and others (n 1) 58.

addicted or otherwise comorbid defendants, would lead to even more dissatisfying results. Consider, for instance, whether severely addicted defendants should still be considered voluntarily intoxicated; or how to conceptualise prior fault in cases whereby the defendant's intoxication gives rise to insanity claims, such as in cases of substance-induced psychoses. These issues are explored across the collection, and in the remainder of this introduction, we briefly outline some of these complexities in prior fault situations.

III. Exploring the Complexities of Intoxication and Prior fault

In what follows, we provide an overview of the issues that arise when prior fault rules are considered in the context of an addicted defendant. The brief legal overview in the previous section and earlier scholarly work highlight that even in paradigm cases of *sec* intoxication, prior fault rules are complex at best and a legal fiction at worst.[32] When D suffers from an underlying addiction, whereby their intoxication can be understood as a result of this disorder, various new and even more complex issues arise. In order to illustrate these issues, let us consider three hypothetical, contrasting cases.

First is Paul, who committed an offence whilst intoxicated. One evening, he went to the pub with his friends and simply had a pint too many, and consequently, he engaged in risky behaviour which he would not have done when sober.
By contrast, we can consider Frank, who is a frequent visitor to the same pub as Paul. He would regularly meet his friends there, but contrary to Paul, however, his alcohol use became excessive to the point that he developed an alcohol use disorder and experienced various behavioural and psychological consequences as a result. When abstaining, Frank is preoccupied with alcohol to the extent that it impairs his focus and leads him to prioritise the short-term rewards of drinking over the long-term benefits of abstaining. Moreover, he experiences withdrawal symptoms and strong cravings, which all contribute to a continuous cycle of substance abuse. One evening, he became excessively drunk, and consequently, he engaged in risky behaviour which he would not have done when sober.
And lastly, there is Marc, who also committed an offence whilst intoxicated, which he would not have done when sober. However, Marc has been addicted to amphetamines (speed) for years: what started as a way for him to self-medicate his ADHD symptoms has spiralled into compulsive use. Marc experiences similar consequences of his addiction as Frank, including the withdrawal symptoms, impairments in his natural reward systems, and cravings.

[32] Goldberg and others (n 1).

Intuitively, different issues arise in the cases of Paul, Frank and Marc in the assessment of prior fault. Using substances recreationally (Paul) or out of strong urges (Frank and Marc) may *feel* different to the reader; and the reader may also have intuitive thoughts about substance use disorders that originated from recreational use (Frank) and those that can be traced back to an underlying mental disorder (Marc). These differences in perceptions are illustrative of the specific attention that ought to be paid to cases of addicted defendants. If, for instance, Marc commits an offence in either a state of anticipation and craving, or in an intoxicated state after the drugs have been consumed, an important question would be how these factors ought to be accounted for when determining Marc's criminal responsibility, if at all.

At first glance, the answer may appear self-evident. A lack of *mens rea* in English law can be substituted by the act of voluntarily becoming intoxicated, and in most civil law systems, *mens rea* cannot be negated by mental impairments.[33] Moreover, across common and civil law jurisdictions, substance addiction is not typically accepted as a valid ground for an insanity plea, or even a defence of diminished responsibility.[34] The reason for this is threefold. First, the specific requirements of those defences may not include the *types* of impairments that are associated with addiction. The M'Naghten rules,[35] for instance, seem to have an exclusive cognitive focus, meaning that only cognitive impairment (for instance, a psychosis) can lead to a successful appeal to the insanity defence.[36] This tends to prevent addiction-related impairments from being considered, as these impairments are mainly control-based (ie, volitional), as exemplified by the strong cravings mentioned above.[37] This is different from continental systems, which seem more lenient in accepting volitional impairments as a basis for the defence, in addition to cognitive incapacities.[38] However, that does not automatically mean that addiction exculpates. A second reason that prevents addiction from being used as a defence is that most systems require a near complete *absence* of capacities in order for a defence to apply.[39] Arguing that addiction impairs cognitive capacities or even volitional capacities is not a controversial argument, but suggesting a complete lack thereof

[33] See s II and also fn 15 of this chapter.

[34] AE Goldberg and D Roef, 'Addiction, Capacities and Criminal Responsibility – a Comparative Analysis' in A Waltermann and others (eds), *Law, Science and Rationality* (Den Haag, Eleven International Publishing, 2019). As opposed to England and Wales, where diminished responsibility is specific to the offence of murder, it is a mitigating defence applicable to all offences in both Germany and the Netherlands. Ch 2 of this collection further elaborates on the diminished responsibility 'defence'.

[35] *M'Naghten* [1843] 10 Cl & Fin 200, 8 Eng Rep 718 (HL).

[36] RD Mackay, 'Righting the Wrong? Some Observations on the Second Limb of the M'Naghten Rules' (2009) 2 *Crim Law Rev* 80.

[37] Goldberg and Roef (n 33).

[38] G Meynen, 'Legal Insanity Standards: Their Structure and Elements' in *Legal Insanity: Explorations in Psychiatry, Law, and Ethics* (Basel, Springer, 2016).

[39] Goldberg and Roef (n 33).

proves much more difficult.[40] Previous research shows that even severely addicted individuals retain an element of choice and control over their behaviour and/or retain at least some (cognitive) connection to reality.[41] This can also be corroborated by addiction neuroscientists and clinicians who, despite their understanding of the significant impact of addiction on volitional capacities, still consider the addict to be at least partially responsible for their behaviour.[42] Hence, reaching the near-absolute benchmark of a loss of capacities that the law employs is rare in cases of addiction.[43]

The exculpatory framework of the insanity defence, therefore, does not seem to accommodate the peculiarities of addiction very well. And even where addiction may be found to apply, ie, when the defendant's addiction impairs the required capacities to a large enough extent, a third reason for preventing exculpation exists in many jurisdictions: the prior fault in acquiring and maintaining the addiction. The continuous consumption of psychoactive substances, leading to an addiction, may function as a substitute to re-establish liability and/or block defences. This mechanism is uncontroversial in common intoxication cases, for instance, when a defendant – such as previously mentioned Paul – has consumed large amounts of alcohol and has consequently committed an offence. Although Paul's capacities at the time of the offence (T2) can be considered seriously impaired, his prior conduct at T1 is considered culpable and will block any applicable defence and/or establish liability.[44] His prior conduct is culpable because we consider his alcohol abuse to be voluntary, thereby warranting responsibility for the consequences of intoxication.

Looking back at the case of Frank and Marc (ie, the addiction-fuelled intoxication case), however, it seems that their intoxication is not straightforwardly voluntary. Should the law be applied to Frank and Marc in the same way as to Paul? Although Frank's initial substance use can be considered voluntary, one may wonder whether this is still the case, now that his alcohol use has become compulsive. For Marc, there are even more factors at play: he has a long history of use, many symptoms – extending beyond impaired capacities during acute intoxication – and an underlying psychiatric disorder explaining the usage in the first place. Yet what the law means by 'voluntary' in the context of voluntary intoxication seems to be as broad as *any* intoxication, except for spiked drinks or unexpected side effects of properly administered medications.[45] Therefore, Marc's intoxication, which is

[40] A Carter and others, 'Control and Responsibility in Addicted Individuals: What Do Addiction Neuroscientists and Clinicians Think?' (2014) 7 *Neuroethics* 205.

[41] GM Heyman, *Addiction: A Disorder of Choice* (Cambridge, Harvard University Press, 2009).

[42] Carter and others (n 17).

[43] This is one of the central themes discussed in ch 5 of this collection, which provides an overview of addiction research on the topic of voluntariness in voluntary intoxication.

[44] As mentioned before, the difference between blocking defences and establishing liability is not merely semantic. It is further elaborated upon in Child (n 3).

[45] A Ashworth and J Horder, *Principles of Criminal Law* (Oxford, Oxford University Press, 2013). The meaning and difference between voluntary and involuntary intoxication are further explored in later chapters as well, such as in chs 4, 7 and 8.

a result of a complex interplay between addiction and other psychiatric conditions, risks being considered (legally) identical to Frank's addicted intoxication and Paul's straightforwardly voluntary intoxication, when it comes to the application of prior fault rules. This exemplifies that fundamental differences between defendants, such as the absence or presence of an underlying addiction, as well as co-existing other (ie, comorbid) mental disorders, are rarely considered when addressing the rules pertaining to prior fault.

Our examples aim to highlight how a discussion of prior fault cannot be had in the legal domain alone. It requires an understanding of the consequences of intoxication, the effects of substance use disorders, the interplay of mental disorders and substance use, and the meaning of voluntariness, just to name a few. Consequently, we strongly contend that evaluating prior fault frameworks requires a multidisciplinary approach.

IV. The Need for an Interdisciplinary Approach

Due to its multifaceted nature, criminal behaviour generally captures the interest of numerous disciplines, each with unique and valuable insights, leading to a more comprehensive understanding of criminality.[46] Delinquency, in turn, is strongly related to substance use and abuse, as the vast majority of offences are committed whilst intoxicated.[47] Hence, to comprehend the intricacies of criminal behaviour, especially when related to addiction and substance use, we must also acknowledge its multifactorial nature and study it accordingly. Similarly, we believe that an understanding of prior fault also requires such a multidisciplinary approach.

This collection seeks to remedy the often mono-disciplinary approach of legal research by exploring the complexities of addiction and prior fault from various disciplines. While it is not surprising that studying multifaceted phenomena like prior fault and addiction necessitates a multidisciplinary approach, there is a potential challenge that arises, namely the ability of different disciplines to effectively communicate and collaborate with one another.[48] This collection aims to contribute to such effective communication through the use of co-authored chapters by scholars from different disciplines.[49] Below, we provide some examples that

[46] eg, A Raine, 'Biosocial Studies of Antisocial and Violent Behavior in Children and Adults: A Review' (2002) 30(4) *Journal of Abnormal Child Psychology* 311; FT Cullen, R Agnew, and P Wilcox, *Criminological Theory: Past to Present: Essential Readings* (Oxford, Oxford University Press, 2014).

[47] HR White, J Brick and S Hansell, 'A Longitudinal Investigation of Alcohol Use and Aggression in Adolescence' [1993] *Journal of Studies on Alcohol* 62; EP Shulman and others, 'The Dual Systems Model: Review, Reappraisal, and Reaffirmation' (2016) 17 *Developmental Cognitive Neuroscience* 103.

[48] R Frodeman and A Briggle, *Socrates Tenured: The Institutions of 21st-Century Philosophy* (Lanham, Rowman & Littlefield, 2016); AF Repko, R Szostak, and MP Buchberger, *Introduction to Interdisciplinary Studies* (Thousand Oaks, Sage Publications, 2019).

[49] Such as law, psychology and criminology (chs 4 and 6); and psychology and neuroscience (chs 5 and 7).

highlight how disciplines such as psychology, neuroscience, and philosophy may aid our understanding of addiction and prior fault. In the upcoming chapters of this book, these aspects are the basis of further in-depth exploration.

As discussed, the law generally holds the presumption that substance users retain (enough) control over their behaviour, such that addiction, in itself, will rarely satisfy exculpatory mechanisms.[50] In addition, any associated intoxication is likely to be treated as voluntary in the context of prior fault.[51] For this reason, addicted defendants are often considered to have prior fault over their addiction-driven behaviour.[52] Insights from neuroscience and other socio-scientific disciplines, however, raise questions regarding the legitimacy of this legal position. Research indicates that addiction can significantly impact an individual's control over their actions and cognitive functioning, thereby questioning whether it is appropriate to minimise the influence of addiction on criminal responsibility. The weight of such evidence suggests that addiction warrants careful examination and that perhaps, such research should prompt a re-evaluation of the legal framework to better account for the complexities and potential impact of addiction on an individual's culpability. In other words, the *intuitive* differences between Paul, Frank and Marc may be *empirically* explained and substantiated by looking at scientific evidence outlining the consequences of addiction on capacities.

A. Examples of Non-Legal Discussions Relevant to the Law

It is clear that the law benefits from interdisciplinary research and empirical evidence on addiction and intoxication, yet these non-legal aspects are unfortunately not simple and uncontested. Thus, the issue is not simply how the law can incorporate scientific insights, but rather how the law should deal with areas of *contested* science. The sometimes contested nature of certain scientific insights further demonstrates the necessity of an interdisciplinary approach. In what follows, we provide some examples of scientific discussions relevant to prior fault.

Some of the more prevalent points of contention in understanding the consequences of addiction on responsibility lie in the varied models of addiction. Insights into the various responsibility questions seem to depend on the model, and on the consequent underlying perspective on addiction.[53] Oftentimes, the discussion of

[50] J Kennett, NA Vincent and A Snoek, 'Drug Addiction and Criminal Responsibility' in L Neil and C Jens (eds), *Handbook on Neuroethics* (Dordrecht, Springer, 2014); SJ Morse, 'Addiction, Choice and Criminal Law' in N Heather and G Segal (eds), *Addiction and Choice: Rethinking the Relationship* (Oxford, Oxford University Press 2017); Goldberg and Roef (n 33).

[51] M Cusick, 'Mens Rea and Methamphetamine: High Time for a Modern Doctrine Acknowledging the Neuroscience of Addiction' (2016) 85 *Fordham Law* Review 2417. See also an exception to this premise mentioned on page 18 of S Dimock, 'What are Intoxicated Offenders Responsible For? The "Intoxication Defense" Re-examined' (2011) 5 *Criminal Law and Philosophy* 1.

[52] Goldberg and others (n 1).

[53] G Winger and others, 'Behavioral Perspectives on the Neuroscience of Drug Addiction' (2005) 84 *Journal of the Experimental Analysis of Behavior* 667; Heyman (n 41).

addiction oscillates between two prevalent models: the 'brain disease' model and the 'choice' model. The 'brain disease' model frames addiction as a chronic medical condition that alters the brain, leading to compulsive drug-seeking behaviour.[54] Critics of this perspective argue that it overlooks the personal reasons behind initiating drug use, neglects the element of choice, and ignores the influence of incentives to abstain from drugs.[55] On the other hand, the 'choice and motivation' model upholds the significance of personal agency in addiction.[56] It posits addiction as a result of individual choices and poor self-control, viewing recovery as attainable through conscious decisions. Critics of this model, however, argue that it fails to acknowledge the significant neuroscientific evidence supporting the distortion of normal wanting processes that addiction instigates.[57] It seems fair to note that the consequences of addiction on human behaviour, choice, and thus legal responsibility seem different depending on the stance taken.[58]

A related question is how the law should deal with, or account for, specific insights from other areas of study. For example, although behavioural evidence may be able to demonstrate points of difference between defendants in terms of control and voluntariness, at what stage (and on what basis) should these differences translate into different legal outcomes? As an example, addressing the capacity for control from a behavioural perspective requires assessment of empirical notions of, eg, impulsivity or decision-making capacity.[59] This in itself is not an easy feat, as there is much variability between as well as within individuals, rendering the assessment of a specific capacity *at the time of the offence* – often relatively far in the past – a difficult one.[60] Moreover, the law employs a binary notion of voluntariness, whereby intoxication is either voluntary or it is not. This does not align with the behavioural sciences, whereby volitional capacities can

[54] GF Koob and ND Volkow, 'Neurobiology of Addiction: A Neurocircuitry Analysis' (2016) 3 *The Lancet Psychiatry* 760.

[55] N Heather and others, 'Challenging the Brain Disease Model of Addiction: European Launch of the Addiction Theory Network' (2018) 26 *Addiction Research & Theory* 249.

[56] B Foddy and J Savulescu, 'A Liberal Account of Addiction' (2010) 17 *Philosophy, Psychiatry, & Psychology* 1.

[57] KC Berridge, TE Robinson and JW Aldridge, 'Dissecting Components of Reward: "Liking", "Wanting", and Learning' (2009) 9 *Current Opinion in Pharmacology* 65.

[58] AE Goldberg, 'The (In)Significance of the Addiction Bebate' (2020) 13 *Neuroethics* 311. This interesting avenue of debate is explored in ch 5, where the limitations of opposing these two models are discussed and the possibility to more accurately account for the consequences of addiction is explored: one that considers addiction's severity as well as environmental factors.

[59] A Bechara, 'Decision Making, Impulse Control and Loss of Willpower to Resist Drugs: A Neurocognitive Perspective' (2005) 8 *Nature Neuroscience* 1458. A thorough overview is provided in ch 7 of this collection.

[60] JD Jentsch and JR Taylor, 'Impulsivity Resulting from Frontostriatal Dysfunction in Drug Abuse: Implications for the Control of Behavior by Reward-Related Stimuli' (1999) 146 *Psychopharmacology* 373; M Field and others, 'Acute Alcohol Effects on Inhibitory Control and Implicit Cognition: Implications for Loss of Control over Drinking' (2010) 34 *Alcoholism: Clinical and Experimental Research* 1346; MJ Fernández-Serrano, M Pérez-García and A Verdejo-García, 'What Are the Specific vs. Generalized Effects of Drugs of Abuse on Neuropsychological Performance?' (2011) 35 *Neuroscience & Biobehavioral Reviews* 377.

be measured on a continuum. A more fundamental question that is raised, additionally, is whether heightened impulsivity indicates an inability to control one's actions, or whether it merely shows a defendant giving in to the impulse. In other words, was there an irresistible impulse, or was the impulse not resisted?[61] These challenges highlight the need to further delve into the mechanisms of addiction and intoxication, and the insights from psychology and the neurosciences therein. In the next three paragraphs, we provide a brief literature review on the consequences of addiction on brain and behaviour.

Substance use can compromise judgment and decision-making, leading to impulsive and risky behaviours that are intricately linked to criminal actions.[62] Neuroscientific research similarly reveals that substances often affect the brain's reward system, particularly the dopamine pathways within the basal ganglia.[63] This alteration can lead to heightened impulsivity and diminished cognitive control, factors contributing to criminal behaviours.[64] Individuals under the influence can be more prone to crimes like theft or vandalism due to altered inhibitory functions.[65] Furthermore, substance use can elevate the risk of aggressive behaviours.[66] Financial challenges, intensified by substance abuse, can lead to unemployment and instability, pushing some towards criminal activities to sustain their addiction. For instance, a vicious interplay often exists between drug use and property offences. Socially, substance abuse has associations with domestic violence and child maltreatment.[67] Antisocial networks contribute to substance initiation and persistence, while prosocial environments foster recovery and lawful behaviours.[68] It demonstrates that

[61] Famously said by SJ Morse: 'If or to what degree a person's desire or impulse to act was controllable is not determinable: there is no scientific test to judge whether an impulse was irresistible or simply not resisted' in SJ Morse, 'Excusing the Crazy: The Insanity Defense Reconsidered' (1985) 58 *South California Law Review* 777, 817. Relatedly, see also HG Frankfurt, 'Freedom of the Will and the Concept of a Person' in JM Fischer (ed), *Free Will: Free Agency, Moral Responsibility, and Skepticism* (Milton Park, Routledge, 2005); C Quoilin and others, 'Neural Bases of Inhibitory Control: Combining Transcranial Magnetic Stimulation and Magnetic Resonance Imaging in Alcohol-Use Disorder Patients' (2021) 224 *NeuroImage* 117435; R Guzulaitis, L Godenzini and LM Palmer, 'Neural Basis of Anticipation and Premature Impulsive Action in the Frontal Cortex' (2022) 25 *Nature Neuroscience* 1683; H Li, O Turel and Q He, 'Neural Basis of Altered Impulsivity in Individuals With Internet Gaming Disorder: State-of-the-Art Review' [2023] *Current Addiction Reports* 1.

[62] RZ Goldstein and ND Volkow, 'Dysfunction of the Prefrontal Cortex in Addiction: Neuroimaging Findings and Clinical Implications' (2011) 12 *Nature Reviews Neuroscience* 652.

[63] ND Volkow, GF Koob and AT McLellan, 'Neurobiologic Advances from the Brain Disease Model of Addiction' (2016) 374 *New England Journal of Medicine* 363.

[64] BJ Everitt and TW Robbins, 'Drug Addiction: Updating Actions to Habits to Compulsions Ten Years On' (2016) 67 *Annual Review of Psychology* 23.

[65] RD Baler and ND Volkow, 'Drug Addiction: The Neurobiology of Disrupted Self-Control' (2006) 12 *Trends in Molecular Medicine* 559.

[66] AJ Heinz and others, 'Cognitive and Neurobiological Mechanisms of Alcohol-Related Aggression' (2011) 12 *Nature Reviews Neuroscience* 400.

[67] DM Fergusson, JM Boden and LJ Horwood, 'Exposure to Childhood Sexual and Physical Abuse and Adjustment in Early Adulthood' (2008) 32 *Child Abuse & Neglect* 607.

[68] D Best and others, 'Cannabis Use in Adolescents: The Impact of Risk and Protective Factors and Social Functioning' (2005) 24 *Drug and Alcohol Review* 483; E Westling and others, 'Pubertal Timing and Substance Use: The Effects of Gender, Parental Monitoring and Deviant Peers' (2008) 42 *Journal*

multiple factors contribute to the defendant's mental state and behaviour, further highlighting the need to consider these insights when discussing prior fault.

Additionally, a range of unconscious or less deliberate processes – such as priming effects, cue reactivity, and learned expectancies – can influence the initial decision to use a substance. These processes may reduce the truly voluntary nature of the choice to drinking or drug use, as individuals may respond automatically to environmental or internal cues rather than engaging in fully conscious deliberation.[69] In chronic users, metacognitive judgments about their capacity to regulate consumption can be skewed, exhibiting overconfidence in their ability to manage or limit substance use, coupled with inaccurate or overly optimistic expectancies regarding its effects.[70] Such factors intensify the risk of continued use and escalation into criminal behaviours.

These effects of intoxication or addiction can be highly dependent on factors such as the type of substance and the moment in the addiction cycle. The cycle of addiction, comprising stages of craving, intoxication, withdrawal, and reinstatement, reveals a persistent pattern.[71] During the craving stage, an individual may exhibit a heightened focus on obtaining the substance, possibly leading to criminal activities like theft or fraud.[72] The intoxication stage, the actual consumption of the substance, often impairs judgment and inhibitory control, further predisposing individuals to delinquent behaviour.[73] At this stage, metacognitive processes may also falter, with users misjudging their level of impairment and making risky decisions because they believe they can 'handle' the substance's effects.[74] The withdrawal stage, usually marked by an array of negative physiological and

of Adolescent Health 555; T Wojciechowski, 'A Life-Course Approach to Understanding Differential Relevance of Deviant Peers for Predicting Cocaine/Crack Use' (2021) 67 *Crime & Delinquency* 2114.

[69] JA Bargh and TL Chartrand, 'The Unbearable Automaticity of Being' (1999) 54 *American Psychologist* 462.

[70] See, for instance, MS Goldman, 'Expectancy and Risk for Alcoholism: The Unfortunate Exploitation of a Fundamental Characteristic of Neurobehavioral Adaptation' (1999) 26 *Alcoholism: Clinical and Experimental Research* 737.

[71] Koob and Volkow (n 54).

[72] RF Anton, 'What Is Craving?: Models and Implications for Treatment' (1999) 23 *Alcohol Research & Health* 165; AR Childress and others, 'Prelude to Passion: Limbic Activation by "Unseen" Drug and Sexual Cues' (2008) 3 *PLoS ONE* e1506; D Eddie, ME Bates and JF Buckman, 'Closing the Brain–Heart Loop: Towards More Holistic Models of Addiction and Addiction Recovery' (2022) 27 *Addiction Biology* e12958.

[73] Goldstein and Volkow (n 62); AM Herman and T Duka, 'Facets of Impulsivity and Alcohol Use: What Role Do Emotions Play?' (2019) 106 *Neuroscience & Biobehavioral Reviews* 202; S De Pirro and others, 'Effect of Alcohol on the Sense of Agency in Healthy Humans' (2020) 25 *Addiction Biology* e12796.

[74] K Fromme, EC Katz and EJ D'Amico, 'Effects of Alcohol Intoxication on the Perceived Consequences of Risk Taking' (1997) 5(1) *Experimental and Clinical Psychopharmacology* 14; K McCarty, 'The Effect of Acute Alcohol Intoxication on Risk Attitude' (PhD dissertation, University of Missouri-Columbia, 2021); Y Liu and others, 'How Drug Cravings Affect Metacognitive Monitoring in Methamphetamine Abusers' (2022) 132 *Addictive Behaviors* 107341; D Delonca and others, 'Relationships Between Attentional Bias and Craving in Alcohol Use Disorder: Role of Metacognitions' (2021) 117 *Addictive Behaviors* 106846.

psychological symptoms, might drive desperate actions to alleviate discomfort.[75] Reinstatement, or relapse, can result from the interplay of various triggers, including overconfidence in one's ability to remain abstinent, potentially re-initiating criminal behaviours linked to substance acquisition and consumption.[76]

Finally, aside from acute intoxication, substance use can be considered an addiction when it disrupts major life functions and persists despite negative repercussions and cessation attempts, as per the DSM-5.[77] Chronic use can also remodel neural connections and reduce the volume of regions like the prefrontal cortex, which is crucial for decision-making and impulse control.[78] These impairments are necessary to understand addiction-driven intoxication and the legal consequences thereof. Hence, neuroscientific insights, which attempt to reveal the brain mechanisms underlying addiction cycles and impairments in mental capacities, can be pivotal for legal discussions, particularly in the contexts of defence applicability and sentencing deliberations.[79]

To conclude our rational for an interdisciplinary approach towards prior fault is necessary, we want to highlight not only the influence of addiction on brain and behaviour but also the underlying philosophical implications.[80] This query should be approached from a philosophical viewpoint too, amongst others, by discussing the meaning of voluntariness, control or agency in the context of addiction, and how these concepts interrelate.[81] Additionally, it is important to understand what it is that the law holds the addict accountable for. Is it the behaviour at the time of the offence, ie, T2? Or rather at T1, the moment when the choice to engage in substance use is made? Or even an earlier time, ie, T0, for instance, when the defendant became addicted? In understanding which actions justify criminal responsibility, we need to understand how different behaviours at different points

[75] GR Breese and others, 'Stress Enhancement of Craving During Sobriety: A Risk for Relapse' (2005) 29 *Alcoholism: Clinical & Experimental Research* 185.

[76] Y Shaham and others, 'The Reinstatement Model of Drug Relapse: History, Methodology and Major Findings' (2003) 168 *Psychopharmacology* 3; AL Milton and BJ Everitt, 'The Psychological and Neurochemical Mechanisms of Drug Memory Reconsolidation: Implications for the Treatment of Addiction' (2010) 31 *European Journal of Neuroscience* 2308.

[77] American Psychiatric Association, *Diagnostic and Statistical Manual of Mental Disorders: DSM-5* (Washinton, American Psychiatric Association, 2013).

[78] M Zhang and others, 'Shared Gray Matter Alterations in Subtypes of Addiction: A Voxel-Wise Meta-Analysis' (2021) 238 *Psychopharmacology* 2365; AO Ceceli, CW Bradberry and RZ Goldstein, 'The Neurobiology of Drug Addiction: Cross-Species Insights into the Dysfunction and Recovery of the Prefrontal Cortex' (2022) 47 *Neuropsychopharmacology* 276.

[79] J Greene and J Cohen, 'For the Law, Neuroscience Changes Nothing and Everything' (2004) 359 *Philosophical Transactions of the Royal Society B: Biological Sciences* 1775; OD Jones, 'Seven Ways Neuroscience Aids Law' in A Battro, S Dehaene and W Singer (eds), *Neurosciences and the Human Person: New Perspectives on Human Activities* (Vatican City, Scripta Varia, 2013) 13; OR Goodenough and M Tucker, 'Why Neuroscience Matters for Law' in A D'Aloia and MC Errigo (eds), *Neuroscience and Law: Complicated Crossings and New Perspectives* (Cham, Springer, 2020). These insights are further discussed in chs 5 and 7 of this collection.

[80] S Wolf, 'Sanity and the Metaphysics of Responsibility' in F Schoeman (ed), *Responsibility, Character, and the Emotions* (Cambridge, Cambridge University Press, 1987); Frankfurt (n 61).

[81] Frankfurt (n 61). This is discussed further in ch 8 of this collection.

in time relate to each other and how far back in time the law can justifiably go.[82] Often, criminal responsibility is based on behaviour or acts at a single moment in time. Discussions on prior fault demand a normative discourse on the justification for prior fault rules, raising the question of on what basis prior conduct is allowed to impact responsibility questions, ie, when and how responsibility can be extended beyond singular time events.[83]

V. Novelty of the Collection

The novelty of this collection is threefold. First of all, there has not been an integrated piece of work on the complexities of prior fault, as of yet. The chapters interact with all the interesting debates that were highlighted in the previous sections. Previous research has addressed these various questions around prior fault in separate contributions, and such studies are discussed in more detail in the respective chapters, but this collection is novel by engaging in all these topics and combining them into one coherent book. This allows for an integrated understanding of prior fault on a conceptual and practical level.

Second, connecting the different aspects of prior fault results in an exciting variety of disciplines. The core legal questions on how to engage with prior fault are addressed from legal, psychological, neuroscientific and philosophical approaches. Previous research has devoted time and space to the complexities of prior fault rules from these monodisciplinary perspectives, but this collection is the first of its kind to engage with these disciplines concurrently. Not just by addressing a wide variety of disciplines, but specifically by pairing experts from different fields in the writing of the interdisciplinary chapters. A unique feature of this collection is that six out of the nine chapters are co-authored by researchers from different disciplines or legal backgrounds, and that many contributing authors in this collection come from interdisciplinary backgrounds themselves. Ultimately, not only the combination of disciplines but also the pairing of authors creates truly multidisciplinary output.

Finally, the topics discussed here are relevant for practitioners and academic scholars alike, and the discourse often reflects on practical implications or suggestions. Due to the co-authored nature of most chapters, the discussion can transcend specific disciplines and jurisdictions, thereby addressing fundamental critiques towards prior fault, and providing legal scholars and practitioners food for thought.

[82] L Alexander and KK Ferzan, 'Culpable Acts of Risk Creation' (2007) 5 *Ohio State Journal of Criminal Law* 375; T Nadelhoffer, 'The Threat of Shrinking Agency and Free Will Disillusionism' in M Balaguer, J Goll and S Nichols (eds), *The Oxford Handbook of Free Will* (Oxford, Oxford University Press, 2011).

[83] RA Duff, 'Towards a Modest Legal Moralism' (2014) 8 *Criminal Law and Philosophy* 217.

2

Prior Fault Insanity and Diminished Responsibility: Comparing English and Dutch Approaches

JOHN J CHILD AND MICHIEL JF VAN DER WOLF

I. Introduction

This chapter provides a comparative examination of the *real and/or potential* application of prior fault to legal rules of insanity and diminished responsibility. In particular, we focus on cases where D's prior conduct (at T1) causes or exacerbates an internal condition (eg, a mental disorder), leading D to commit (potentially criminal) harms at T2. If we analyse the T2 event in isolation, it may be possible for D to avoid liability, either because his mental disorder led to a lack of culpability/*mens rea* or to the application of an exculpatory defence (typically, within common law systems); or to an excuse, relevant to D's blameworthiness (typically, within civil law systems). The question is whether, in such circumstances, the criminal law will provide for prior fault analysis: expanding its lens to include D's conduct across T1–T2, and creating a route to liability on this basis. The circumstances of T1 prior fault that we are concerned with might include, for example, D's failure to take prescribed medication; D's failure to seek medical assistance following symptoms of disorder; and even conduct leading to disorder, such as drug taking resulting in addiction. We refer to these throughout as our 'target cases'.

In order to investigate current approaches to prior fault in this area, and to provide evaluative critique, we will focus on two primary jurisdictions: England and Wales and the Netherlands.[1] The comparison is useful because of the *apparently* very different ways in which the two jurisdictions approach our target cases. Both jurisdictions provide relatively expansive rules of prior fault where D's voluntary intoxication at T1 leads to a disordered state at T2 (we refer to this as the

[1] Referred to hereafter as English law and Dutch law.

'paradigm case of intoxication').[2] However, doctrinally at least, there appears to be a marked shift regarding our target cases (ie, where D's prior fault does not arise from intoxication at T1, or intoxication merely triggers a pre-existing disorder at T2).

In English law, there is a hard doctrinal division between categories. Prior fault intoxication rules will apply to the paradigm case of intoxication, regardless of whether D's intoxicated state at T2 might be *scientifically* described as a mental disorder; and insanity or diminished responsibility rules will apply to non-intoxicated mental disorders at T2, even where that disorder is prompted or exacerbated by D's conduct at T1. Our target cases, therefore, are located *exclusively* within this second category; and, as we will see, this makes them immune from prior fault analysis in English law. Dutch law, in contrast, makes no such distinction. Rather, where D's mind is disordered at T2, legal analysis will engage with *both* an assessment of impairment (ie, insanity and diminished responsibility) *and* an assessment of prior fault. In this manner, what we have referred to as the 'paradigm case of intoxication' comes within the same broad category as our 'target cases'.

The comparison between our two jurisdictions allows us to highlight similarities and differences in approach between contrasting common law and civil law traditions, and to analyse how different legal foundations (as well as differences in contemporary approach) impact the application of prior fault rules. As we will discuss, the potential for prior fault analysis of our target cases raises unique problems for both systems, and the efforts of each system to engage with these problems (from contrasting doctrinal positions) provide a unique and valuable comparative insight. We structure this discussion across three sections. Section II provides further legal context, setting out in more detail how insanity and diminished responsibility rules are understood within our two primary jurisdictions, including the potential role for prior fault analysis. Following this, in section III, we explore how each jurisdiction engages with prior fault regarding our target cases; we unpack academic debates about the potential application (and/or exclusion) of prior fault for our target cases; and we draw comparative conclusions. Finally, in section IV, we discuss the challenge of comorbidity as a sub-set of cases which seem to overlap categories of paradigm intoxication and our target cases (ie, cases where D's capacity is impacted by a pre-existing mental disorder *and* another factor, most commonly drug intoxication).

II. Understanding the Law and Context

Prior fault rules do not operate in isolation but rather apply to existing offence and defence (-like) constructions. Thus, for example, where T1 prior fault leads to incapacity and/or delusions at T2, these effects are only relevant to the extent that they

[2] For a comparative analysis of these paradigm cases, see AE Goldberg and others, 'Prior-Fault Blame in England and Wales, Germany and the Netherlands' (2021) 8 *Journal of International and Comparative Law* 53.

provide reasonable doubt as to an offence element (eg, a *mens rea* requirement), or provide the basis for a potential defence (eg, capacity based, or of mistaken belief).[3] In each case, prior fault rules apply (at least potentially), to create a unique path to liability, regardless of D's lack of *mens rea* and/or otherwise available defence.

The relational nature of prior fault rules makes a clear understanding of their legal context essential, and that is our focus here (ie, before discussing prior fault rules directly in section III). We provide a brief explanation of insanity and diminished responsibility as they are understood in English and Dutch law. In each case, it is vital to understand the standard application of these rules in order to appreciate the potential differences created through prior fault analysis.

A. Defence of Insanity

Insanity represents a claim of irresponsibility; a claim that D's internal disorder and/or cognition – when committing potentially criminal harms – should excuse them from the standard application of criminal law rules. Where insanity is satisfied, D will be acquitted, meaning that no *punishment* will follow. However, a hospital order or safety measure is still an option if D satisfies the relevant criteria.

In England and Wales, and across much of the common law world, the law continues to follow a set of judicial pronouncements from 1843 (ie, the 'M'Naghten Rules').[4] The Rules apply where, at the time of the alleged offence, it is proven that D was suffering a defect of reason caused by a disease of the mind (understood simply as an internal cause); where this leads D either not to understand the nature or purpose of his actions, or not to understand their legal and moral wrongfulness.[5] If satisfied, the special verdict of 'not guilty by reason of insanity' will apply. The special verdict provides a qualified acquittal: D avoids liability, but the court is left with a series of disposal options, including compulsory treatment and/or supervision.[6]

Although typically referred to as a defence, the insanity rules provide for a unique *dual* diversionary function. Insanity can apply as a supervening defence in the standard way, where D has committed the elements of an offence and then appeals to insanity by way of exculpation. However, insanity can also apply where D has not committed an offence, where D's denial of *mens rea* (for example) relies on a delusional or other state that satisfies the insanity rules. Here, insanity is not exculpating D from an offence (ie, because there is no completed offence), but is

[3] JJ Child, 'Prior Fault: Blocking Defences or Constructing Crimes' in A Reed and M Bohlander (eds), *General Defences in Criminal Law* (Milton Park, Routledge, 2014).

[4] Emanating from debate in the House of Lords following the case of *M'Naghten* [1843] 10 Cl & Fin 200.

[5] See JJ Child and others, *Simester and Sullivan's Criminal Law* (Oxford, Hart Publishing, 2022) ch 19.2.

[6] Criminal Procedure (Insanity and Unfitness to Plead) Act 1991, s 5, as amended by the Domestic Violence, Crime and Victims Act 2004.

applying simply to divert D via the special verdict to a series of potentially restraining disposal options.[7]

Understanding the dual functionality of insanity rules is vitally important for the analysis of prior fault in the context of English law, though it has been unfortunately neglected within current debates. It is important because, if prior fault rules were to apply to insanity – creating a route to liability – the functions of insanity would provide two fundamentally different contexts for that application. Where insanity operates as a supervening defence, the question would be whether D's prior fault at T1 is sufficient to undermine D's claim to that defence: if D's prior fault were deemed sufficient, insanity will be disapplied as a defence, and D would be liable for the completed offence. In contrast, where D has *not* committed an offence and insanity rules operate simply as a diversion to the special verdict, the application of prior fault would be quite different. Here, simply blocking the application of insanity would be insufficient as a route to criminalisation: D has not committed all the elements of a crime, and so there is no default to liability. Rather, prior fault rules would have to apply *both* to block the application of insanity and to substitute for those offence elements missing at T2. The second part of this equation, which is not relevant to insanity as a defence, would require rules that demonstrate an equivalence of fault between D's conduct at T1 and those offence elements missing at T2 (ie, a unique, particularly difficult challenge for the law).

Dutch law provides a quite different substantive context. Within the civil tripartite structure of criminal liability, a staged analysis focuses on: (i) the elements of the offence, as defined in statute and case law; (ii) the wrongfulness of the conduct, which may be negated by a justification; and (iii) the blameworthiness or guilt of the actor, which may be denied by an excuse.[8] Although it is *possible* for insanity-like circumstances to lead to a denial of *mens rea*, the extremely high bar for this (bordering on unconsciousness) makes it highly unlikely; and, subsequently, it is not discussed in the practice or academic literature.[9] Rather, the discussion and application of insanity rules are focused on the final limb alone, the requirement of blameworthiness.

In the Netherlands, the doctrine equivalent to insanity – codified in article 39 of the Dutch Criminal Code – is '*ontoerekeningsvatbaarheid*', which translates literally to 'no susceptibility for attribution' and is commonly referred to as 'non-accountability' or 'non-responsibility' in international literature. Attribution has a broader meaning within criminal law in light of the question of whether an offence can be attributed to the defendant, also underlining the legal competence in

[7] For discussion and critique of this second function, see C Hogg and JJ Child, 'Not Guilty by Reasons Other than Insanity' in AP Simester (ed) *Modern Criminal Law* (Oxford, Hart Publishing, 2024) 155.

[8] J Keiler, 'Actus Reus and Mens Rea' in J Keiler and D Roef (eds), *Comparative Concepts of Criminal Law* (Cambridge, Intersentia, 2019) 115.

[9] It is accepted in case law that a mental disorder can negate intent if the defendant 'at the time of the act lacked any understanding in the range of his conduct and the possible consequences': see Supreme Court of the Netherlands 09-06-1981, *NJ* 1983, 412.

deciding on the matter in relation to behavioural experts' advice.[10] The doctrine of insanity is embedded in criminal procedure and is therefore not called a defence.[11] In this inquisitorial system, 'insanity' – or the lack of criminal responsibility/culpability due to a mental disorder – is seen as an excuse negating the blameworthiness of the offence. It is an issue that procedurally only arises after an offence has been established, including its *mens rea* elements.

The framework of the non-accountability excuse consists of the presence of a mental disorder, a causal connection between this mental disorder and the offence, and a test of 'attribution', in which all factors together are considered by the judge, who determines whether non-accountability applies.[12] Interestingly, article 39 lacks a specific test as to this final criterion, the attribution test, and does not specify which capacities should be impaired. In fact, until recently, no consensus has been reached on the subject by the legislator nor in jurisprudence. Yet last year, in the high-profile case of a triple murderer, a criterion was formulated. The defendant was considered non-responsible by behavioural experts as his actions were based on delusional beliefs, but this advice was not followed by two separate courts (in first instance and upon appeal). In upholding these decisions, the Supreme Court formulated a specific test for insanity for the first time, which includes a volitional prong in addition to a cognitive requirement similar to the M'Naghten rules: 'the defendant's inability to understand that his acts were legally wrongful or his inability to act in accordance with his understanding of the legal wrongfulness'.[13] In the Dutch insanity structure, prior fault functions as a tool to deny the 'attribution' part of the excuse. While the disorder (induced by substance use) would still have to be established and could have influenced the offending behaviour as described in the test, the judge may decide that despite meeting the test, the offence is still attributed to the defendant due to his fault in bringing about the disorder.

Two important comparative observations may be highlighted at this stage, relating to the function and scope of insanity rules (relevant to the potential for prior fault analysis). First, in terms of function, the Dutch insanity rules are not split across the dual functions that we observed in their English equivalent. Thus, because the Dutch insanity rules do not apply as a diversion where no offence is committed, the potential for prior fault need not engage with *mens rea* (or other offence element) equivalence. Rather, the potential application of prior fault within

[10] As the wording suggests, in establishing psycholegal concepts like disorder, responsibility and dangerousness the court relies on the advice of behavioural experts, but is not bound to it. In general, however, the advice is followed, although exceptions to this custom tend to receive more attention. See MJF van der Wolf and others, 'The Dutch perspective' in MJF van der Wolf (ed), *Safeguarding the Quality of Forensic Assessment in Sentencing: A Review Across Western Nations* (New York, Routledge, 2022).

[11] MJF van der Wolf and HJC van Marle, 'Legal Approaches to Criminal Responsibility of Mentally Disordered Offenders in Europe' in K Goethals (ed), *Forensic Psychiatry and Psychology in Europe. A Cross-Border Study Guide* (Cham, Springer International Publishing, 2018) 31.

[12] G Meynen, *Legal Insanity: Explorations in Psychiatry, Law, and Ethics* (Dordrecht, Springer, 2016) ch 2.

[13] Supreme Court of the Netherlands 07-10-2023, ECLI:NL:HR:2023:1295.

Dutch law focuses on D's disorder as an excusatory claim alone: the question becomes whether evidence of prior fault at T1 is sufficient to displace D's claim of excuse. Whilst this helps narrow the potential focus of prior fault analysis in Dutch law, the second observation on scope rather pulls in the opposite direction. This is the fact that insanity, in Dutch law, applies (at least potentially) to all forms of mental disorder at the time of offending, including those directly caused by voluntary intoxication. Thus, within this broader conception of insanity, it is more difficult for prior fault rules to distinguish our target cases for special treatment from the paradigm cases of intoxication (ie, should this be deemed necessary). We return to this issue in the sections that follow.

B. Diminished Responsibility

Diminished responsibility applies in a similar way to insanity but represents a claim of only *partial* irresponsibility. D remains criminally liable, within both systems, but with a reduced sentence.

Diminished responsibility operates as a partial substantive defence in English law, applicable only to the offence of murder.[14] Thus, where D commits murder, if he also satisfies the elements of diminished responsibility when doing so, D's liability will be reduced to manslaughter (and, crucially, D will thereby avoid the mandatory life sentence for murder). Diminished responsibility requires D to demonstrate an abnormality of mental functioning, arising from a recognised medical condition; leading to a substantial impairment of D's ability to understand the nature of his conduct, form a rational judgement, or exercise self-control; and, additionally, the abnormality must provide an explanation (or cause) for the killing.

Unlike the insanity rules, the English diminished responsibility defence operates a single exculpatory function. In all cases, D will have committed the offence of murder at T2, so the potential application of prior fault will be as a block to the partial defence only. This requires us to consider the appropriateness of such blocking, in both normative and practical terms, but it does not require the reconstruction of missing offence elements.

The role of diminished responsibility in English law, as a substantive partial defence, is largely a product of the mandatory life sentence for murder. Essentially, where D's sentence for murder is fixed by law, any mitigation must be translated into a partial defence. This is why we do not see diminished responsibility applying as a general defence across other crimes: similar levels of mitigation may be expected at sentencing, but these can be left to the sentencing court and need not be re-located to the liability stage.[15]

[14] Homicide Act 1957, s 2 (as amended).

[15] The anomaly here is the lack of partial defence for other fixed-term offences, where (as with murder) there is a lack of discretion at sentencing. Murder may still be a special case, however, with fixed-life sentences. For discussion of prior fault considerations at sentencing, see ch 3 of this collection.

In the Netherlands, diminished responsibility applies more broadly as a spectrum measure of responsibility related to the practice of sentencing. Unlike the narrow English equivalent, diminished responsibility in Dutch law aims to assess and assign degrees of responsibility and is applicable to all offences. There is a tradition of viewing diminished responsibility due to a mental disorder[16] as part of a dimensional, or rather gradual, concept of criminal responsibility with non-responsibility (equal to legal insanity) as its outer manifestation. The Dutch legislator chose not to mention diminished responsibility in the criminal code, but in practice, it plays an important role.

The gradual approach to responsibility may have more 'face validity' than a dichotomous view, but automatically raises problems in the reliability of assessment. Indeed, the Dutch experience has shown that even something like 'percentage responsibility' can be developed in practice, leading to far too many gradations than can scientifically be distinguished.[17] For a decade, the debate has focused on whether to accept five or three gradations of responsibility. The guideline from the Dutch Association of Psychiatry in 2013 seemed to suggest that five gradations (including severely diminished and somewhat diminished responsible) cannot reliably be distinguished by behavioural experts and thus should not be used.[18] However, the succeeding guideline from 2024 leaves more room for using five gradations, as a lack of nuance was felt by both forensic experts and judges, possibly leading to harsher sentencing.[19] In diagnostic terms, non-responsibility is generally reserved for cases of psychotic motivations, while many personality-disordered or sexually deviant offenders are considered to be (somewhat) diminished responsible.[20] Additionally, as we discuss further in section III, in cases of psychosis where the threshold for non-responsibility is not reached (possibly due to prior fault), diminished responsibility offers an 'escape' from complete liability.

Originally, both 'no punishment without guilt/culpability' and 'punishment to the extent of guilt' were considered principles of Dutch criminal law. However, after a ruling of the Supreme Court in 1957, the latter principle was not adopted as binding for legal practice.[21] Rather, forward-looking assessments of dangerousness were recognised as factors to be explicitly balanced against and/or alongside assessments of responsibility. It has meant that in the case of a diminished responsible dangerous criminal, the prison sentence could be extended on grounds of

[16] In a way the juvenile criminal justice rules, with lower sentences for non-adults, can also be seen as derived from a broader concept of diminished responsibility, with the non-liable under aged being viewed as non-responsible.

[17] See M Zeegers, 'Diminished Responsibility. A Logical, Workable and Essential Concept' (1981) *International Journal of Law and Psychiatry* 433.

[18] NVvP (2013), *Richtlijn psychiatrisch onderzoek en rapportage in strafzaken*. Utrecht: NVvP.

[19] Federatie Medisch Specialisten/NVvP (2024), *Psychiatrisch onderzoek en rapportage in strafzaken*. Utrecht: NVvP.

[20] Van der Wolf (n 10).

[21] Supreme Court of the Netherlands 10-09-1957, ECLI:NL:HR:1957:2.

public protection, in addition to a safety measure (tbs-order: the 'entrustment' measure). Diminished responsibility was the pivotal concept in the coming about of the tbs-order in 1928, with the safety measure originally compensating for what a mitigated sentence could not do for public protection in a case of someone who had apparently committed an offence under the influence of a mental disorder.

In short, diminished responsibility is related to sentencing both as an optional, albeit not obligatory, mitigating factor in determining the levels of the sentence and a relevant, albeit not required, factor in imposing a tbs-order. Even though it is not considered something equivalent to a defence, there is, however, potential for prior fault reasoning here to weigh against the diminishing of responsibility, but this would practically hinder the availability of the tbs-order in case of dangerousness. Despite the substantive differences between the jurisdictions then, it appears that there is perhaps more common ground than may first appear, with the role of prior fault in diminished responsibility cases weighing as one of many factors in the calculation of D's appropriate sentence.

III. Prior Fault and Mental Disorder

In this section we discuss the current law and reform debates concerning the application of prior fault rules to insanity and diminished responsibility. We are concerned with cases (ie, our 'target cases') where D's incapacity at T2 is caused by a mental disorder, itself caused or exacerbated by D's blameworthy conduct at T1.

A. England and Wales

English law explicitly rejects the application of prior fault to insanity, whether applied as a defence or diversion, as well as to the partial defence of diminished responsibility.[22] As a result, a strict distinction is drawn between states of voluntary intoxication and/or *externally* caused states of automatism, where prior fault analysis is permitted,[23] and *internally* rooted states of insanity or diminished responsibility that apply to our target cases.[24] The exclusion of prior fault was clearly articulated in the case of *Davies* in 1881,[25] quoted with approval in the seminal case of *Beard* in 1920:[26]

> … drunkenness is one thing and the diseases to which drunkenness leads are different things; and if a man by drunkenness brings on a state of disease which causes such a

[22] Child (n 3).

[23] Automatism is discussed in ch 8 of this collection.

[24] On the internal/external distinction, and the problems this creates in practice, see Child (n 5) ch 18.4.

[25] *Davies* (1881) 14 Cox CC 563.

[26] *Beard* [1990] AC 479, 500.

> degree of madness, even for a time, which would have relieved him from responsibility if it had been caused in any other way, then he will not be criminally responsible.

Indeed, speaking categorically, the House of Lords in *Beard* state that 'the law takes no notice of the cause of insanity'.[27] Thus, regardless of D's blameworthy conduct at T1, in cases where the insanity rules apply at T2, D will be diverted to the special verdict of 'not guilty by reason of insanity'; and in cases where diminished responsibility applies, D's liability will be reduced from murder to manslaughter.

Despite the longstanding exclusion of prior fault rules, however, much lies behind these headlines. In the sub-sections that follow, we explore the principal areas of debate regarding the potential application of prior fault analysis to insanity and diminished responsibility within our target cases, focusing on issues of public policy, culpability, and consistency. Our task here is twofold. We are concerned with arguments as to the potential *future* application of such rules and whether this would be a positive development for the law. But we are also concerned with the *present* law and how the current exclusion of prior fault is understood and applied by the courts in practice. The picture that emerges is one of a legal system struggling for coherence in the face of legal, normative, and scientific uncertainties.

i. Public Policy

We begin with issues of public policy (ie, concerns about public safety and dangerousness) in recognition of the central role played by such concerns within the wider prior fault debate. Particularly in relation to voluntary intoxication, the willingness of courts (and commentators) to prioritise a perception of public policy ahead of 'strict logic' has been truly striking;[28] with repeated assurance that 'no wrong is done' when labelling and punishing a defendant for an offence the elements of which she has not (due to absent *mens rea*) completed;[29] and that this is warranted by 'criminal recklessness',[30] and by intuitions of 'order' and 'justice'.[31] It becomes vital to ask, therefore, what role these same policy concerns have played in debates about prior fault insanity and diminished responsibility regarding our target case group.

In answering this question, it is clear that the internal cause conditions relevant to insanity and diminished responsibility are not uniquely immune from intuitions about prior fault and dangerousness. Quite the opposite, in fact. In the context of insanity and mental disorder, criminal law rules have developed to explicitly engage with forward-looking questions of dangerousness. However, rather than

[27] ibid.
[28] *DPP v Majewski* [1977] AC 443, 482.
[29] ibid 474.
[30] ibid 475.
[31] On the problematic appeal to intuition, see also M Shain and G Higgins, 'The Intoxication Defence and Theories of Criminal Liability: A Praxeological Approach' (1997) 24 *Contemporary Drug Problems* 731.

seeking to identify a sub-set of cases involving prior fault (ie, such as our target cases), here we mean the general application of the special insanity verdict. The special verdict provides for an acquittal, but one that can give rise to a significant restriction of liberty in the interests of public policy. As stated in *Bratty*:[32]

> Suppose a crime is committed by a man in a state of automatism or clouded consciousness due to a recurrent disease of the mind. Such an act is no doubt involuntary, but it does not give rise to an unqualified acquittal, for that would mean that he would be left at large to do it again. The only proper verdict is one which ensures that the person who suffers from the disease is kept secure in a hospital so as not to be a danger to himself or others. That is, a verdict of guilty but insane.

The role for insanity rules here in 'clutching' and restraining a potentially dangerous person – explicitly focused on issues of public policy – has been consistently reiterated by the appellate courts, including within the now leading case of *Sullivan*.[33]

The application of insanity and subsequent diversion of D to the special verdict have clear implications for the prior fault debate. The special verdict provides the court with powers of compulsory restraint, and so public policy aims can be achieved without recourse to prior fault criminalisation; just as liability for manslaughter (in the context of diminished responsibility) retains sentencing powers. And so, arguably, public policy becomes less of a concern for internally caused conditions, and debate moves to the related but distinct issue of culpability.

ii. Culpability

The question of culpability is separate from issues of public policy, asking whether – although D satisfied the elements of insanity or diminished responsibility – would it be *fair* to use her prior fault at T1 to create a route to liability. Historically, culpability claims have been constructed upon the crude (mis)association of madness and badness; on the premise that mental disorder represented (or was punishment for) moral failing.[34] Demonisation of this kind, of course, has no place within an informed modern debate. But the opposite premise – that mental disorder is *always* absent of fault – may also be resisted. Certainly, where D intentionally (or even recklessly) fails to take medication, knowing that this is likely to lead to incapacity and potential harms at T2, it seems plausible to blame D where those harms are caused in fact. In doing so, D is not blamed for causing harms involuntarily (ie, singling him out for punishment because of his disorder), but rather for

[32] *Bratty v Attorney-General for Northern Ireland* [1963] AC 386, 410.

[33] *Sullivan* [1984] AC 156: 'The purpose of the legislation relating to the defence of insanity, ever since its origin in 1800, has been to protect society against recurrence of the dangerous conduct' per Lord Diplock at 182. On the concept of 'clutching', see J Feinberg, *Doing and Deserving: Essays in the Theory of Responsibility* (Princeton, Princeton University Press, 1970) ch 10.

[34] See discussion in, eg, EW Mitchell, *Self-Made Madness: Rethinking Illness and Criminal Responsibility* (Milton Park, Routledge, 2003) 20–23; see also A Loughnan, *Manifest Madness: Mental Incapacity in the Criminal Law* (Oxford, Oxford University Press, 2012).

his choice to avoid treatment at T1 leading to those harms. Mitchell refers to this phenomenon – blaming D across T1 and T2 – in terms of meta-responsibility[35] and provides some useful clinical insights into its appearance in practice.[36] Where this is most forceful, it challenges the appropriateness of the special verdict, which may provide public protection, but may be insufficient in that it fails to *blame* D.

Claims of culpability here – and the potential move to criminalisation – have not been entirely lost on the courts, even whilst maintaining the headline exclusion of prior fault. We see this, for example, where the potential for prior fault insanity is accepted by lower courts, only to be overturned on appeal.[37] Such cases, it should be acknowledged, are extremely rare. But much more common, in the context of co-morbidity, are examples of courts emphasising prior fault blame; and then foregrounding intoxication causes (which provide a route to liability) and backgrounding alternative causes based on mental disorder (which, of course, do not currently provide a route to liability).[38] Indeed, where alternative routes to prior fault criminalisation are not available,[39] or may be contested,[40] we see the appeal courts increasingly willing to criticise the exclusion of prior fault insanity (and to marginalise it through the expansion of intoxication rules[41]). As Hughes LJ stated in *Harris*, for example, having concluded that the intoxication rules were not applicable:[42]

> We agree that there is scope for the argument that an illness caused by his own fault ought as a matter of policy to be treated in the same way as is drunkenness at the time of the offence … But in the present state of the law, *Majewski* applies to offences committed by persons who are then voluntarily intoxicated but not to those who are suffering mental illness.

Beyond this, in the context of sentencing, where judges have considerably more discretion, we see evidence that blameworthy conduct at T1 leading to mental disorder is likely to have an aggravating effect.[43]

[35] Mitchell (n 34).

[36] ibid ch 3.

[37] See, eg, the US case *State v McCleary* No. CR49471 (Ohio 1979); No. CR42116 (Ohio Ct. App. 1980): D had been taking medication for schizophrenia for 11 years, but stopped doing so days before the incident. The lower court sought to distinguish 'insanity and insanity that can be controlled' (at 44). And, more recently, *State v Eager*, 398 P.3d 756 (Haw. 2017), discussed in C Caveney and C Cooper-Lehki, 'Improper Application of Self-Induced Intoxication' (2019) 47 *Legal Digest* 105.

[38] See, eg, *Oye* [2013] EWCA Crim 1725. Discussed in JJ Child and GR Sullivan, 'When Does the Insanity Defence Apply? Some Recent Cases' (2014) *Crim LR* 787. We see a similar approach being taken across common law jurisdictions: see, eg, recent Australian cases *Stefanski v Western Australia* [2022] WASCA 5; *R v Scott (No 3)* [2021] NSWSC 164.

[39] See, eg, *Harris* [2013] EWCA Crim 223.

[40] See, eg, *Taj* [2018] EWCA Crim 1743.

[41] Discussed in JJ Child, H Crombag and GR Sullivan, 'Defending the Delusional, the Irrational, and the Dangerous' [2020] *Criminal LR* 306.

[42] *Harris* [2013] EWCA Crim 223, [25].

[43] See N Sinclair-House, JJ Child and H Crombag, 'Addiction Is a Brain Disease, and It Doesn't Matter: Prior Choice in Drug Use Blocks Leniency in Criminal Punishment' (2019) 26 *Psychology, Public Policy, and Law* 36.

Culpability claims have also triggered academic and reform debates, suggesting the recognition of prior fault insanity as a route to liability alongside intoxication and prior fault automatism. However, it is notable that such debates have not progressed much beyond familiar appeals to intuition, highlighting compelling examples rather than setting out a principled basis for criminalisation. Mitchell's case for prior fault criminalisation, for example, focuses on medication non-compliance only.[44] In this context, he distinguishes T1 blame in terms of 'consensual meta-responsibility', where D avoids medication in pursuit of other ends (eg, avoiding unwanted side-effects), and 'purposive meta-responsibility', where D avoids medication in preference for a disordered state.[45] He argues that each may warrant criminalisation, though he does little to explain the move from meta-responsibility to crime, beyond a simple analogy to intoxication rules and appeals to 'common sense notions of justice'.[46] Indeed, Mitchell's accompanying empirical work – which does not establish a clear preference for criminalisation in such cases – rather exposes the omission.[47]

A similar approach is adopted by the Law Commission when discussing positively the potential expansion of prior fault to insanity in our target cases. The following example is illustrative:[48]

> N has a recognised medical condition and has a total loss of capacity but that total loss of capacity is caused by his own culpable fault. The only significant difference between N and L (who has unreasonably ingested a substance when he was aware, or ought to have been aware, of the likely consequences) is that N failed to do something he ought to have done and L did something he ought not to have done. *We believe that the culpability is the same in this context and therefore the outcome should be the same.*

Like Mitchell, rather than making the case for criminalisation directly, the Commission constructs an indirect claim through broad allusions to the intoxication rules.

The issue here is not simply the lack of detail in the analysis of D's culpability at T1, but – perhaps more importantly – it is also the lack of engagement with the two functions played by insanity rules. As we set out in section II, the application of insanity rules (in English law) provides both for: (i) a supervening defence where D has committed a crime; as well as (ii) a diversion to the special verdict where D lacks *mens rea* or voluntariness due to an internal condition.[49] This distinction should be foundational for any culpability claim in favour of criminalisation. This is because, where prior fault is employed as a route to criminalisation within the second category at least, it is not enough to show T1 blame; it is necessary to demonstrate that D's fault at T1 was *equivalent* to the

[44] Mitchell (n 34).
[45] ibid ch 3.
[46] ibid 49. See also p 30, for a general appeal to 'common sense'.
[47] ibid Part II: Mock Juror Study.
[48] Law Commission, *Insanity and Automatism* (Discussion Paper, 2013) [6.77], emphasis added.
[49] Diminished responsibility falls within this second functional category only.

missing offence elements at T2. In this regard, we do not believe that the case for culpability equivalence has been convincingly made in the context of intoxication or prior fault automatism,[50] and so – by extension – the simple analogy to those rules cannot provide for equivalence here. Specific case examples may demonstrate blameworthiness, and perhaps to the point that criminalisation becomes appropriate, but this is not the same as principled equivalence: it does not demonstrate that D's T1 culpability is of the same 'weight' as that missing at T2 (ie, foresight of risks in action vs foresight of potential future harms); nor that it is similarly 'connected' to the harms caused at T2 (ie, as identified specific risks vs unidentified non-specific risks).[51]

It is also important to acknowledge concerns about assessments of culpability in the context of insanity (and by extension, other internal cause conditions). In order to establish prior fault in our target cases, it is necessary to scrutinise the *causal route* of D's internal condition at T1. This means we must distinguish blameworthy causes of internal conditions from non-blameworthy causes, as we do (however imperfectly) when distinguishing externally relevant factors such as voluntary/involuntary intoxication and dangerous/non-dangerous drugs. It is here that we encounter a dual critique, questioning the moral appropriateness of scrutinising the causal routes of mental disorder in general (ie, a dignity critique), as well as the clinical uncertainty of such causal route distinctions in practice (ie, a scientific critique).[52] Criticisms of this kind are most prevalent within addiction debates, where questions of fault in becoming addicted can be drawn back over years and are likely to be complicated with factors such as additional co-morbid mental disorders.[53] However, even with the most 'simple' cases of medication non-compliance, important questions arise about the many and varied factors that may contribute to such non-compliance, only some of which may be legitimate targets of blame.[54] This is not to say that certain *specific* cases may not be identified where

[50] JJ Child, HS Crombag and R Fortson, 'Understanding the "Fault" in Prior-Fault Intoxication' in A Reed and M Bohlander (eds), *Fault in Criminal Law* (Milton Park, Routledge, 2022) 86.

[51] Unlike in the context of intoxication, it is notable that we do not see academics or others engaged in the kind of work necessary to provide a basis for equivalence. See, eg, G Yaffe's work on how culpability equivalence might be established for intoxication. G Yaffe, 'Intoxication, Recklessness and Negligence' (2012) 9 *Ohio State Journal of Criminal Law* 545.

[52] See, eg, M Wondemaghen, 'Evaluating Predominant Causes of Insanity in Cases of Drug-Induced Psychoses' (2015) 14 *International Journal of Forensic Mental Health* 76; H Crombag and others, 'Drunk, Dangerous and Delusional: How Legal Concept-Creep Risks Overcriminalization' (2020) 115 *Addiction* 2200 (including responses).

[53] See, eg, N Heather and G Segal, *Addiction and Choice* (Oxford, Oxford University Press, 2017); and a useful discussion of causal routes and disposition to addiction in S Nemerson, 'Alcoholism, Intoxication and the Criminal Law' (1988) 10 *Cardozo LR* 393, 411–419. See also ch 5 of this collection.

[54] See, eg, R Mackay and D Hughes, 'Insanity and Blaming the Mentally Ill: A Critique of the Prior Fault Principle in the Law Commission's Discussion Paper' (2022) *Crim LR* 21, 29–32; R Mackay, 'The Insanity Defence in English Law' in R Mackay and W Brookbanks (eds) *The Insanity Defence* (Oxford, Oxford University Press, 2022) 37; and A Loughnan and N Wake, 'Of Blurred Boundaries and Prior Fault: Insanity, Automatism and Intoxication' in A Reed and M Bohlander (eds), *General Defences in Criminal Law* (Milton Park, Routledge, 2014) 113, 127–132.

T1 blame is tolerably clear,[55] but we should be mindful of a change that is likely – outside of isolated examples – to engage courts with significant factual and scientific uncertainty, with a risk of inappropriate criminalisation.

iii. Consistency and Coherence

Within more recent academic and policy debates, arguments in favour of expanding prior fault rules to insanity and diminished responsibility for our target cases have tended to focus on issues of consistency and coherence. The argument here is enticingly simple: if we accept the application of prior fault rules for intoxication and automatism, then it is incoherent to exclude their similar application to insanity cases; and removing this exclusion (creating consistency) will also remove the need to distinguish internal and external causes for the purpose of prior fault assessments. It is an argument that features prominently in the Law Commission's most recent project on insanity and automatism, where the Commission sets out proposals for extending prior fault rules to insanity,[56] as well as within associated academic writing.[57]

But are arguments of this kind enough? Claims of current *incoherence* may be effective in burden shifting, asking those who support the exclusion of prior fault to justify that position, but the special features of internal cause conditions discussed above (ie, in terms of public policy and culpability) provide a coherent response. Arguments concerning *inconsistency* are perhaps more effective. It is certainly true that current inconsistencies create a scientifically artificial distinction between internal and external cause conditions.[58] However, proposals for prior fault insanity regarding our target case group do not represent a panacea, even in terms of consistency. Prior fault insanity is still likely to operate with different substantive requirements from other prior fault rules (eg, as we see currently between prior fault intoxication and prior fault automatism), requiring distinction;[59] and, as discussed above, the application of prior fault insanity will require new (and perhaps even *more* problematic) points of distinction to be made in the assessment of D's causal route to insanity. Indeed, as Mackay and Hughes rightly observe,[60] the pursuit of consistency could also take us in the other direction, abolishing prior fault rules across cause conditions. Abolition of prior fault rules would also

[55] A point emphasised in Mitchell (n 34) 57–62, and accepted in principle by the Law Commission when proposing the expansion of prior fault.

[56] Law Commission, *Insanity and Automatism* (Discussion Paper, 2013) ch 6.

[57] See, eg, D Ormerod and M Dsouza, 'Reforming the Insanity Defence in England and Wales' in R Mackay and W Brookbanks (eds), *The Insanity Defence* (Oxford, Oxford University Press, 2022) 45.

[58] A central and convincing message within Law Commission, Insanity and Automatism (Discussion Paper, 2013).

[59] The Law Commission seek to limit inconsistencies in its proposals, within a broader 'recognised medical condition' set of rules, but it will still be necessary to distinguish intoxication cases, for example. See, Law Commission, *Insanity and Automatism* (Discussion Paper, 2013) ch 6.

[60] Mackay and Hughes (n 54).

remove the need to distinguish internal and external causes for the purpose of fault attribution and would do so without introducing new points of scrutiny in the causal route to insanity.

B. The Netherlands

The headline position in Dutch law begins from the opposite premise to English law, allowing for the prior fault analysis of insanity cases. The position here is not the product of a specific debate, however, of the kind discussed in relation to the bespoke insanity provisions in English law. Rather, because prior fault rules apply in general to the assessment of wrongfulness (justifications)[61] and blameworthiness (excuses) in the Dutch system, they are applied (effectively in default) to insanity as a subset of cases raising issues of blameworthiness and potential irresponsibility.

The substance of the English debate, however – engaging unique concerns for public policy, culpability, and coherence in the context of our target cases – are not absent from the Dutch system. It is clear that our target cases (ie, T1 conduct which causes or exacerbates an existing mental disorder) are also recognised, at least tacitly, as a case apart from paradigms of intoxication. Indeed, it is here that our comparison may be most enlightening, to see how a system that embraces the potential for prior fault insanity (defined broadly to include our target cases alongside intoxication causes) grapples with the same range of legal, factual, and scientific challenges.

We explore this question across two sub-sections. The first explores the current interpretation and application of prior fault in Dutch law, illustrating how prior fault as a generalised concept has been skewed in practice by its focus on intoxication cases. Following this, in the second sub-section, we focus on our sub-set target cases. The question here is whether, given the skewing of prior fault analysis towards the paradigm of intoxication, any doctrinal flexibility is maintained to deal with the particular challenges of prior-fault insanity based on causes other than intoxication.

i. Prior Fault Insanity (Including Intoxication Causes)

In Dutch criminal law, the concept of prior fault is referred to as '*culpa-in-causa*'. *Culpa-in-causa* can be defined as the exclusion of an a priori applicable justification or excuse, normally negating liability, because the defendant themself culpably contributed to the creation of these circumstances.[62] Prior fault insanity

[61] In relation to justifications, prior fault is mainly discussed in relation to self-defence, most commonly because of a 'sought confrontation'.

[62] Goldberg and others (n 2).

is therefore only a factual subset of a more general legal rule, with potential application to any denial of responsibility or blameworthiness. Such denial requires that the state of mind of D at T2, when committing the offence, can be seen as psychopathology or mental disorder. As in the legal context the concept of mental disorder is interpreted very broadly, including, for example, disturbances in mental functioning (possibly as an effect of intoxication), this is not that big of a hurdle.[63] Simple drunkenness, however, is explicitly excluded by the legislator – and in other aspects of criminal law considered to be more of an aggravating than a mitigating factor in terms of responsibility and sentencing.[64]

Despite the *potential* general application of the culpa-in-causa doctrine to the broad insanity/responsibility concept, it is notable that the doctrine has developed in almost exclusive reference to the effects of intoxication. In the jurisprudence of the Supreme Court, two factors seem to be central in assessing culpa-in-causa. These are: (i) voluntariness and awareness of ingestion of the substance on the one hand; and (ii) foreseeability of the consequences of such ingestion on the other.[65] Voluntariness and awareness of ingestion are generally assumed, unless there are indications to the contrary. For example, cases in which a person is forced to take a drug or consumes a drink that is unknowingly spiked. The second factor of foreseeability was, therefore, originally the most important criterion, according to the Supreme Court. In the so-called '*Culpa-in-Causa*' judgment from 1981, D stabbed his grandmother whilst under the influence of cocaine.[66] Despite possible mental disturbances, the Court of Appeal considered that the offence should be attributed to the defendant, and the insanity defence denied, because the mental disorder was self-induced. D was familiar with using cocaine and had previously experienced hallucinations as a result. It was also stressed that it was a fact of common knowledge that heroin and cocaine, when used, could affect moral reasoning. Finally, when using cocaine, D had previously had violent fantasies of bank robberies and firearms. Therefore, the Court concluded that the defendant:[67]

> (…) must be deemed to have had such an insight into the dangers of cocaine and its effect on his mental faculties that it must be judged that the pathological disturbance of his mental faculties – occurring at the time of the commission of the proven offence – should be blamed on the defendant, so that the acts committed in that state must be attributed to the defendant.

[63] See MJF van der Wolf and J Bijlsma, 'Het Stoornisbegrip in het Strafrecht en de Pro Justitia Rapportage' in HJC van Marle and others (eds), *Gedragskundige Rapportage in het Strafrecht* (Deventer, Kluwer, 2022) 263: more difficult is qualifying for the additional cognitive and volitional impairment-criteria for non-responsibility.

[64] See RJ Verkes and E Fechner, 'Middelengebruik, Verslaving en Culpa in Causa' in HJC van Marle and others (eds), *Gedragskundige Rapportage in het Strafrecht* (Deventer, Kluwer, 2022) 379.

[65] See, eg, AE Goldberg, 'Foreseeability and Prior Fault: Examining the Assessment Framework for Intoxication, Blame and Criminal Responsibility' (2024) 29 *Bialystok Legal Studies* 69.

[66] Supreme Court of the Netherlands 10-06-1981, ECLI:NL:HR:1981:AC0902.

[67] Court of Appeal Amsterdam 29-12-1980, referred to in the Supreme Court judgment (ibid).

The Supreme Court upheld the judgment. After all, from an individual foreseeability point of view, D had previously experienced hallucinations and violent fantasies. Moreover, cocaine is clearly identified by the government as risky and harmful by unequivocally prohibiting its possession, distribution and use. In the literature, foreseeability – in the sense of knowing the possible consequences from individual experience – is generally considered to be the most relevant criterion for prior fault.[68]

The position of the law has advanced further in a more recent landmark case, the so-called '*Cannabis Psychosis*' judgment. Here, D was acting from an acute psychosis induced by the use of cannabis. The court held that a psychotic state was not a commonly known or frequently seen consequence of cannabis use. Also, unlike D in the Culpa-in-Causa judgment, the defendant here had no previous negative experiences with cannabis of his own. Nevertheless, according to the Court of Appeal, D knew that the use of that intoxicant has an effect on the general mental state, and, therefore, D could have known that its use would be risky and that this drug could affect functioning in such a way that risky behaviour could arise from it.

The Supreme Court considered that this reasoning was not incomprehensible: prior fault rules should still apply, despite the fact that a psychotic state is generally a rare and unforeseen consequence of cannabis use.[69] Hence, in this case, foreseeability seems to be interpreted in a much broader and more objective sense. After all, the defendant does not have to foresee any concrete negative consequences, and it is sufficient to assume that one could (read: should) have known that cannabis has an effect on the general psychological state. The fact that cannabis use is legally tolerated in the Netherlands – at least not unequivocally prohibited – further completes the shift from the prior Culpa-in-Causa judgment. As a result, the Cannabis Psychosis judgment seems to set a low requirement for the attribution of prior fault: voluntary and fully aware consumption of a substance seems sufficient, as there is no further need for concrete foreseeability of risky behaviour. As a result, substance use seems to be seen as a form of abstract endangerment that is sufficiently culpable to constitute prior fault.[70]

It is perhaps also understandable from a public policy perspective that all substance use is, in principle, a form of prior fault. In the annotation of the Culpa-in-Causa case, Van Veen argues that substance use should not become 'a free pass' – or an a priori excuse – to commit criminal acts.[71] This fear may be aimed at the possible inclusion within insanity of cases of 'prior intent', where D becomes intoxicated *in order to* commit crimes in a disordered state. When focused on avoiding precedent, courts seem to prefer communication towards the general

[68] See, eg, J Bijlsma, 'Drank, Drugs en Culpa. Zelfintoxicatie en Culpa in Causa: Pleidooi voor een Voorzienbaarheidseis' (2011) 44 *Delikt & Delinkwent* 654.

[69] Supreme Court of the Netherlands 12-02-2008, ECLI:NL:HR:2008:BC3797.

[70] See AE Goldberg, *Blaming the Addicted Brain: Building Bridges between Criminal Law and Neuroscientific Perspectives on Addiction* (Den Haag, Eleven International Publishing, 2022) 48.

[71] Supreme Court of the Netherlands 09-06-1981, *NJ* 412 (annot. Th. W. van Veen).

public over the culpability of the individual in finding responsibility for (potentially unwanted, but harmful) consequences of voluntary substance use. In this communication of general interests, they emphasise the risks of substance use and provide restoration of damages done to victims and society through attributing accountability. Finally, from a public policy perspective, considering all voluntary substance use to be sufficient for prior fault is relatively easy to apply, representing an efficient and pragmatic approach for the judiciary. This is generally valued in the Netherlands and also seems to underlie the existence of common objective approaches to establishing *mens rea* elements.[72]

This interest in communicating the harms of substance use and thus prior fault responsibility to the general public, is supported by research on legal decision-making in cases of intoxication. A study demonstrated that courts mainly deviate from the behavioural experts' advice on non-responsibility in cases of severe offences, often on grounds of intoxication, while in cases of severe offences, experts already tend to advise a higher degree of responsibility.[73] Arguably, the limitations of behavioural science to reliably assess the causal effects of substance use in symptomatology, involving criminal acts in an individual case, allow for and warrant the shift to a more normative approach. These limitations become apparent through increased disagreement among behavioural experts' opinions on insanity in cases of substance use, both in adversarial and inquisitorial systems.[74] A famous Dutch homicide case related to possible side effects of (withdrawal from) prescribed psychopharmacological drugs led to a record of six deviating expert opinions.[75]

In effect, the approach of the courts has been to simplify the assessment of prior fault, looking for readily identifiable factual markers (such as voluntary drug taking) and eschewing more fine-grained points of scientific distinction. This is understandable for the policy reasons already acknowledged, but it is much less clear that it is *fair*. The Supreme Court jurisprudence above is concerned with the relatively straightforward situation of the assessment of non-responsibility in the case of an indirect effect of drug use on crime through inducing or aggravating psychopathology. However, situations of intoxication during offending behaviour are often of a different or more complex nature. Nevertheless, similar prior fault reasoning, without mentioning the culpa-in-causa doctrine explicitly, is also used in situations of more direct effects of substances (such as aggressive behaviour, not stemming from psychopathology), the (incorrect) use of legal or even prescribed substances, or in case of withdrawal symptoms (after abrupt abstinence).[76] Also,

[72] *cf* Goldberg and others (n 2).

[73] AE Goldberg and others, 'Verslaafd en Verantwoordelijk? Complexe Culpa in Causa Kwesties in Rapportage Pro Justitia en Jurisprudentie' (2024) 10 *Delikt & Delinkwent* 833.

[74] See MJF van der Wolf and M de Vries Robbé, 'Contemplations and Discussions on the Quality of Forensic Assessment in Sentencing: Puzzling Pieces for Decision Makers' in MJF van der Wolf (ed), *Safeguarding the Quality of Forensic Assessment in Sentencing. A Review Across Western Nations* (New York, Routledge, 2022) 6.

[75] See Court of Appeal Arnhem-Leeuwarden, 11-12-2014, ECLI:NL:GHARL:2014:9618.

[76] See, for case law, Verkes and Fechner (n 64) 379.

in assessing the situation at T1 a wide variety of reasons and causes for substance use can exist, which may be overlooked when focusing on aware and voluntary intoxication as a requirement only.[77] For instance, there seems to be an intuitive difference between the defendant who uses recreationally, the defendant who uses from a very severe addiction, and the defendant who uses substances for self-medication for an underlying disorder.[78] An abstract foreseeability requirement, as was formulated in the Cannabis Psychosis case, would be satisfied in all these circumstances, although one may feel that the 'weight' of (anterior) culpability differs. Consequently, further examination of the time of the substance use is necessary to understand whether this prior behaviour is truly culpable.

As mentioned in section II.A, jurisprudential criteria were recently adopted for insanity, involving both cognitive and volitional impairments. It has been argued that this should mean that for an anterior assessment of fault at T1, similarly a cognitive and volitional test should apply.[79] However, both the Supreme Court jurisprudence and case law from lower courts show that the judiciary has a strong cognitive focus: D knew, could know, or should have known that using this substance could induce mental disorder. Conversely, behavioural experts do incorporate volitional impairments in their assessment of responsibility at T1. This line of reasoning is more fairly tailored to the addicted defendant, as her impairment is more of a volitional than a cognitive nature.[80]

ii. Prior Fault Insanity (Our 'Target Cases' Only)

The cases discussed in the previous sub-section can all be rooted back to voluntary intoxication, where D's choice to become intoxicated led to psychosis and harmful conduct. In this manner, although it is D's disordered state at T2 that gives rise to the claim of insanity/non-responsibility, it is his voluntary intoxication at T1 that grounds the assessment of prior fault; and this becomes the foreground issue at trial. But what of cases where there is *no* intoxication at T1, such as our target cases of medical non-compliance or failure to seek medical assistance exacerbating or inducing mental disorder? Does the culpa-in-causa doctrine apply in the same way, representing the major point of doctrinal distinction between English and Dutch law?

The answer, it seems, is unclear; and the lack of clarity here is crucially important. Two points may be observed. First, the answer is unclear because of a lack of relevant case law. It may be possible to explain this absence on the basis that the factual circumstances – medical non-compliance leading to disordered conduct, etc – are simply less common in practice; though it is difficult to determine the empirical validity of this claim. It may also be observed that, within the Dutch

[77] Discussed in ch 6 of this collection.
[78] Goldberg (n 70).
[79] Goldberg and others (n 73).
[80] ibid.

system, non-intoxication cases of this kind are more likely to be diverted to assessments of diminished (rather than absent) responsibility, allowing for greater flexibility in sentencing and disposal as discussed in section two (ie, all without explicit recourse to prior fault in terms of culpa in causa). In this manner, similar to the English courts, facts within our target cases are not immune from public policy considerations and outcomes, but these ends are achieved through alternative legal mechanisms.

It has been reported in the Netherlands that in almost 10 per cent of cases in which a substance use disorder is assessed, defendants are (still) being found non-responsible by the courts. This is generally due to a pre-existing (not substance use induced) psychotic disorder, in which the substance use that triggered later offending behaviour is considered to be taken as self-medication.[81] Similar reasoning has also been followed in a case of discontinuation of (anti-psychotic) medication and simultaneously starting cannabis use, which eventually contributed to the manifestation of psychosis and the subsequent offence, as 'inherent to the defendant's disorder'.[82] Despite the reporting psychiatrist recommending diminished responsibility because of prior fault reasoning, the judge instead followed the psychologist's advice and considered the defendant non-responsible. This exemplifies that courts may very well incorporate underlying reasons for substance use in their decisions. And when the threshold for non-responsibility is not reached, diminished responsibility can offer an escape. This may also be the outcome of cases of co-morbid personality disorder, which in theory may lead to a lack of inhibition of the impulse to use substances.

The second observation is more profound for the future of culpa-in-causa and/or in the non-intoxication target cases relevant to this chapter. It seems that the current interpretation of culpa-in-causa, defined through the paradigm of intoxication, may have placed the broader doctrine on the horns of a three-part dilemma. It may be that (i) the culpa-in-causa doctrine, although interpreted by the courts with reference to intoxication, remains a test of general application to non-intoxication cases as well. However, if this were true, the current objective construction of that test would appear unacceptably broad for our target cases: it is one thing to assume knowledge of dangerous drugs, but quite another to equate objective foresight of psychiatric symptoms with comparable fault in all cases (eg, in cases of medical non-compliance, or unhealthy or addictive use). A response might claim that (ii) the culpa-in-causa doctrine should not be understood in this way and that the broad assessments of fault are only relevant to intoxication cases; leaving other cases to be decided differently, perhaps on the basis of subjective foresight. This response, however, seems to require a bright-line distinction between intoxication and non-intoxication cases of the kind we see in English law and of the kind doctrinally absent from Dutch law. Finally, extending the previous

[81] ibid.
[82] Court of Noord Holland 11-12-2023, ECLI:NL:RBNHO:2023:12623.

option, it may be that (iii) the culpa-in-causa doctrine should only be considered as a doctrine of prior fault intoxication, with our target cases falling outside. This final option, of course, would effectively bring into alignment the Dutch and English approaches, even though the Dutch prior fault intoxication is set within the broad framework of insanity/responsibility.

IV. The Challenges of Comorbidity

In this final section, we provide some additional analysis of comorbidity (ie, a status of reduced capacity at T2 owing to a *combination* of psychopathological factors). We have already highlighted challenges associated with comorbidity in this chapter, particularly where D is impacted by mental disorder as well as drug intoxication; and it is an issue that will be discussed elsewhere in this collection.[83] The principal challenge here is one of factual/scientific uncertainty: where we cannot isolate the causal factors leading to D's reduced capacity at T2, or weigh those factors with any certainty, should we continue to apply legal rules that require such distinctions in practice?

The obvious answer is that we should not, and it is therefore no surprise to see arguments about removing causal distinctions being foregrounded in prior fault debates. Our point here is not to rehearse such debates again but rather to clarify the difficulty for both sides. Essentially, whether prior fault is applied to our target cases within insanity and diminished responsibility or not, so long as it exists elsewhere (eg, intoxication and automatism), problematic causal distinctions will remain. Where prior fault is excluded, as it currently is in English law, a hard causal distinction is required between internal causes of T2 incapacity (where prior fault is excluded) and external causes of T2 incapacity (where prior fault analysis may be possible). One response is to apply prior fault more generally, as we see debated in English law, and as we see (in theory at least) in Dutch law. The problem with this, however, is that even if we accept a broader application of prior fault, we might still sensibly want to apply different rules between intoxication and non-intoxication cases, leading to a reemergence of the problem of separation. And this is what we have seen in the Dutch context.

It is important to recognise in practice that comorbidity is the standard – and not the exceptional – case. A Dutch study shows that in behavioural reports written about defendants with a substance use disorder, over 95 per cent also had a co-morbid mental disorder (about 50 per cent psychotic, about 40 per cent personality, and about 30 per cent developmental disorders).[84] The challenge for both

[83] See also the discussion in ch 6, s VI of this collection.

[84] Goldberg and others (n 73). The selection of reports was based on the fact that they were part of a multidisciplinary assessment, which is generally only used in cases of severe offences as it is a formal requirement for imposing the tbs-order. Thus, these estimates may not be representative for defendants

criminal law systems should be viewed in the face of this reality, and the factual and scientific uncertainty that will be a feature of many of these cases. The law is right to seek doctrinal and normative coherence, but it cannot do so on the basis of an unreality in the science, and so the use of bright-line causal distinctions within the law should be resisted.

V. Conclusion

This chapter has detailed and discussed two *apparently* very different legal systems, both struggling to understand and account for the potential of prior fault analysis. The similar substance within these debates is perhaps unsurprising, with public policy concerns of dangerousness, culpability, and consistency all featuring prominently across both systems. And in so doing, there is acknowledgement of some of the unique aspects of the *non-intoxication* prior fault debate and particularly the difficult and uncertain causal pathways that may result in (resurfacing of) mental disorder in our target cases. Where insanity is qualified or consumed through prior fault attribution, the potential uncertainty of this causal path must be acknowledged, and rules designed to minimise the chance of inappropriate criminalisation.

What has been more surprising, for the authors at least, has been the similarities of substance between approaches to our target cases that began with such polarised doctrinal positions. Whilst English law headlines the exclusion of prior fault insanity, the practical reality is a system that finds other means to secure similar (at least public policy) ends: through stretching the definition of intoxication (and associated prior fault); foregrounding circumstances of intoxication in cases of comorbidity; and utilising the liberty-restricting disposal powers associated with the special verdict. Similarly, within Dutch law, despite the broad headlines of culpa-in-causa, we see a doctrine applied almost exclusively within the factual confines of intoxication; and non-intoxication cases (our target cases) are diverted to alternative assessments of diminished responsibility. The blurring of lines within each system is readily understandable, but the concern – explored throughout this chapter – is that this blurring represents an unprincipled avoidance rather than engagement with the problem.

And the problem is stark. Whether we return to our opening examples of prior fault insanity (ie, medication non-compliance, etc), or more common examples of comorbidity, neither system provides a simple answer in terms of potential liability; and just as importantly, neither system provides a test designed to engage with the complexity and uncertainty inherent in these target cases. The challenge now is less for the courts to make sense of current rules, and rather more for the theorist in providing new ways forward in terms of reform.

with substance use disorders in general, as minor offending behaviour, including possession of drugs, were excluded from this sample.

3

A Penology of Prior Fault: Reflections on Penal Context, Aims and Opportunities

GAVIN DINGWALL

I. Introduction

Criminal law scholarship has devoted considerable attention to whether prior fault should determine or impact substantive liability or the availability of a defence. Comparative analysis demonstrates a marked inconsistency of approach, indicative perhaps of broader differences in determining liability as well as the overarching (and universal) complexity of reconciling legal doctrine with the legitimate aim of reducing harm.[1] In prior-fault cases resulting in conviction, the relevance (if any) of prior fault re-emerges. Even where prior fault did not affect substantive liability, it may sometimes be appropriate for prior fault to influence the penal response. Yet, penal theorists have given the issue scant attention. This constitutes a major omission, as appropriate punishment requires an assessment of offence severity, which, as will be shown, should incorporate both the seriousness of the harm and the offender's culpability. Prior fault clearly has the potential to impact (positively or negatively) on culpability. It is a topic that should, therefore, engage theorists and, given the frequency with which addiction and intoxication arise in criminal courts, demands a considered policy response.

At the outset, it is vital to note that it is impossible to divorce substantive law from sentencing, as the substantive law on intoxication will often directly impact the penalty imposed. Accordingly, substantive liability and sentencing cannot simply be viewed sequentially. An example, in the English and Welsh context, is that offences of specific intent, where evidence of intoxication can be considered in determining whether *mens rea* was satisfied,[2] are often underpinned by basic

[1] AE Goldberg and others, 'Prior-Fault Blame in England and Wales, Germany and the Netherlands' (2021) 8 *Journal of International and Comparative Law* 53.

[2] The seminal authority is *Director of Public Prosecutions* v *Majewski* [1976] UKHL 2. See chs 1 and 2 for a consideration of the decision and the substantive law of intoxication in England and Wales.

intent offences. Evidence of intoxication remains relevant to basic intent offences, but in a different way. Where the prosecution cannot prove *mens rea*, the individual will nonetheless be held liable if there is evidence of intoxication. The 'lesser' offence often carries a lower maximum penalty. For example, serious violence will usually be charged as either wounding/causing grievous bodily harm with intent[3] or unlawful wounding/inflicting grievous bodily harm.[4] The former, a crime of specific intent, carries a maximum penalty of life imprisonment, whilst the latter, a crime of basic intent, has a maximum of five years' imprisonment. With regards to homicide offences in England and Wales, the desire to avoid the mandatory penalty of life imprisonment for murder[5] in certain situations has led to tortuous and complicated developments in the criminal law, both by Parliament and by the courts. Whilst this inter-relationship between substantive law and sentencing should be recognised, this chapter will not explore how sentencing issues have impacted on the criminal law further.

The relevance of prior fault to sentence should depend on the broader sentencing aim(s) of a criminal justice system. The upcoming section II provides an overview of sentencing in England and Wales – the jurisdiction most familiar to the author – to show that sentencers have to balance several sentencing aims. In practical terms, such an approach may be sensible and may accord with the thought processes of sentencers. Nonetheless, having several concurrent aims complicates the process and, subsequently, any discussion of punishing prior fault. One of the central arguments underpinning this chapter is that, if prior fault should affect sentence, this must be justified both on sound penology and on acceptable policy grounds. Stating that sentences should depend on multiple concerns compromises these twin objectives. Sections III and IV will consider in turn the relationship between prior fault and four universal justifications for punishment: retribution; deterrence; public protection; and rehabilitation. In each case, the rationale will be explained before generic concerns will be raised. Specific attention will be given to the relevance of intoxication and addiction with regards to each of these aims. It will be seen that the relevance varies markedly and that this matters in a criminal justice system with multiple sentencing aims.

After considering individual sentencing aims, section V will turn to the relevance of the offender's behaviour *after* committing the offence. Specifically, does meritorious behaviour after the offence counterbalance prior fault? Or should such behaviour be viewed more prosaically as evidence to bolster a belief that the offender recognises that they need help and will respond positively to an intervention designed to help address addiction or intoxication? The section will assess the value of a mechanism available in English law for delaying imposing sentence for a period of time to monitor an offender's behaviour. Deferring sentence offers the potential for offenders to address an underlying cause of their offending and to

[3] Contrary to the Offences against the Person Act 1861, s 18.
[4] ibid s 20.
[5] Murder (Abolition of the Death Penalty) Act 1965, s 1(3).

divert offenders from environments, such as prison, which may increase the likelihood of relapse.[6] It is an approach which should be encouraged, particularly when intoxication or addiction are present, as it offers an incentive for individuals to seek assistance and, where appropriate, for this to be reflected in the sentence. The conclusion will return to the need to reconcile just punishment with the expectation that society will be protected from the (sometimes serious) harm that can follow prior-fault behaviour.

II. Penal Justification and Prior Fault

When sentencing adults,[7] section 57(2) of the Sentencing Act 2020[8] lists the following purposes of sentencing, which courts must have regard to:

(a) the punishment of offenders;
(b) the reduction of crime (including its reduction by deterrence);
(c) the reform and rehabilitation of offenders;
(d) the protection of the public; and
(e) the making of reparation by offenders to persons affected by their offences.

These aims are not prioritised, which leaves ample scope for the discrepancy associated with individual sentencers' general beliefs in the purpose(s) of sentence and in what they perceive as the priority when dealing with the offender before them.[9] When addiction or intoxication is present, such differences may be even more marked. This conflict is tempered, theoretically at least, by the 'disposition threshold' tests contained in the Sentencing Act 2020 and, especially, in offence-specific sentencing guidelines. It will be suggested that the combined effect of the

[6] HM Inspectorate of Prisons, *HM Chief Inspector of Prisons for England and Wales Annual Report 2023 – 24* (London, HMIP, 2024) 23: 'In men's prisons around one-third (32%) of prisoners told us that it was easy to get illicit drugs; in women's prisons, it was around a fifth (21%). Nine per cent of men said they had developed a problem with illicit drugs since arriving in jail, rising to a shocking 21% at Lindholme.'

[7] Two provisions are relevant to sentencing offenders under the age of 18. Section 37 of the Crime and Disorder Act 1999 stipulates that the principle purpose of the youth justice system is 'to prevent offending by children and young people'. There is also a duty in s 44 of the Children and Young Persons Act 1933 to have regard to the welfare of the child or young person.

[8] The Sentencing Act 2020 is sometimes referred to as the Sentencing Code, although it has the same legal status as any other primary legislation. The Act, which comprises 420 sections and 29 schedules, largely consolidated previous law found mainly in the Powers of Criminal Courts (Sentencing) Act 2000 and the Criminal Justice Act 2003. The Sentencing Act 2020 has already been revised in subsequent legislation, most notably the Police, Crime, Sentencing and Courts Act 2022.

[9] The Sentencing Council perceive the role as a balancing exercise. Sentencing Council, *General Guideline: Overarching Principles* (London, Sentencing Council, 2019): 'The court should consider which of the five purposes of sentencing it is seeking to achieve through the sentence that is imposed. More than one purpose might be relevant and the importance of each must be weighed against the particular offence and offender characteristics when determining sentence.'

threshold tests and the structure of sentencing guidelines de facto prioritises retribution, or, as section 57(2)(a) of the Act defines it, 'the punishment of offenders'.[10]

In order to impose particular penalties in England and Wales, thresholds have to be reached. The thresholds relate to the seriousness of the offence. For example, a discretionary[11] custodial sentence can only be imposed for adult offenders if '(a) the offence, or (b) the combination of the offence and one or more offences associated with it, was so serious that neither a fine alone nor a community sentence can be justified for the offence'.[12] Imprisonment should then be reserved as a punishment for the most serious offences.[13] A similar threshold test exists for community sentences, which provides that a 'court must not make a community order unless it is of the opinion that (a) the offence, or (b) the combination of the offence and one or more offences associated with it, was serious enough to warrant the making of such an order'.[14] Other penalties, particularly financial penalties, are imposed where these disposition thresholds are not satisfied. A final point to make about disposition thresholds is that, even if the threshold is reached, courts usually retain the discretion to impose a lesser penalty if specific mitigating factors are present.[15]

Courts must then start by determining how serious an offence is. Section 63 of the Sentencing Act 2020 stipulates how offence-severity is to be quantified:

> Where a court is considering the seriousness of any offence, it must consider –
>
> (a) the offender's culpability in committing the offence, and
> (b) any harm which the offence –
>
> (i) caused,
> (ii) was intended to cause, or
> (iii) might foreseeably have caused.[16]

[10] G Dingwall, 'Deserting Desert? Locating the Present Role of Retributivism in the Sentencing of Adult Offenders' (2008) 47(4) *Howard Journal of Criminal Justice* 400.

[11] There are some situations where an immediate custodial sentence is mandatory. This generally depends upon a combination of the severity of the current offence and previous convictions. The law is not consistent and appears driven by political will rather than empirical evidence. There are, for example, provisions relating to repeat domestic burglars (Sentencing Act 2020, s 314) but none for those who commit repeated acts of moderate violence.

[12] Sentencing Act 2020, s 230.

[13] Sentencing Council, *General Guideline: Imposition of Community and Custodial Sentences* (London, Sentencing Council, 2017).

[14] Sentencing Act 2020, s 204(2).

[15] Sentencing Council (n 13): 'Passing the custody threshold does not mean that a custodial sentence should be deemed inevitable. Custody should not be imposed where a community order could provide sufficient restriction on an offender's liberty (by way of punishment) while addressing the rehabilitation of the offender to prevent future crime.'

[16] Although s 63 does not discuss the relative weight that should apply to culpability and harm, there is debate about the legacy of the unlawful act manslaughter case of *Attorney-General's Reference (No 60 of 2009) (Appleby)* [2009] EWCA Crim 2693 where the court held that, without diminishing the relevance of culpability, 'far greater weight' should be given to the fatal harm occasioned by his actions. The decision precedes the establishment of the Sentencing Council but in another manslaughter case, *Attorney-General's Reference (No 36 of 2015) (Nicholles)* [2015] EWCA Crim 1174, the Court of Appeal noted an increase in the length of sentences to reflect a focus on harm.

When analysing how prior fault, particularly in the context of addiction or intoxication, should impact on a sentence, it is the first factor – culpability – that is paramount. This will be reviewed fully when discussing retribution, as culpability is integral to desert. The harm occasioned by the offence would appear constant regardless of whether or not there was prior fault. Harm, as defined in the Act, requires more comment nonetheless. Offences generally specify a particular harm as part of the *actus reus*. But appropriate penalties have to be determined for 'conduct crimes'[17] and for inchoate offences where the harm associated with the completed offence does not materialise. In such cases, it may be necessary to assess whether prior fault is relevant to any assessment of whether harm was intended or might foreseeably have been caused.[18] This chapter will not develop this further, partly due to space constraints and partly because it would entail a broader discussion about criminalising conduct and inchoate action.

Sentencing guidelines are also vital to criminal justice in England and Wales, although they are a comparatively recent development. The Coroners and Justice Act 2009 created a Sentencing Council for England and Wales.[19] The Act requires the Council to prepare sentencing guidelines which either address general sentencing principles ('overarching guidelines') or particular offences or categories of offence ('offence-specific guidelines').[20] Offence-specific guidelines should specify an 'offence range' appropriate for that offence and, where a guideline categorises the offence on the basis of harm and/or culpability, should specify a 'category range'.[21]

Section 59 of the Sentencing Act 2020 provides that:

> (1) Every court –
>
> (a) must, in sentencing an offender, follow any sentencing guidelines which are relevant to the offender's case, and
>
> (b) must, in exercising any other function relating to the sentencing of offenders, follow any sentencing guidelines which are relevant to the exercise of the function,
>
> unless the court is satisfied that it would be contrary to the interests of justice to do so.

[17] With regards to conduct crimes, the consequences of the defendant's behaviour has no bearing on liability. Indeed there may be no consequence. The defendant's behaviour may satisfy the *actus reus* even if it fails to achieve the consequence intended (or any consequence). *R v Pogmore* [2017] EWCA Crim 925 establishes, for example, that, in English law, blackmail is a conduct crime as it is satisfied when the defendant, with a view to gain for himself or another or with intent to cause loss to another, makes an unwarranted demand with menaces; the Theft Act 1968, s 21.

[18] When harm materialises, this can be quantified, however the harm may not have been intended and may indeed have been exceptionally unlikely. Moral luck plays a part. For example, a single punch may cause no injury, significant injury or even death. Conduct crimes are sometimes appropriate because of the latent harm associated with the prohibited conduct, for example dangerous driving. The Sentencing Act 2020 states that harm includes foreseeable harm. However, an offender who is intoxicated may not be able to foresee such harm. Penalising intended harm that does not materialise raises similar questions about the extent to which an intoxicated offender intended the harm. This may be an issue of substantive liability, but assuming the offender is found liable, the issue resurfaces when calculating the harm associated with the offence.

[19] Coroners and Justice Act 2009, s 118(1).

[20] Coroners and Justice Act 2009, s 120(2).

[21] Coroners and Justice Act 2009, s 121.

Where an offence-specific guideline exists, the requirement to 'follow any sentencing guideline' means that the court should impose a sentence which falls within the 'offence range' specified. The range from the top of the highest category to the bottom of the lowest category can be considerable and will often include different types of sentences (eg, custody and community) as well as different sentence lengths. The guidelines are framed in such a way that a variety of penalties can often be imposed based on legitimate interpretations of the circumstances of the offence and/or the characteristics of the offender.

Courts retain a statutory right to depart from a guideline where adherence would be 'contrary to the interests of justice'. As this is an exceptional power and inherently fact-specific, it is difficult to glean any sense of when departure is used and on what basis departure is justified. An example of a case where departure was held to have been appropriate on appeal suggests that the circumstances have to be atypical and that departure from a guideline is necessary to reflect this appropriately when sentencing the offender. *R v Maxwell*[22] concerned an assault committed by someone with a history of violence which resulted in catastrophic brain injury. In order to reflect the gravity of the injury, it was seen as appropriate for the judge to exceed the top end of the category range when determining a proportionate sentence. It is clear that departure cannot be justified because a judge dislikes the effect of a guideline[23] or preferred guidance that pre-dated the Sentencing Council.[24]

Guidance on sentencing cases where addiction and intoxication are present can be found both in an 'overarching' guideline and in many 'offence-specific' guidelines, which replicate the principles in the 'overarching' guideline. Courts are bound to follow both, unless it would be contrary to the interests of justice. The *General Guideline: Overarching Principles* states that the commission of an offence whilst under the influence of alcohol or drugs is generally to be regarded as an aggravating factor. The principles are stated in full:[25]

> The fact that an offender is **voluntarily** intoxicated at the time of the offence will tend to increase the seriousness of the offence provided that the intoxication has **contributed to the offending**.
>
> This applies regardless of whether the offender is under the influence of legal or illegal substance(s).

[22] *R v Maxwell* [2019] EWCA Crim 130.

[23] *R v Taylor* [2012] EWCA Crim 630; *R* v *Umoh* [2013] EWCA Crim 1260.

[24] *R v Healey* [2012] EWCA Crim 1005. Prior to the establishment of the Sentencing Council, the Court of Appeal issued 'guideline' judgments which listed factors to be considered by sentencing courts as well as indicative sentences. The system suffered from its dependency on appeals from the lower courts, especially as these usually concerned the most serious, and thus infrequent, cases that came before the courts. There was not a 'guideline' judgment for how courts should sentence offenders who had been intoxicated at the time of the offence, but there are authorities where the courts treated it as a neutral factor (eg, *R v Parkhouse* [1999] 20 Cr App R(S) 206) or as a mitigating factor (eg, *R v Spence* [1982] 4 Cr App R(S) 175).

[25] Sentencing Council (n 9).

> In the case of a person addicted to drugs or alcohol the intoxication may be considered not to be voluntary, but the court should have regard to the extent to which the offender has sought help or engaged with any assistance which has been offered or made available in dealing with the addiction.
>
> An offender who has voluntarily consumed drugs and / or alcohol must accept the consequences of the behaviour that results, even if it is out of character. (emphasis in original)

It can be observed that the general principle that alcohol or drug intoxication aggravates a sentence is subject to various qualifications. The first is that the intoxication has to be voluntary. For the purposes of this chapter, this suggests that prior fault is relevant in determining whether or not intoxication should be regarded as relevant in determining sentence; it would be inappropriate to aggravate where there was no prior fault. Causation also matters. This further emphasises the importance of prior fault when it comes to whether intoxication should be regarded as aggravating.

Addiction is to be treated differently, but with the important proviso that the court should look for evidence that the offender has tried to address the addiction. Here the wording is careful in that it would appear that, in cases of addiction, intoxication may still be considered involuntary even though an offender may not have taken steps to address the addiction. Presumably, attempts to address addiction provide supporting evidence that the offender's behaviour was not blameworthy. The overarching guideline goes further and states that attempts to address addiction should be regarded as mitigation:[26]

> Where offending is driven by or closely associated with drug or alcohol abuse (for example stealing to feed a habit, or committing acts of disorder or violence whilst drunk) a commitment to address the underlying issue (including where the offender has actively sought support but, for reasons outside their control, it has not been received) may justify a reduction in sentence. This will be particularly relevant where the court is considering whether to impose a sentence that focuses on rehabilitation.

These principles are replicated in guidelines for sentencing particular offences.[27] Assuming courts do follow the guidelines, intoxication should, save in limited circumstances, aggravate an offence. The clear implication here is that, in most situations, an intoxicated offender is seen as more culpable than a sober offender. In previous work, discussed in the next section, I have challenged this assumption.[28] The fact that the intoxication must be voluntary and there must be a causal link between the intoxication and the offence recognises (correctly) that prior fault must be present if it is appropriate to aggravate the sentence. Addiction is to be

[26] ibid.

[27] See, eg, Sentencing Council, *Assault Occasioning Actual Bodily Harm / Racially or Religiously Aggravated ABH* (London, Sentencing Council, 2021).

[28] G Dingwall, *Alcohol and Crime* (Cullompton, Willan Publishing, 2006); G Dingwall and L Koffman, 'Determining the Impact of Intoxication in a Desert-Based Sentencing Framework' (2008) 8 *Criminology & Criminal Justice* 335.

treated differently, on the basis that the intoxication was involuntary (and hence there was no prior fault).[29] Where there is a link between the addiction and the type of offending and, critically, where the offender has sought help, this may be seen as mitigation. Mitigation may allow the courts to impose a lesser penalty even where a disposition threshold has been reached.

What is known about how the guidelines are applied in practice? The Sentencing Council has not reviewed how courts sentence addiction and intoxication, but there was an interesting finding from research into how three offence-specific guidelines were being applied. With regards to domestic burglary, theft from a shop or stall, and the supply or possession with the intent to supply a controlled drug, the research found that the guidance on addiction and intoxication was being applied inconsistently.[30] In other research which focused on addiction, intoxication and violence, Lightowlers and Pina-Sánchez found that the Crown Court did impose more severe sentences where the offender had been intoxicated but that this was moderated where the intoxication was deemed out of character.[31] (The guideline states that this is irrelevant.) The study also found that addiction decreased the severity of sentences imposed, in keeping with the guideline. A later study by Lightowlers found evidence of gender disparity.[32] Females who had committed a violent offence whilst intoxicated were likely to receive a greater increase in sentence than males who committed violence whilst intoxicated. This raises the spectre that the interpretation and effect of the guideline may be gendered. Summing up the evidence base in a report for the independent Sentencing Academy, Lightowlers concluded:

> Given its prevalence in cases coming before the courts and potential impact, intoxication as a sentencing factor has not been subject to as much scrutiny, monitoring and research as it warrants. It remains a contentious factor in sentencing and there is only a limited body of research and scholarship in the English and Welsh context which examines its impact across types of offence and offenders. This is hampered further still by the lack of detailed data collection and ongoing monitor of the use of intoxication as a mitigating factor.[33]

This section has shown that sentencers have to balance several aims when determining an appropriate sentence in England and Wales. There is also an obligation to follow overarching guidelines and offence-specific guidelines, unless it would be contrary to the interests of justice to do so. The guidelines articulate how courts should deal with cases involving addiction or intoxication, and, though empirical

[29] This differs significantly from the law with regard to substantive prior fault rules.

[30] Sentencing Council, *The Impact of Three Guidelines on Consistency in Sentencing* (London, Sentencing Council, 2021) 17.

[31] C Lightowlers and J Pina-Sánchez, 'Intoxication and Assault: An Analysis of Crown Court Sentencing Practices in England and Wales' (2017) 58(1) *British Journal of Criminology* 132.

[32] C Lightowlers, 'Drunk and Doubly Deviant? Gender, Intoxication and Assault' (2019) 59(3) *British Journal of Criminology* 693.

[33] C Lightowlers, *Intoxication and Sentencing: A Review of Policy, Practice and Research* (London, Sentencing Academy, 2022) 16.

analysis is sparse, it would appear to be the case that courts do act consistently with the guidelines subject to the provisos above. How prior fault should impact sentence can also be assessed normatively with regard to individual sentencing aims. Broadly, punishment can be justified on retributive or consequentialist grounds, and these will be considered in the upcoming sections III and IV.

III. Punishment, Prior Fault and Culpability

It is convenient to start our assessment of how prior fault should influence sentences with retribution given it is the first statutory aim of sentencing and, in the author's opinion, central to the structure of English sentencing law and practice.[34] Two seemingly straightforward notions are central to retribution. The first is that offenders 'deserve' punishment, and the second is that the punishment that is deserved should reflect the seriousness of the offence.[35] This is reflected in the approach taken in the Sentencing Act 2020 and in the guideline judgments in England and Wales. Retributivism requires no future benefit; though no doubt, rehabilitation or deterrence would be a welcome consequence, they do not serve as a justification. To many, the idea that punishment should follow offending is obvious and requires no exploration, but why the infliction of harm, in the form of a penalty, should follow a criminal harm can be debated if it serves no future benefit.

Judith Rumgay's research shows how evidence of intoxication could be framed to argue that the offender's culpability was reduced, though it is important to note that the research took place prior to the sentencing guideline. The following plea in mitigation was observed:[36]

> These offences were clearly committed under the influence of drink and my client can remember very little of the events. He has been shown statements and evidence to the effect that it was he who did these things and no-one else and he accepts that this must be so. This particular behaviour is out of all character to him.

It should be noted that the plea makes no reference to addiction. Reliance is made of the fact that the behaviour is uncharacteristic, a factor the overarching guideline states is irrelevant.[37] Whether prior convictions should affect culpability and hence

[34] This section draws upon work previously published by the author: Dingwall (n 28); Dingwall and Koffman (n 28).

[35] M Bagaric, 'Proportionality in Sentencing: Its Justification, Meaning and Role' (2000) 12(2) *Current Issues in Criminal Justice* 143; A von Hirsch, *Past or Future Crimes: Deservedness and Dangerousness in the Sentencing of Criminals* (Manchester, Manchester University Press, 1986).

[36] J Rumgay, *Crime, Punishment and the Drinking Offender* (London, Palgrave Macmillan, 1998) 154.

[37] More generally, the fact that the offender has no previous convictions is seen as strong mitigation. This could offset the aggravating effect of intoxication, even if the intoxication was uncharacteristic.

sentence has troubled retributivists. Andrew von Hirsch articulates the practical problem:[38]

> The issue of prior criminality is critical to a desert-based theory of sentencing, because it influences the structure of the penalty scale so much. If prior record is irrelevant, then penalties can be ranked unidimensionally to reflect the comparative seriousness of offenders' current crimes. If it is relevant, a two-dimensional grid is required, in which penalties are ordered to reflect not only the gravity of the current act but the extent of the criminal record as well. It then becomes essential to decide how much weight the record should carry. Should the emphasis remain on the current crime, or should it shift primarily to record?

A retributive argument can be framed that prior offending (as opposed to prior fault in the current offence) whilst intoxicated is of relevance when committing another similar offence. A first-time intoxicated offender should receive a lesser sentence than an individual who consistently engages in crime whilst intoxicated. Their culpability is reduced on the basis that their intoxication in the past has not led to a criminal conviction. (It may have resulted in criminal conduct that did not result in prosecution or conviction.) However, repetition makes this claim untenable. Culpability is increased when an offender is aware of the potential consequences of intoxication yet continues. There is a decision from the New South Wales Court of Criminal Appeal which adopts this reasoning.[39] The appellant argued that his intoxication should mitigate the sentence. However, the Court of Criminal Appeal argued that he could no longer claim that intoxication should mitigate because he had continued to offend whilst intoxicated. Yet, as well as saying that his pattern of offending whilst intoxicated could no longer act as mitigation, the Court held that it should not aggravate the sentence. Repeated offending whilst intoxicated should, by implication, be seen as no more or less culpable than repeated offending.

Addiction should be dealt with differently. Here the sentencing guideline accords with retributive theory. A recognition that intoxication in such cases was involuntary implies that there was no culpability associated with prior fault.[40] The guideline states that the intoxication should generally have a neutral impact (in contrast to voluntary intoxication). Credit in the form of mitigation should be given to those who take proactive measures to address an addiction. If one were to

[38] Von Hirsch (n 35) 77–78. Most retributivists believe that prior convictions should have some bearing on culpability but that the effect should be limited. The preference is for the lack of prior convictions to serve as mitigation as opposed to the existence or prevalence of prior convictions to aggravate sentence. Section 65(2) of the Sentencing Act 2020 states that 'the court must treat as an aggravating factor each relevant previous conviction that it considers can reasonably be so treated, having regard to – (a) the nature of the offence to which the relevant previous conviction relates and its relevance to the current offence, and (b) the time that has elapsed since the relevant previous conviction'.

[39] *R v Coleman* [1990] 47 A Crim R 306.

[40] Whether or not addiction can be considered a culpable state and thus relevant for the assessment of prior fault is further discussed in ch 6 of this collection.

focus on other sentencing objectives, most notably rehabilitation, this stance may be easier to justify, but the author has argued in earlier work that this approach can be accommodated in a retributive sentencing model:[41]

> The offender's culpability is arguably enhanced in such cases both because of a willingness to take appropriate steps to avoid repetition and because his intoxication did not have the usual degree of voluntariness. The fact that the offender was an addict in itself may not suffice. It could be argued that credit can only be given when the offender takes the additional step of addressing his addiction. In such a case he could be said to be doing something additional and positive that should be favourably reflected when it comes to imposing a sentence. Conversely, one could argue that the sentence should depend upon his culpability *at the time of the offence*. If one were to adopt this stance then credit would not be given for action taken after the commission of the offence. There is a logic to this position, but one can cite other situations where creditworthy activity after the offence, for example helping the authorities or pleading guilty, are recognised in mitigation.

Reviewing this observation, I wonder if it misses a simpler point. Namely, an addict's culpability is reduced first and foremost because the intoxication was involuntary. Mitigation should not be dependent on whether subsequent help is sought. Perhaps it is better to regard help-seeking as a separate ground of mitigation under a retributive model.

A final point regarding retributivism relates to proportionate punishment. In some instances, this will be obvious; the most serious offences can only be dealt with by a lengthy custodial sentence, whilst minor offences will result in a financial penalty. There are situations, though, where different sentences can have a similar penal impact. The best example are community sentences, where different requirements can be attached, all of which have consequences for the offender. A community sentence can thus be tailored in such a way that it maximises the potential for rehabilitative success whilst ensuring that it remains a proportionate punishment. The chapter will return to this point in the conclusion, where it will be argued that retributive concerns are vital to ensuring that punishments remain proportionate to the offence for which the offender is before the court. However, within these constraints, there is scope to design a sentence to rehabilitate.

When it comes to determining a proportionate penal response, which is essential to retributivism, regard must be had to addiction and intoxication, as they may affect the offender's culpability. But addiction and intoxication can affect culpability in various ways, and this is reflected in the sentencing guidelines in England and Wales. One could argue that the distinctions drawn remain too blunt. The next section considers the relevance of addiction and prior fault to consequentialist sentencing justifications.

[41] Dingwall (n 28) 132.

IV. Consequential Punishment, Addiction and Intoxication

Most sentencing aims require consequential benefit. Classic utilitarian theory stipulates that harm (in this context, punishment) cannot be justified unless it will lead to a greater good.[42] Punishment cannot be 'deserved' without this benefit, unlike retributivism. However, provided the benefit exists, even severe sanctions can be acceptable. To take an example with popular resonance, lengthy terms of imprisonment should be imposed where necessary to protect the public. Deterrence, Rehabilitation and Public Protection share a common aim of stopping, or at least reducing the frequency and severity, of future offending and, for this reason, are consequentialist. The means for achieving this end differ. Put simply, deterrence rests on the notion that the penalty will be of a severity that will make either the offender[43] or the population more broadly[44] resist offending in similar circumstances.[45] Rehabilitation is more problematic to define, but for current purposes it can be taken to mean imposing a sentence that seeks to modify the offender's behaviour to address the root cause(s) of their offending. Public protection is easier to define; the aim of the punishment is to put the offender in a position where they are unable to re-offend for a period of time, usually in the contemporary context by imprisoning them.

Just as retributivists have to answer some fundamental questions, consequentialism raises some conceptual problems which have far-reaching practical effects. First, a sentence can only be justified on consequential grounds if the subsequent benefit outweighs the harm of the penalty. How does one assess this? Second, there is a definitional issue. What amounts to 'success'? Complete desistance sets a high bar. Temporal measures appear relevant. An extended period without offending should perhaps be seen as a success. Offence-severity should also arguably have some bearing. If a serious offender becomes a minor offender, even if a repeat minor offender, that too should be considered a satisfactory consequentialist intervention. Third, there is a causal difficulty. Desistance is a complex process, and the impact of a punishment may play only a marginal part. One must not conclude that a future decision not to offend was the consequence of punishment. Finally, this is an apposite time to raise a retributive objection. Focussing on potential benefit can legitimise differential treatment. To a retributivist, two individuals who commit offences of like seriousness (depending on culpability and harm) deserve like sentences. That is not the case if sentences are based on deterrence,

[42] M Bagaric, 'Incapacitation, Deterrence and Rehabilitation: Flawed Ideals or Appropriate Sentencing Goals?' (2000) 24(1) *Criminal Law Journal* 21.

[43] Often referred to as specific deterrence.

[44] Often referred to as general deterrence.

[45] The retributive objection is that the penalties used to this end are disproportionate to the seriousness of the offence.

rehabilitation and public protection, where there is the potential to lose sight of proportionality and impose draconian penalties.[46]

A. Deterrence

Penological research suggests that punishment-severity has negligible effects on crime rates.[47] Deterrence has an intuitive logic, which is why it is important to stress the lack of an evidence base to support imposing harsher penalties. Taking a step back, it is easy to see a number of flaws in the reasoning behind deterrence. First, it supposes the decision to offend is rational. It is suggested that this may be the case on occasion, but that often offending is spur-of-the-moment. Second, for a punishment to deter, potential offenders have to know what it will be. Third, in the context of addiction and intoxication, rational decision-making about whether the impact of a particular punishment should lead to a change in behaviour is even more tenuous.[48]

In the mid-2000s, the UK government launched a 'blitz' on alcohol-related crime and disorder 'to ensure that the system of offences and penalties works so as to discourage unacceptable alcohol-fuelled behaviour'.[49] The statement suggests that part of the approach would be to increase sentencing levels where intoxication was present. No sentencing guidelines existed at the time and one needs to be wary of reading too much into remarks in Court of Appeal sentencing decisions. In *R v Bradley*[50] the court stated that the offender's intoxication should not be considered mitigating, but did not provide a rationale based either on deterrence or on retribution. All that can be said is that the stance is consistent with a deterrent policy. Consistency can also be found in a couple of decisions where the offences were described either as a 'drunken frolic'[51] or out of character.[52] It will be recalled that the Sentencing Act 2020 stipulates that deterrence is one of the aims which courts should consider in determining sentence. However, the framework of the Act is designed in such a way to ensure that sentences are proportionate to the seriousness of the offence.

[46] See further N Sinclair-House, JJ Child and HS Crombag, 'Addiction is a Brain Disease, and it Doesn't Matter: Prior Choice in Drug use Blocks Leniency in Criminal Punishment' (2020) 26(1) *Psychology, Public Policy, and Law* 36.

[47] Home Office, *Making Punishment Work: Report of a Review of the Sentencing Framework for England and Wales* (London, Home Office, 2001).

[48] In this collection, ch 5 further discusses the conceptualisation of addiction and the consequences on (legally relevant) capacities. Moreover, ch 7 delves into the consequences of alcohol intoxication and the potential relevance for prior fault arguments.

[49] Department for Culture, Media and Sport, Home Office and Office of the Deputy Prime Minister, *Drinking Responsibly: The Government's Proposals* (London, Department for Culture, Media and Sport, 2005) para 4.2.

[50] *R v Bradley* [1980] 2 Cr App R (S) 12.

[51] *R v Abrahams* [1980] 2 Cr App R (S) 10.

[52] *R v Spence* [1982] 4 Cr App R (S) 175.

B. Public Protection

The need to protect the public from violence has influenced the substantive law in both England and Scotland. In *DPP v Majewski*,[53] the leading English case, the House of Lords maintained that '[to] accede to the argument on behalf of [Majewski] would leave the citizen legally unprotected from unprovoked violence where such violence was the consequence of drink'.[54] In Scotland, allowing an offender to escape liability on the basis of intoxication would be a 'perilous doctrine'.[55] The correct principle can perhaps be found in the Australian High Court decision in *R v O'Connor*.[56] Society needs protecting from many people, and the question is whether a departure from the usual rules of substantive law in the case of intoxication can be justified on this basis.

Most of the concerns about sentencing on the basis of public protection are not particular to prior fault. A general concern relates to how risk is to be assessed; again, as a consequentialist justification, a greater good has to be shown to justify the punishment. It is impossible to know how an incarcerated offender would have behaved if at liberty. It is also worth reflecting on public protection over a wider timescale. Whilst an offender is in prison, it is true that they pose no risk to the general population (though there is a potential risk to other prisoners and to prison staff). However, if prison increases the risk of reoffending when the offender is released, its crime-prevention function demands more consideration. This is not the place for further comment on 'dangerous' offenders and the circumstances in which lengthy terms of imprisonment can be justified on that basis. Prisons often run courses for offenders with drug and alcohol dependency issues, and prisoners can avail themselves of specialist assistance, although resources are typically stretched. Unfortunately, however, prison inspection reports in England and Wales frequently find extensive drug use in prisons[57] and instances of prisoners developing a drug habit whilst serving their sentence.

Public protection can be served in ways other than imprisonment. Curfews and banning orders serve as examples. Technology provides the scope for additional methods to be employed, such as a home detention curfew. Again, caution is necessary to ensure that the use of such measures is proportionate and that there is evidence that the offender does present a risk to the public.

[53] *DPP v Majewski* [1977] AC 443.

[54] ibid, Lord Simon of Glaisdale, 476.

[55] *HM Advocate* v *Savage* [1923] JC 49, 50.

[56] *R v O'Connor* [1980] 146 CLR 64.

[57] See, eg, HM Inspectorate of Prisons, *Report of an Independent Review of Progress at HMP Durham 6–8 January 2025* (London, HMIP, 2025) and HM Inspectorate of Prisons, *Report of an Unannounced Inspection of HMP Winchester 7–18 October 2024* (London, HMIP, 2025) p 3: 'In our survey, 47% of prisoners said that it was easy to get illicit drugs, yet despite the prison identifying the supply of illicit items as a serious security risk, all drug testing had been suspended for five months during 2024. Random drug testing only recommenced during August, returning a positive rate of 41%.'

C. Rehabilitation

There is a long history of specific measures being used when an offender's actions were attributed to drinking. The history of probation in England and Wales is linked to the church and to the temperance movement. Police Court Missionaries were established by the Church of England Temperance Society in 1875,[58] and their role became formalised in the Summary Jurisdiction Act 1879. The Act allowed magistrates to conditionally discharge a person convicted of a minor offence provided they remained of good character; if they reoffended, they could be recalled for sentence. Other religious groups, including the Church Army, the Federation of Local Free Church Councils, the Roman Catholic Westminster Education Fund, the National Temperance Association and the Reformatory and Refuge Union, became involved. The Criminal Justice Act 1914 gave the courts specific powers to require abstinence as a requirement for discharge.

Historically, a distinct approach was taken to those with addiction. The Habitual Drunkards Act 1879 provided for the voluntary treatment of habitual drunken offenders instead of the more usual forms of punishment. Voluntariness no longer became essential after the enactment of the Inebriates Act 1898. Provided specified criteria were met, then the offender could be compulsorily detained for up to three years in state or Certified Inebriate Reformatories. All 15 reformatories had closed by 1921.[59] There has been little subsequent call for offenders with addiction to receive treatment against their wishes.

Although penal reformers and many academic commentators advocate for rehabilitation, its prominence in official discourses has varied since. Confidence in the ability of penal interventions to rehabilitate was arguably lowest in the mid-1970s. Robert Martinson published a seminal paper in 1974 which came to the infamous conclusion that 'nothing works'.[60] In retrospect, rehabilitative schemes may not have been given the opportunity to succeed. For example, the Home Office announced a pilot scheme to respond to public drunkenness by setting up detoxification units with a clear medical and therapeutic purpose.[61] The pilots in Leeds and Manchester were unsuccessful, but issues of funding, confusion of departmental responsibility, and lack of clarity of the aims were cited as impediments.

It is fair to say that in the English context at least, the focus now is on what works. Community sentences may be determined by the severity of the offence,[62] but the requirements of the sentence are chosen in part with rehabilitation in mind. Where intoxication or addiction is a factor in the offending, the following

[58] D Bochel, *Probation and After-Care: Its Development in England and Wales* (Edinburgh, Scottish Academic Press, 1981).

[59] B Thom, *Dealing with Drink: Alcohol and Social Policy from Treatment to Management* (London, Free Association Books, 1999).

[60] R Martison, 'What Works – Questions and Answers about Prisoner Reform' [1974] *The Public Interest* 22.

[61] Home Office, *Habitual Drunken Offenders: Report of the Working Party* (London, HMSO, 1971).

[62] Sentencing Act 2020, s 203.

requirements are particularly relevant: programme requirement; prohibited activity requirement; curfew requirement; drug rehabilitation requirement; drug testing requirement; alcohol treatment requirement; alcohol abstinence and monitoring requirement.[63] Rehabilitation programmes for those with alcohol or drug issues also take place in prisons.

By shifting the focus to a future benefit, consequentialist justifications should treat addiction and intoxication differently from retribution. It is essential to remember that the harm associated with punishment must be outweighed with a future benefit under a consequentialist model; therefore, interventions, however well-intentioned, can only be justified if the benefit (here desistance or a reduction in offence-frequency or offence-severity) outweighs the harm associated with the punishment. This differs from the retributive concern that consequentialist justifications can justify the imposition of disproportionate punishment relative to the seriousness of the offence – which remains a valid concern. There is also the issue that consequentialist aims may seek to achieve the same result, but, as the means differ, so does the relevance of addiction and intoxication.

V. Deferring Sentence

The preceding section cautions against over-optimism and unrealistic expectations when criminal justice responses are justified on a rehabilitative basis. However, a criminal justice system which fails to consider whether underlying factor(s) explain the offence and/or makes no attempt to encourage desistance is doomed to entrench recidivism. Punishing with no expectation or regard to consequential benefit sets a low benchmark, especially when criminologists caution that the harms associated with criminal justice involvement (and imprisonment in particular) are often criminogenic. Addressing the cause(s) of offending should factor in sentencing. The potential benefit is both personal and societal if offending ceases or reduces in frequency or severity. Determining whether an intervention may prove successful at the time of sentence is problematic, particularly as many offenders present complex histories which may include addiction and problem drinking.

Sentencers find themselves in a difficult position. They may be receptive to imposing a sentence designed to address underlying addiction or problematic intoxication but want evidence that an offender will engage, particularly if there is a pattern of non-compliance. Deferring sentence until a later date provides the space for engagement and progression to be monitored over a defined timeframe before a decision is taken about the appropriate disposal. Put simply, deferring sentence provides an evidence base where individuals have sought to address issues that have led to their offending. Where this proves successful (and one can

[63] Sentencing Act 2020, s 201.

debate what this means), such conduct should influence both a proportionate punishment and help determine whether and what rehabilitative intervention is appropriate. Admittedly, deferring sentence is easier to justify purely on rehabilitative grounds. With regards to retribution, deferring sentence stretches traditional notions of culpability beyond culpability at the time of the offence to encompass character-based culpability. There is also an implicit deterrent: failure will result in a more punitive option being imposed. Deferring sentence can then be justified on policy grounds and on a penological basis.

Scotland introduced deferred sentencing in 1963[64] followed by England and Wales in 1972.[65] The current law is found in the Sentencing Act 2020.[66] There is no overarching guideline about the use of deferred sentencing. The Court of Appeal has stated that, even where an offender has made exceptional progress during the deferment period, the court retains the option of imposing a custodial sentence when sentencing.[67] The Act specifies two grounds for deferring sentencing. The first, which is potentially relevant to this discussion, is to have regard to the offender's conduct after conviction.[68] The second is because of changes to the offender's circumstances.[69] A deferment order can include specified requirements.[70] When the offender returns to the court for sentencing, the sentencer can consider the offender's post-conviction conduct.[71]

It is important to distinguish between deferring a sentence and suspending a sentence. A deferment order is not a sentence; rather it delays sentencing. The offender comes before the court for sentence at a later date.[72] A suspended sentence differs in that it is a disposition. The offender will not serve the sentence in custody unless they fail to comply with specified requirements or reoffend during the time of their suspended sentence.[73] Possible requirements could include undertaking a treatment programme for alcohol or drugs. A drug rehabilitation requirement can be imposed where the court is satisfied that the offender is dependent on or has a propensity to misuse drugs which requires or is susceptible to treatment.[74] Treatment can be residential or non-residential and requires the offender's

[64] Criminal Justice (Scotland) Act 1963, s 47.

[65] Criminal Justice Act 1972, s 22.

[66] Sentencing Act 2020, s 3.

[67] *Attorney General's Reference No. 1 of 2006 (R v P)* [2006] EWCA Crim 3335, para 17.

[68] Sentencing Act 2020, s 3(1)(a).

[69] Sentencing Act 2020, s 3(1)(b).

[70] Sentencing Act 2020, s 3(2).

[71] Sentencing Act 2020, s 6(1)(a).

[72] In England and Wales, the maximum period of deferment is six months: Sentencing Act 2020, s 5(2).

[73] The Sentencing Council stress that '[a] suspended sentence is a custodial sentence. Sentencers should be clear that they would impose an immediate custodial sentence if the power to suspend were not available. If not, a non custodial sentence should be imposed': Sentencing Council (n 13). It is worth noting in the context of this chapter that two of the factors indicating that it may be appropriate to suspend a sentence listed in the guideline are a realistic prospect of rehabilitation and strong personal mitigation.

[74] Sentencing Act 2020, Sch 9, Pt 10.

consent. An alcohol treatment requirement requires the court to be satisfied that the offender is dependent on alcohol and that the dependency is susceptible to treatment.[75] The treatment can again be residential or non-residential and requires consent.

VI. Conclusion: Context, Aims and Opportunities

One can criticise sentencing law and practice in England and Wales, as in other jurisdictions, but this conclusion will focus on the current context and how there are real, meaningful opportunities for sentencing offenders who have addiction issues or who offend whilst intoxicated. It will be argued, with slight trepidation, that a principled response to sentencing prior fault can be accommodated within the sentencing framework in England and Wales. At times, reliance will be made on provisions which should be invoked exceptionally. One has to be very cautious. Departure from guidelines and principles should not be undertaken lightly, as consistency of approach in sentencing is essential if arbitrariness, inconsistency and injustice are to be reduced.

An initial, and obvious, contextual concern is that multiple statutory aims of sentencing are present in England and Wales. These aims potentially conflict, and there is no prioritisation (save with regard to provisions for 'dangerous' offenders). An argument has been advanced in this chapter that the sentencing framework prioritises retribution given the 'threshold' tests for different punishments and the way in which sentencing guidelines are structured. Both require an assessment of the seriousness of the offence. The Sentencing Act 2020 states that this is to be calculated with reference to the offender's culpability and the harm associated with the offence. Prior fault evidently can affect culpability, even if there may be debate about what amounts to prior fault and the effect that prior fault should have on culpability and hence the seriousness of the offence and a proportionate sentence.

It is suggested that the retributive demand for proportionality between the seriousness of an offence and the sanction imposed is of particular relevance when sentencing cases involving intoxication or addiction. Individualised sentences calculated on assessments of risk, need and likely compliance can marginalise the gravity of the offence and lead to disproportionate punishment. Proportionality should serve a limiting function, ensuring that any intervention is acceptable.

Once a disposition has been selected on the basis of offence-severity and with regard to sentencing guidelines, sentencers must consider addiction and intoxication. The guideline is clearer on intoxication; assuming it is voluntary and led to the offence, it should aggravate the sentence. It has been argued that this lacks nuance; it is unclear, for example, why an intoxicated offender is more culpable than a sober offender. Addiction, conversely, is treated carefully and in an appropriate manner.

[75] Sentencing Act 2020, Sch 9, Pt 11.

The overarching guideline recognises both that addiction may make intoxication involuntary (and hence it should not aggravate the sentence) and that attempts by the offender to address the addiction are creditworthy (and hence should mitigate the sentence). In addiction cases, sentencers are not afforded the discretion to do whatever they feel is just. Rather, the discretion is guided by: (a) is the intoxication voluntary and (b) has the offender taken proactive steps to address the addiction? Where the offender receives a community sentence, the requirements can focus on measures designed to tackle addiction or problem drinking. This is a classic example of how an assessment of rehabilitative need can be accommodated within a proportionate penal response. Moreover, guidelines can be disregarded where it would be contrary to the interests of justice if they were followed. This right must be exercised rarely, but it does present an opportunity to avoid injustice *in extremis*. The concern from the limited available research is that the guidelines may not always be followed correctly.

Sound policy would encourage offenders with drug and alcohol problems to avail themselves of support. Sentencers may also want evidence about an individual's willingness and ability to address addiction or problem drinking. Deferring sentence provides space for such an evaluation, and the threat of a punitive response may aid compliance. It is a valuable option, and this is a plea to make more use of it. Sentencing should not only take account of addiction and intoxication but should also provide avenues for offenders to take proactive steps to address these behaviours and should reward those who do.

A wholly individualised system, where the penal response depends upon subjective assessments of need, risk and likely compliance, should be rejected. The seriousness of the offence must provide parameters which limit the penal response, save in exceptional cases where someone has committed a serious violent or sexual offence and there is compelling evidence that they pose immediate danger if at liberty. There is no compelling evidence base to justify deterrent sentencing, especially as deterrence tends to escalate sentencing levels. It should be robustly rejected. Rehabilitation is fraught with difficulty in criminal justice settings, but meaningful interventions exist and must be sought. Best practice should be shared. Critically though, rehabilitative measures can be a proportionate outcome.

Some of these conclusions are generic and go beyond prior-fault scenarios. The issue here does not relate to punishment but to the nebulous and contested nature of prior fault. Prior fault should always be considered when sentencing, but, because of the factual scenarios that arise, it can be appropriate to regard it on occasion as aggravation, a neutral factor, or as mitigation. Sentencing, above all, is about achieving justice in individual cases, and that means recognising difference and giving courts the discretion to respond.

4

Bridging the Gap: The (In)Compatibility of Legal and Behavioural Perspectives on Prior Fault, Intoxication and Addiction

ANNA GOLDBERG AND NICHOLAS SINCLAIR-HOUSE

I. Introduction

The mechanism of prior fault in cases of intoxication and addiction in this collection thus far has been discussed predominantly from doctrinal and normative perspectives. Prior fault is a mechanism allowing a defendant's previous conduct outside of an offence or defence definition to be included in the overall assessment of their liability. In the context of intoxication, prior fault rules operate to find liability for the intoxicated offender who may lack the required mens rea or fulfil the criteria for a defence at the time of the offence because of their voluntary choice to consume the substance. Prior fault *rules*, as such, are highly normative constructs. Prior fault rules are frequently subjected to debate or criticism.[1] Yet such challenges are often legitimised by the argument that without prior fault, voluntary behaviour – such as intoxication – would allow the defendant to get away with crime. Evidence of the concern such exculpation may ignite is clear from the reaction to the case of Nadruku:[2] a defendant's acquittal of assault charges, because he was not capable of forming the required intent due to his severe intoxication, later caused public and political criticism. Hence, it is safe to say that prior fault rules are derived – at least in part – from some sort of intuitive prior fault logic.

[1] See, eg, J Child, 'Prior Fault: Blocking Defences or Constructing Crimes' in A Reed and M Bohlander (eds), *General Defences: Domestic and Comparative Perspectives* (Farnham, Ashgate, 2014). For further discussion, see also ch 2 of this collection.

[2] *SC Small v Noa Kurimalawai* [1997] Australian Capital Territory Magistrates' Court, Matter No CC97/01904.

It seems only fair that one's reckless intoxication must not lead to exculpation or mitigation, which explains the intuitive rationale of prior fault.[3]

Importantly, throughout this chapter we sometimes differentiate between prior fault rules and prior fault logic: the former being the formal or doctrinal set of rules and criteria, and the latter being the more colloquial perception that individuals may have about anterior culpability, from which those rules are drawn. Please note that the rules and their underlying logic are not juxtaposed here: we merely differentiate between these concepts to indicate that we do not always discuss the exact legal rules, but rather a more generalised concept of prior fault. Our reason for making this distinction is twofold. First, it allows us to deviate from doctrine-specific intricacies that complicate the discussion on prior fault. After all, each jurisdiction will have different approaches towards the exact prior fault rules, each with its own challenges. Accounting for all these possibilities distracts from a more overarching discussion this chapter aims to set out, ie, a discussion on how multi-disciplinary perspectives may benefit our understanding of prior fault. Second, discussing prior fault *logic* allows us to explore more informal perceptions around prior fault, which may not be incorporated into formal prior fault rules but affect the application of such rules. Especially in section III, which discusses the effects of bias and stigma on prior fault, this serves as an important distinction.

A legal application of such prior fault logic can be traced back as far as the twelfth century, when canon law employed the term *versari in re illicita* ('to be engaged in an unlawful activity') to hold priests liable for all consequences stemming from an impermissible act, even when (some of) these consequences are unforeseen and/or unintended.[4] As behavioural sciences were essentially non-existent before the late nineteenth century,[5] we can argue that, at its core, prior fault has much less to do with mental states and much more with the necessities of legal doctrine. Yet, as also discussed in other chapters of this collection, the application of prior fault rules continues to face criticism from scholars on the basis that they fail to fully and adequately distinguish between different prior fault scenarios. Equally intuitive as the existence of prior fault logic is the difference between recreational and excessive substance use versus the use of substances as a form of self-medication to moderate underlying psychological distress. Yet, prior fault rules can fail to differentiate (sufficiently) between these circumstances.[6] Given advances in behavioural

[3] The exact mechanisms by which intoxication may lead to exculpation or mitigation depend on the jurisdiction and are not discussed in this chapter. See AE Goldberg and others, 'Prior-Fault Blame In England And Wales, Germany And The Netherlands' (2021) 8 *Journal of International and Comparative Law* 53 for an introduction to prior fault mechanisms in England & Wales, Germany, and the Netherlands.

[4] HB Vos, 'Het "Versari in Re Illicita" Speciaal Bezien in Verband met het Leerstuk van de Poging' (1931) 41 *Tijdschrift voor Strafrecht* 111, 113.

[5] RM Young, 'Scholarship and the History of the Behavioural Sciences' (1966) 5 *History of Science* 1.

[6] AE Goldberg and others, 'Verslaafd en Verantwoordelijk? Complexe Culpa in Causa Kwesties in Rapportage pro Justitia en Jurisprudentie' (2024) 10 *Delikt & Delinkwent* 833; see also the discussion by Browning and Goldberg in ch 6 of this collection.

science over recent decades, it would appear there are increased opportunities for interactions between legal and behavioural disciplines that may help us better distinguish between prior fault situations and, in turn, more accurately assess the true scope of an agent's culpability. This can consequently aid the development of the scientifically – and ethically – justified application of such prior fault rules.

This chapter aims to identify how different disciplines outside the law are relevant, perhaps even necessary, to understand prior fault rules in the context of addiction and substance use. Our focus here is on the so-called 'BCN sciences': behavioural, cognitive and neurosciences. Over the course of this chapter, we build bridges between these different disciplines by highlighting discrepancies between prior fault rules and logic with insights from BCN sciences. Additionally, we discuss whether these two different perspectives are compatible at all.

To do so, this chapter first provides a brief historical perspective on the origins of prior fault rules in section II. This lens puts the establishment of prior fault rules in its historical context, helping us identify the (legal) rationale of prior fault rules. As a result of this legal background, some may argue that other disciplines are not relevant at all to the concept of prior fault. As a fundamental legal, normative concept, perhaps prior fault rules do not need to consider advances in BCN sciences. If this is truly the case, and prior fault doctrine ought to be considered a purely normative-legal concept, this would mean that the defendant's mental states are supplementary.[7] Yet even then, we still cannot deny that the law is a social construct and that cases of addiction and intoxication are assessed by human judges. It has been well-documented that drug use and addiction can be highly stigmatised conditions. These perceptions undoubtedly affect the application of prior fault rules. Hence, without contesting the *nature* of prior fault rules as being normative, we can still consider the general *application* thereof from a socio-scientific perspective. The third section, therefore, discusses how interdisciplinary research is fundamental to understanding how prior fault logic in the context of addiction influences legal decision-making.

In the remainder of the chapter, however, we contest the view that the nature of prior fault rules is exclusively normative. Despite a strong legal basis, and a normative justification for the presence of prior fault rules, it cannot be ignored that prior fault rules ultimately address various levels of culpability in (previous)

[7] In our opinion, normative concepts are by definition not behavioural, ie, they are mutually exclusive. A recent discussion in a landmark Supreme Court case explains this decision (Supreme Court of the Netherlands 17-10-2023, ECLI:NL:HR:2023:1295, *Thijs H.*). The Court emphasised that determining legal insanity is the judges' decision and as such, although they may be informed by information from behavioural experts, the judge is ultimately responsible in establishing whether all requirements for the insanity defence are fulfilled. This includes the determination of the presence of a mental disorder. Consequently, this case exemplifies how the legal and the behavioural are juxtaposed: one may inform the other, but ultimately, the legal doctrines are normative decisions, whereby the judge is responsible, even though the concept is seemingly behavioural in nature. To extend this reasoning to our current context, we believe that if prior fault rules are considered normative in nature, they are by definition not behavioural concepts.

mental states.[8] As such, BCN sciences become highly relevant, as they provide evidence of mental functioning and impairment. As a case study to address the relevance of interdisciplinary perspectives on prior fault, the fourth section looks at volitional aspects in prior fault rules. Although not necessarily a formal requirement of prior fault, anterior culpability often presupposes the *voluntary* nature of previous conduct, ie, the voluntary consumption of a substance. Importantly, contemporary socio-scientific research has advanced our knowledge on the meaning of voluntariness, or similar control-based capacities, which does not necessarily align with the legal meaning of voluntary intoxication.[9] Hence, it is imperative to address the discrepancy between the law's perspective towards control – often a synchronous outlook – and social scientific advancements identifying different types and degrees of (diachronous) control.[10] This begs the question of whether prior fault rules need to be updated to better incorporate such developments in socio-scientific research.

If prior fault rules indeed require an update, then the question moves from 'if' to 'how'. Specifically, how can the law change normative doctrines to accommodate empirical findings? This leaves us with a challenge akin to the historical is-ought problem, whereby Hume identified a problem in trying to incorporate facts ('what is') into norms ('what ought to be'). We briefly reflect on the challenges that arise when BCN-related developments, ie, empirical findings, are applied to legal doctrine, ie, norm-setting, in the fifth and final section of this chapter.

All in all, this chapter connects the legal frameworks from the previous chapters with the upcoming discussions by identifying the different areas of prior fault rules that call for a more nuanced, multidisciplinary approach than one rooted strictly in normative legal doctrine. Importantly, our task is not undertaken with a jurisdiction-specific approach and instead discusses features of prior fault in more universal, generalist terms, which are consequently relevant to both common and civil law systems. Fundamental features of prior fault (such as the meaning of voluntariness or anterior culpability) are sometimes better discussed without focussing on specific legal doctrine. Nonetheless, examples from the authors' origins – the Netherlands and England and Wales – are used sporadically in this work to illustrate these more universal arguments.

[8] We acknowledge that the ultimate decision regarding prior fault remains a legal one.

[9] Such a discussion may easily be extended into other concepts whereby terms are understood differently from legal versus (socio-)scientific lenses. Legal concepts do not necessarily need to be compatible with behavioural equivalents. We merely aim to show that once meanings from different disciplines diverge greatly, we may want to carefully assess the reason for such divergence and analyse whether the law may need to be updated, as it remains a social construct and thus reflective of scientific developments.

[10] Synchronous control focuses on the immediate exercise of individual agency, centred on the ability to exercise choice and control over actions in the moment, whereas diachronous control emphasises the temporal dimension of behavioural regulation, with account taken of self-governance over time and the potentially cumulative effects of decisions and behaviour. See, eg, ZC Irving, 'Will-Powered: Synchronic Regulation is the Difference Maker for Self-Control' (2022) 225 *Cognition* 105154.

II. Historical Perspectives

The idea that an individual accused before the law cannot rely on exculpatory or mitigatory circumstances they have themselves had a hand in creating is by no means a novel concept. Though the formalisation of prior fault in legal systems such as England and Wales[11] or the Netherlands took place over the course of the nineteenth and early twentieth centuries,[12] the notion that self-induced impediment or impairment could not be used to absolve oneself of liability for acts committed in their wake has had a place in the common law going back at least as far as the medieval period, in turn drawing on the judicial philosophy of Ancient Greece. The purpose of this section is to briefly outline the development of prior fault rules in order to identify the types of questions that the law is concerned with when it comes to intoxicated states and prior fault. This provides a basis to discuss the potential roles of other disciplines, but also solves the issue of whether prior fault ought to be concerned with mental states at all (as opposed to being a purely legal notion). As we outline, we believe that despite normative justifications of prior fault rules, the legal underpinnings of the rules have clear behavioural components to them in which BCN-sciences can prove useful.

In Nicomachean Ethics, Aristotle argued that actions resulting from a state of ignorance caused by negligence cannot be excused, as such ignorance arises from within. Using the example of voluntary intoxication to illustrate this principle, he outlines that

> we punish a man for his very ignorance, if he is thought responsible for the ignorance, as when penalties are doubled in the case of drunkenness; for the moving principle is in the man himself, since he had the power of not getting drunk and his getting drunk was the cause of his ignorance.

The same principle can be found in various legal codes and guiding moral philosophies across the ancient world. The Code of Hammurabi (c. 1750 BC) outlines liability for harm done through previous negligence or wrongdoing.[13] The concept of 'aitia' found in Ancient Greek law recognised the contribution of an individual's prior actions to their liability for subsequent crime. Roman law contained the concept of 'culpa' (fault or negligence), holding individuals responsible for the unintended but foreseeable consequences of their actions. Under the

[11] From hereon referred to as 'England' or 'English law' only.

[12] The first time that the Dutch notion of prior fault ('culpa in causa', fault in its cause) was formally introduced into the law was around 1930. See CJ van Netburg, 'Eigen Schuld!? "Culpa in causa" bij Wettelijke Strafuitsluitingsgronden' [1994] *WODC Den Haag*. In England and Wales, the formalisation of prior fault rules took place gradually over the course of the 19th and into the 20th century, established through developing caselaw rather than any specific act of codification.

[13] For instance, Laws 229 to 233 of the code outlined the subsequent liabilities attached to a housebuilder where improper construction leads to collapse causing death or damage, whilst Law 251 addressed the fault attached to ox-related deaths where, though the threat was known, the owner had failed in enacting measures to contain it.

Brehon Law of Ancient Ireland, determinations of liability and compensation were influenced in part by consideration of prior conduct.

The Digest, a compendium of Roman jurisprudence compiled on the orders of the Byzantine emperor Justinian I in the sixth century AD, draws on similar principles, establishing that ignorance should be classed as a form of negligence (50.17.132), and that an individual who sustains damage through their own fault is not considered to have been injured (50.17.203). This Corpus Juris Civilis, as it came to be known, was at the heart of subsequent legal codes such as the Basilika and the Prochiron, and remained the basis for the eastern Roman Empire's law into the fifteenth century. In western Europe, the rediscovery of the Digest in the twelfth century renewed interest in Roman law and ultimately led to the Corpus Juris Civilis being a foundational work for all civil law systems.[14]

Later, Canon law, which governed the Christian Church in medieval Europe and significantly influenced secular legal systems in the period, placed an emphasis on personal moral responsibility. Voluntary intoxication was held as no excuse for sinful behaviour, as individuals were regarded as having a duty to avoid putting themselves into compromising situations. Rather, it represented a wilful relinquishment of faculties, and hence the voluntary invalidation of reason. That these faculties, and the reasoning they informed, were understood to form the basis for rational, and more importantly moral, thought suggested that their willing surrender provided a marker of immorality in itself.[15]

Commonly referenced as the earliest case of precedent in English Common law informing prior fault intoxication, *Reniger v Fogossa* held that:[16]

> if a person that is drunk kills another, this shall be felony, and he shall be hanged for it, and yet he did it through ignorance, for when he was drunk he had no understanding nor memory; but inasmuch as that ignorance was occasioned by his own act and folly, and he might have avoided it, he shall not be privileged thereby.

The judgment proceeds to outline the underlying rationale for this conclusion, offering that: 'Aristotle says, that such a man deserves double punishment, because he has doubly offended, viz. in being drunk to the evil example of others, and in committing the crime of homicide'.

Though the *Reniger* decision drew on the notion that intoxication should potentially aggravate offending, it did not incorporate this principle into the judgment itself, but rather merely established that drunkenness should not excuse. That intoxication might be an inherently aggravating feature of criminal conduct was developed in Beverley's Case of 1603: 'Although he who is drunk is for the

[14] FW Dingledy, 'The Corpus Juris Civilis: A Guide to Its History and Use' (2016) 35 *Legal Reference Services Quarterly* 231.

[15] A Loughnan and S Gless 'Understanding the Law on Intoxicated Offending: Principle, Pragmatism and Legal Culture' (2017) 3 *Journal of International and Comparative Law* 345. See also E Papp Kamali 'The Horrible Sepulture of Mannes Resoun: Intoxication and Medieval English Felony Law' (2022) 30 *Rechtsgeschichte – Legal History* 20.

[16] *Reniger v Fogossa* [1551] PB 1 Plowd 1, 75 Eng Rep 1.

time *non compos mentis*, yet his drunkenness does not extenuate his act or offence nor turn to his avail, but it is a great offence in itself, and, therefore aggravates his offence.' That, during the protracted transition from medieval to modern jurisprudence, voluntary intoxication was understood not as an excuse but rather as a malfeasance in itself is encapsulated in the passage through Parliament of the 1606 Act for repressing the odious and loathsome Sin of Drunkenness. Indeed, the notion that being intoxicated in a public place is an offence in its own right is still enshrined in English, Welsh and Northern Irish law. Section 12 of the Licensing Act 1872 provides for punishing any person intoxicated 'in any highway or other public place, whether a building or not, or on any licensed premises'. Albeit, there is little evidence of this law being broadly enforced in English pubs today.

As this brief historical overview demonstrates, the arbitration of the principles underlying prior fault intoxication, at least through Anglo-American common law, has therefore focused largely on two questions. The first being not *whether* but rather *how* to prevent intoxication from providing an excuse for criminal acts. The notion that self-induced intoxication should not permit an individual to escape culpability is discussed, established and re-established across many of the foundational legal works of this period, being found, for example, in Coke (1 Inst. 247a), Blackstone (4 Commentaries 26), Hawkins (1 P.C. c. 1, s. 6) and Hale (1 Hale 31). Across civil law jurisdictions, such as the Netherlands, we see a similar discussion on the rationale of prior fault being the prevention of unjust exculpation.[17] The second question, on which there has been less clarity historically in English traditions, is that of whether intoxication should aggravate offending in its own right. Interestingly, in the Netherlands, intoxication is generally considered an aggravating factor predominantly in violent offences, and recent policy changes mandate immediate breath or blood samples from suspects of violent crimes in order to facilitate evidentiary matters therein.[18] If, by virtue of prior fault, intoxication should aggravate offending in its own right, we need to engage in a discussion on whether intoxication is always a blameworthy condition or whether there are situations in which it is not, ie, situations without prior fault, which would reject such an aggravating notion.

However, for the purpose of our chapter, we focus on the first question here, being the way in which prior fault rules can prevent intoxication from becoming exculpatory. There is no reason to question the necessity of having prior fault

[17] For example, 't Hart in Supreme Court of the Netherlands, 28-6-1983, *NJ* 1983 53 annot. AC 't Hart, ECLI:NL:HR:1983:AC8052.

[18] The sentencing guidelines of the Dutch prosecution office indicate a 75% increase in the sentence when the offender committed a violent offence whilst under the influence. Of course, the judge is not obliged to follow the charges brought forward by the prosecution, but the heightened sentencing pleas do affect the final sentencing verdict. Moreover, under art 55d Dutch Code of Criminal Procedure, police officers acquire the right to take blood or breath samples from suspects of violent offences, if there are indications that the suspect is indeed under the influence of substances. Note that these aggravating effects are sentencing-related, and do not change the nature of the offence that the offender is charged with.

doctrines in the first place: we can say that it is not a matter of *whether* prior fault rules ought to exist. Rather, *how* these rules operate is important to examine further, as the conceptualisation of prior fault determines what kind of prior behaviour is considered culpable and how we can adequately distinguish between different forms of prior fault.

Until the late nineteenth century, the position English law took on intoxication was one which reflected a broader societal emphasis on personal responsibility and the rejection of vice. The history of prior fault thinking as it pertains to intoxication has tended towards being one of expediency rather than protracted philosophical debate, being rooted in public policy considerations such as maintaining accountability for criminal actions, deterring individuals from intentionally becoming intoxicated to commit crimes, and avoiding the potential for abuse of intoxication as a defence (including the potential for fabricated claims). Established precedent has been shaped in great part through practical necessity, driven by principle rather than theoretical discourse.[19] Similarly, the Netherlands also appears to employ a perspective towards prior fault that seems more convenience-based, rather than one rooted in clear doctrinal considerations.[20] Yet, in the English common law system, as early as 1678 we see consideration of the distinction between the acute and chronic effects of intoxication and the relevance of this distinction to questions of liability for offences:[21]

> That although the simplex phrenzy occasioned immediately by drunkenness excuse not in criminals, yet if by one or more such practices an habitual or fixed phrenzy be caused though this madness was contracted by the vice and will of the party, yet this habitual and fixed phrenzy thereby caused puts the man into the same condition in relation to crimes, as if the same were contracted involuntarily at first.

Clearly, there is account being taken here of a meaningful difference between aberrance consequent to acute intoxication and that mediated by chronic exposure. This sentiment is echoed two centuries later by Stephen J in *R v Davis*[22] and approved by Lord Birkenhead in *Beard*:[23]

> drunkenness is one thing and the diseases to which drunkenness leads are different things, and if a man by drunkenness brings on a state of disease which causes

[19] See P Handler, 'Intoxication and Criminal Responsibility in England, 1819–1920' (2013) 33 *Oxford Journal of Legal Studies* 243 and see also D Rabin 'Drunkenness and Responsibility for Crime in the Eighteenth Century' (2005) 44 *Journal of British Studies* 457.

[20] This sentiment is nicely summarised in an interview with a public prosecutor: 'I admit that it is forced. I realise very clearly that the moment that somebody's consciousness is greatly reduced, or absent, that you are pulling a trick (doctrinally speaking) by saying 'yes, but this person has used a substance prior, even days prior, to the time of the offence, and with that he factually assumed responsibility for the offence days later'. Of course, I can see that that's somewhat forced. Yet it's something we can hold onto as lawyers, and sometimes, we are just looking for a way to work around the issue.' See AE Goldberg, *Blaming the Addicted Brain: Building Bridges between Criminal Law and Neuroscientific Perspectives on Addiction* (The Hague, Eleven International Publishing, 2022) 274–275.

[21] M Hale, *The History of the Pleas of the Crown* (London, Tonson, 1678).

[22] *R v Davis* [1881] 14 Cox C.C. 563.

[23] *DPP v Beard* [1920] AC 479 (HL).

> such a degree of madness, even for a time, which would have relieved him from the responsibility if it had been caused in any other way then he would not be criminally responsible.[24]

We might speculate, on that basis, about the voluntary nature of intoxication in the example of addicted individuals. Dutch criminal law has differentiated between 'simple' and addicted intoxication:[25]

> The prior fault doctrine does not imply that every kind of self-intoxication is legally irrelevant. Looking at the parliamentary history of article 37 Dutch Criminal Code [the former Dutch insanity defence – AEG], this was never its intention. Generally, I believe that we could differentiate between a couple of scenarios which, under certain conditions, could fall outside the scope [of prior fault – AEG], to be subdivided into three groups: […] (b). A second group of cases are those in which the self-intoxication, even though it was originally initiated voluntarily, has become a coercive act and has led to monomania (for instance 'I took those substances myself, but I could not have acted differently'). This could be the case for addicts.

What we can learn from this is that, historically, there are potentially grounds to differentiate between intoxication-induced brain states on the basis of their aetiology, and potentially even between types of intoxication, such as one fuelled by an underlying dependency.[26] More recently, these distinctions have been very much supported by developments in BCN-sciences, as chapters five and seven of this collection discuss. Whether legal decision-makers also make this discernment between prior fault for addicted and non-addicted defendants in practice is a different question. This draws us to our next section, where we discuss whether perspectives on addiction do indeed affect decision-making.

[24] This distinction has arguably been blurred by the finding in *R v Taj* [2018] EWCA Crim 1743, wherein the defendant was denied a claim of self-defence because s 76(5) of the Criminal Justice and Immigration Act 2008 provides that a defendant may not rely as a basis for their self-defence on a mistaken belief attributable to intoxication which has been voluntarily induced. Though not intoxicated at the time of the offending, the defendant was denied a claim of self-defence. In the subsequent appeal against conviction, it was held that 'the words "attributable to intoxication" in s. 76(5) are broad enough to encompass both (a) a mistaken state of mind as a result of being drunk or intoxicated at the time and (b) a mistaken state of mind immediately and proximately consequent upon earlier drink or drug-taking, so that even though the person concerned is not drunk or intoxicated at the time, the short-term effects can be shown to have triggered subsequent episodes of eg paranoia', concluding that 'the phrase "attributable to intoxication" is not confined to cases in which alcohol or drugs are still present in a defendant's system.' See H Crombag, J Child and G Sullivan, 'Drunk, Dangerous and Delusional: How Legal Concept-Creep Risks Overcriminalization' (2020) 115 *Addiction* 2200.

[25] Supreme Court of the Netherlands, 28-6-1983, *NJ* 1983 53 annot. AC 't Hart, ECLI:NL:HR:1983:AC8052. In 1959, Pompe has also mentioned that 'pathological drunkenness' in principle ought to fall within the realm of the non-accountability excuse (ie, the Dutch equivalent of the insanity defence) contrary to regular, non-addicted intoxication. WPJ Pompe, *Handboek van het Nederlandse Strafrecht* (Zwolle, WEJ Tjeenk Willink, 1959) 193.

[26] It is questionable whether the intended distinction between types of prior fault is upheld in modern judgments. In the Netherlands, addicted intoxication and non-addicted intoxication are often considered or at least treated as being equivalent, with the exception of various sentencing nuances (eg, imposing mandatory addiction treatment as a condition to a suspended sentence).

III. Legal Decision-Making, Bias, and the Application of Prior Fault Rules

History suggests that prior fault rules were generally not concerned with mental states. Let us indeed presume that prior fault is a fundamentally legal concept, to be assessed through doctrinal and normative analyses. The fact that certain legal concepts may mirror some behavioural notion does not mean that it *considers* that behavioural notion in its legal judgment. For example, the concept of 'intent', colloquially speaking, may suggest a behavioural dimension, whereas in most civil law jurisdictions, the assessment of intent is entirely normative.[27] In the Netherlands, for instance, it is barely possible to negate intent on the basis of a mental disorder. Having intent is simply inferred objectively, based on the outward manifestation of behaviour.[28] We acknowledge that common law systems employ much more subjective perspectives towards intent; we merely use this example to clarify how certain legal concepts may have behavioural equivalents, but that legal systems do not always incorporate or acknowledge the behavioural parallels. Moreover, previous research shows that legal professionals oftentimes consider concepts such as insanity or prior fault to be fundamentally normative, meaning they believe that, ultimately, legal decision-making on prior fault or insanity must be reserved exclusively to a judge.[29] In this section, we argue that *even then* it is irresponsible to ignore non-legal factors that influence prior fault rules. After all, legal rules are ultimately applied by human agents. Decisions, legal or otherwise, will always be influenced by features specific to the decision-maker and their situation. Legal professionals are equally affected by biases and other preconceived notions as their non-legal peers. It is, therefore, misguided to presume that any decision in the law is not influenced already by non-legal factors. Perhaps the conceptualisation of prior fault rules themselves are sometimes considered immune to the influence of other disciplines, but the application of these rules certainly is not. It is, consequently, important to address the effects of bias in legal decision-making using empirical

[27] J De Hullu, *Materieel Strafrecht* (Alphen aan den Rijn, Wolters Kluwer, 2018) 233.

[28] For example, consider if somebody stabs another. From the mere act of stabbing the judge may objectively infer that it was his intent to kill, or at least seriously harm, the other: why else would he be stabbing them, if not to harm or kill? If the defendant acts on a psychotic belief that the person he stabs is an evil intruder who must be killed, he is still acting intentionally as to kill the other. Indeed, he may not be blamed for it, because his beliefs were formed by a mental disorder, but this is addressed at the blameworthiness phase, not when establishing intent. As such, the notion of intent has been stripped off its colloquial, behavioural meanings to a large extent.

[29] Goldberg (n 20). Moreover, a recent landmark case in the Netherlands established the criteria which must be met for insanity to apply (Supreme Court of the Netherlands 17-10-2023, ECLI:NL:HR:2023:1295, *Thijs H.*). Although insanity requires the presence of a mental disorder, the Dutch Supreme Court ruled that mental disorder must be understood in a legal sense, and the presence thereof can be established by the judge. Although naturally, in most cases a judge will have themselves been informed by a behavioural expert on this matter, it is not a requirement and judges may also establish a mental disorder without such behavioural expertise, or decide against the experts' advice therein. See also n 7.

research findings as an illustration of how prior fault rules ought to necessarily be addressed in a broader, interdisciplinary socio-legal context. This section discusses evidence of the use of bias in cases of addicted defendants and argues that such biases can be considered a consequence of stigma towards substance use disorders, strongly related to prior fault logic.

Before doing so, we want to clarify the vocabulary used in this section. We discuss research on legal decision-making and the apparent biases that appear here. Moreover, we link those biases to stigma. Bias and stigma are sometimes considered different sides of the same coin but are occasionally also described as distinct concepts. For the purpose of this chapter, we understand bias as it is commonly defined in legal decision-making research: 'When making judgments or decisions, people often rely on simplified information processing strategies called heuristics, which may result in systematic, predictable errors called cognitive biases.'[30] Hence, biases are errors resulting from mental shortcuts. Stigma can be defined as 'a complex multilevel social process that encompasses the elements of labelling, stereotyping, separation, status loss, and discrimination in the context of a power situation.'[31] In our view, the relatively harmless human tendency to have certain biases can lead to stigmatisation, or, vice versa, stigma can be an underlying reason for biases in decision-making to exist.

There is a plethora of research available showing the different biases in decision-making in the legal sphere. There are studies highlighting biases towards the defendant's gender, race, attractiveness and age, just to name a few.[32] Specifically regarding addiction, however, research is more scarce. Two studies are discussed here to illustrate in what way prior fault logic may impact legal decision-making. First is an experimental study demonstrating that Dutch prosecutors tend to perceive an addicted defendant as less responsible when their addiction is framed as a brain disease as opposed to 'just' a substance use disorder.[33] Despite an equal amount of impairment in the mental capacities of the defendant, the label and description of the defendant's condition mattered in the decision by the prosecutor on the degree of accountability. This suggests that not only the case facts and the concrete impairments of or behaviour by the defendant affect the legal decision, but also the nature (or framing thereof) of the disorder. The study hypothesised that prior fault logic caused the difference between the two addiction perspectives: a brain disease notion of addiction may mitigate prior fault logic, by being perceived as a condition that is outside the individual's control, thereby resulting in reduced accountability.

[30] V Berthet, 'The Impact of Cognitive Biases on Professionals' Decision-Making: A Review of Four Occupational Areas' (2022) 12 *Frontiers in Psychology* 1.

[31] G Thornicroft and others, 'The Lancet Commission on Ending Stigma and Discrimination in Mental Health' (2022) *The Lancet Commissions*.

[32] For a well-known study about offender characteristic bias, see for instance D Steffensmeier, JT Ulmer and JH Kramer, 'The interaction of Race, Gender, and Age in Criminal Sentencing: The Punishment Cost of Being Young, Black, and Male' (1998) 36 *Criminology* 763.

[33] Goldberg (n 20).

The second study of interest is a more detailed experiment, addressing decision-making in cases of addicted defendants. Based on a sample of UK-based magistrates, the research examined differences in sentencing administration for a hypothetical case of simple theft.[34] The defendant's disorder was manipulated to either be the result of a substance disorder or a fictional neuropsychiatric condition, and the prior fault of the defendant in acquiring and sustaining these conditions was also altered. The mental impairments and other circumstances of the offence remained equal. Hence, this study allows us to first examine differences between addiction and a non-existent disorder – whereby both disorders resulted in the same impairments in capacities, which technically should result in the same sentencing outcomes. Second, it is possible to draw conclusions about the role of prior fault in the final sentencing discussion, providing insight into the currently unclear sentencing guidelines.[35] For the purpose of this chapter, we address the first outcome. The defendant suffering from addiction was provided with a markedly different sentencing decision compared to the defendant with the fictional disorder: the non-addicted defendant was more than three times as likely to receive a reduction in sentence as the addicted defendant. Again, stressing that the mental capacities and impairments therein were identical for both conditions, it is remarkable that simply the label of addiction compared to a fictional neuropsychiatric disorder had such effects.

The outcome of these studies can be explained by the preconceived notions we apparently have when dealing with defendants suffering from substance disorders. Such perceptions are not exclusive to legal decision-makers. Global research inside and outside the legal arena consistently identifies a substance-related disorder as having one of the most stigmatising effects compared to other behavioural, health and social characteristics.[36] This causes biases whereby individuals are perceived as more dangerous, aggressive and threatening.[37] The effects on the individual cannot be overstated: stigmatisation results in poorer mental health and bars the accessibility of (mental) healthcare.[38] Moreover, qualitative research also indicates that those with an addiction feel treated unfairly in the criminal justice system.[39]

[34] N Sinclair-House, JJ Child and HS Crombag, 'Addiction is a Brain Disease, and it Doesn't Matter: Prior Choice in Drug Use Blocks Leniency in Criminal Punishment' (2020) 26 *Psychology, Public Policy, and Law* 36.

[35] ibid.

[36] R Room and others 'Cross-Cultural Views on Stigma, Valuation, Parity, and Societal Values Towards Disability' in TB Üstün and others (eds), *Disability and Culture: Universalism and Diversity* (Amsterdam, Hogrefe & Huber Publishers, 2001) 276–277.

[37] A Crisp and colleagues, 'Stigmatization of People with Mental Illnesses: A Follow-up Study Within the Changing Minds Campaign of the Royal College of Psychiatrists' (2005) 4 *World Psychiatry* 106; R Ford, 'Interpersonal Challenges as a Constraint on Care: The Experience of Nurses' Care of Patients Who Use Illicit Drugs' (2011) 37 *Contemporary Nurse* 241.

[38] PW Corrigan, BG Druss and DA Perlick, 'The Impact of Mental Illness Stigma on Seeking and Participating in Mental Health Care' (2014) 15 *Psychological Science in the Public Interest* 37.

[39] S Fraser and others, 'Addiction Stigma and the Biopolitics of Liberal Modernity: A Qualitative Analysis' (2017) 44 *International Journal of Drug Policy* 192.

It is not surprising, therefore, that such biases have the effects on legal decision-making that we just described.

The potential effects of stigma on the application of prior fault rules should not be underestimated. As these two examples showed, addiction can be met with prior fault perceptions, which in turn can influence a range of decisions, from the application of defences to the imposition of sentences. It is safe to assume that such *perceptions* also impact the application of prior fault *rules*; ie, cases of addiction trigger prior fault intuition, which in turn affects how prior fault rules are applied. Due to inconsistencies or uncertainties in the application of prior fault rules,[40] prior fault intuitions causing undue bias can more easily go unnoticed. Clear and consistent prior fault rules may help to prevent this.

This conclusion exemplifies that interdisciplinary research is fundamental to understanding the application of prior fault rules. A final example from legal practice allows us to highlight this significance. Based on Dutch case law research, two types of arguments can often be found for defendants who are addicted. First is when the defendant is or has been addicted but failed to seek appropriate help (both professionally and socially). This can be considered indicative of the disorder being 'your own fault': the court argues that you did not do enough to aid recovery and thus can hold you accountable for the consequences of the addiction. This reasoning seems to suggest that the blameworthy aspect of the addiction is the fact that you did not actively try to improve your lot. The second type of argument is, therefore, very interesting. It is common to read that when the addicted defendant did actively seek out help, perhaps even repeatedly, but has relapsed into use, this is equally considered blameworthy. Perhaps surprisingly, multiple previous rehabilitation or treatment attempts, which may suggest a certain severity of the disorder, are not necessarily considered a sign that D's mental disorder was debilitating to such an extent that they had trouble conforming their behaviour to the law. Instead, it is argued that the addiction implies a longstanding experience with the substance and its effects, meaning D knew about the consequences or should have known these. Moreover, the fact that D relapsed also implies that there were periods of remission as well. Here, culpability for the consequences of addiction is found in having awareness and experience, as opposed to the first argument, where it seems that D is blamed for failing to manage their condition.[41]

Hence, it seems that prior fault intuition is implicitly – and nearly automatically – present when the defendant is addicted. This is interesting, as the two arguments outlined above are polar opposite situations, ie, cases where a defendant either did or did not try to get better. The fact that both situations have similar outcomes, in which the defendant is considered responsible for the consequences of their addiction, further suggests that it is not so much behaviour that matters but rather the

[40] For a Dutch perspective, see, eg, AE Goldberg, 'Foreseeability and Prior Fault: Examining the Assessment Framework for Intoxication, Blame and Criminal Responsibility' (2024) 29 *Bialystok Legal Studies* 69.

[41] Goldberg and others (n 6).

addiction itself. As such, although hardly ever mentioned explicitly, it seems that it is the state of being addicted that is sufficient for culpability and consequently liability, due to such ingrained prior fault perceptions. This is a clear marker of bias or even stigma.

This is problematic for two main reasons. First is the general nature of most legal systems' approach towards criminal law. Especially in civil law countries, employing an act-based jurisdiction, the aim is to penalise prohibited behaviour or omissions. Being addicted is neither a behaviour nor an omission. Although courts often refer to the behaviour or consequences caused by the addiction as their basis for culpability, the argument above shows that it essentially boils down to being blamed for the state of being addicted, thereby deviating from the purpose of the law. The second reason, very much related, is namely that a generalised blame for a certain lifestyle is something the law ought to avoid. Referred to by the Germans as *Lebensführungsschuld* (lifestyle blame) or, in the Netherlands, as *karakterschuld* (character blame), this type of generalised culpability without specific related prohibited behavioural markers is problematic.

To briefly conclude this section, we argue that BCN sciences are fundamental to understanding prior fault logic and its consequences in legal decisions, despite possibly arguing prior fault is a doctrinal and/or normative concept with which other disciplines ought not to be concerned. When decisions are made, there is an inevitable human factor, and we demonstrated that this results in bias, stigma, and criminalisation of character in cases of addiction. Prior fault cannot be considered in isolation but ought to integrate other disciplines to fully understand the consequences for legal practice.

Moving to the next section, the necessity to involve other disciplines in the study of prior fault also becomes apparent when discussing whether substance use can be considered voluntary or not, such as in cases of severe substance dependencies. Despite being a central feature in prior fault rules, this is a discussion that can also be had outside the legal arena. The main reason why non-addicted intoxication and addicted intoxication may be distinguished from one another to us seems to be the degree of control the defendant had in using the substances, where a reduced amount of control – or even absent volition – would be indicative of a lower degree of culpability. If this is indeed the main distinction between these two scenarios, then behavioural sciences may play a critical role in differentiating between prior fault situations. Luckily, perspectives on human decision-making capacities, responsibility, and criminal culpability have advanced considerably since the medieval era. Whereas early legal doctrine espoused a rigid binary model of 'voluntary' versus 'involuntary' intoxication, modern behavioural science recognises a more complex reality.[42] Volition and control are multidimensional constructs modulated by internal biology and the external environment, the

[42] R Holton and K Berridge, 'Addiction Between Compulsion and Choice' in N Levy (ed), *Addiction and Self-Control: Perspectives From Philosophy, Psychology, and Neuroscience* (New York, Oup USA, 2013).

nuances of which are not readily captured into simple dichotomies.[43] In the next section, we explore the differences between the legal and behavioural meanings of these constructs further in order to identify how the law can be aided in understanding concepts such as voluntariness and control in the context of prior fault and (in)voluntary intoxication.

IV. Perspectives on Behavioural Control

Volition or control-related capacities are a key concept in many responsibility discussions, such as the volitional prong in some forms of the insanity defence or the lack of control in the requirements for duress. Prior fault rules are no exception: prior fault rules regarding intoxication seem to presuppose that the substances were consumed voluntarily.[44] In the context of prior fault and intoxication, voluntariness is a negatively defined premise, ie, intoxication is generally considered voluntary with certain exceptions, such as spiked or coerced drinks,[45] or unexpected reactions to prescription medications.[46] However, without contraindications suggesting otherwise, intoxication is generally voluntary, even when compulsive use (such as addictions) underlies the reasons for taking the substances.[47] As such, volitional capacities seem to be at the core of prior fault rules: the assumption that intoxication is generally voluntary and that voluntariness is necessary to consider the intoxication culpable.[48] This section aims to explore the concept of voluntariness and address the relevance of non-legal disciplines in understanding it further. In fact, the concept of voluntariness is the perfect case example to highlight discrepancies between legal and non-legal disciplines, highlighting the relevance of behavioural sciences in examining legal doctrine.

In law, voluntariness is clearly a binary notion. A defendant either acted voluntarily, for instance, when consuming substances, or involuntarily, for instance, by having their drink spiked with an unknown drug. Yet human nature and the capacity for control are not binary: behaviour can be considered in degrees of voluntariness and thus best be represented on a scale. This section further discusses the differences in legal and behavioural notions of control. This is relevant for a discussion

[43] ibid.

[44] A Loughnan and S Gless, 'Understanding the Law on Intoxicated Offending: Principle, Pragmatism and Legal Culture' (2017) 3 *Journal of International and Comparative Law* 345.

[45] Q Haque and I Cumming 'Intoxication and Legal Defences' (2003) 9 *Advances in Psychiatric Treatment* 144.

[46] J Piel 'The Defense of Involuntary Intoxication by Prescribed Medications: An Appellate Case Review' (2015) 43 *The Journal of the American Academy of Psychiatry and the Law* 321.

[47] Goldberg and others (n 6).

[48] Note that there seems to be a comparative difference between jurisdictions, whereby the focus in English law is on the voluntariness of the intoxication (ie, the outcome), compared to the Netherlands, which addresses the voluntariness of the substance use (ie, the act). Although in practice these two features are mostly synonymous, we do want to highlight potential differences in legal discussions that may arise because of this distinction.

on prior fault and addiction, as addicted intoxication is often considered voluntary and thereby reason to apply prior fault rules. The section's discussion shows that the conceptualisation of control through a scientific lens is much broader than the definition the law upholds. As such, we argue that developments in BCN-sciences are necessary when evaluating prior fault rules, but also argue that the current binary distinction between voluntary and involuntary is a conceptualisation that is not rooted in human behavioural physiology. Importantly, there are many legal concepts that do not align with more colloquial, behavioural equivalents. Consider, for instance, notions of intent or premeditation, which have a clear legal scope which may not include folk-psychological conceptions.[49] Thus, we do not wish to transform legal concepts into behavioural equivalents, but rather use the behavioural explanations to identify bottlenecks in the law.

The legal assessment of voluntariness does not have a clear behavioural equivalent. With that we mean that other concepts with behavioural parallels, such as the cognitive criterion for insanity ('to *know* what one is doing), are equipped to incorporate such behavioural notions. Consider, for instance, the role of behavioural experts in advising the courts on the defendant's cognitive capacities and the potential for an insanity defence. Even though the judge decides, and thus we may ultimately consider it a legal matter, there is a clear behavioural marker to this legal notion that experts may test: eg, the defendant's sense of reality or presence of psychotic delusions. For voluntariness, there is no such parallel as of yet.[50] This has already led to a legal-behavioural struggle, for instance, when looking at the volitional prong in the insanity defence.[51] Many insanity defence criteria (such as the Model Penal Code, the German *Schuldunfähigkeit*, or the Dutch *ontoerekenbaarheid*) allow for a control-based impairment as a basis for a successful defence.[52] It has been argued that this volitional prong is potentially riddled with complexities. An issue with allowing a control-based impairment is that a lack of control regarding some aspects of behaviour does not eliminate having control in other aspects. For instance, in the case of substance abuse, one may experience irresistible urges as a result of cravings for the drugs. Control over the consumption of substances is substantially diminished or even absent.[53] Yet the consumption of substances is only one action in a potentially endless chain of behaviours, of which not all behaviours are equally captivated by the irresistible urge. As we discuss later when differentiating between synchronous and diachronous control, we can – in the case of the addicted defendant – still argue that the individual had control in decisions leading up to the subsequently uncontrollable craving. Criminal law addresses behaviour integrally, and thus the issue arises of how a lack of control regarding a particular set of actions is assessed in the broader chain of actions that

[49] See also the discussion in fns 7 & 28 of this chapter.

[50] One can think of associated behavioural notions such as impulsivity or inhibition. We discuss these, including its flaws, later this section.

[51] See G Meynen, *Legal Insanity: Explorations in Psychiatry, Law, and Ethics* (Basel, Springer, 2016), especially in ch 2.

[52] ibid.

[53] GF Koob and ND Volkow 'Neurocircuitry of Addiction' (2010) 35 *Neuropsychopharmacology* 217.

comprise the offence. As Meynen put it: 'Within the context of forensic psychiatric evaluations of defendants, this means that the fact that some control was retained cannot in itself justify a conclusion that the defendant retained the legally relevant type of control.'[54]

Aside from this rather practical issue, there is also a more fundamental problem with allowing a volitional prong in a legal criterion. As Morse has put it:[55]

> There appears to be a prima facie case for a compulsion branch of the insanity defense, but is it persuasive and would the test be workable? If or to what degree a person's desire or impulse to act was controllable is not determinable: there is no scientific test to judge whether an impulse was irresistible or simply not resisted. At best, we may develop a phenomenological account of the defendant's subjective state of mind that will permit a common sense assessment of how much compulsion existed.

This criticism towards volitional impairment as a putative basis for a defence is rooted in a fear of under-criminalisation, where potential defendants who are able, but unwilling, to exercise control may be excused.[56] Still, many jurisdictions find themselves working with a volitional prong.[57] This quick detour to the insanity defence shows that control-based criteria for legal concepts can pose problems by not aligning with a clear behavioural counterpart. Yet it also shows that this does not necessarily prevent behavioural sciences from informing the law on potential behavioural substrates of such concepts. A potential feature to be looked at is, for instance, impulsivity. Although not the same as control or voluntariness as it is used in the law, it does provide insight into volitional (in)capacity. Let us explore impulsivity as a concept a little further.

There are different varieties of impulsivity, which are both behaviourally and neurobiologically distinct from one another. As such, it is not a unitary concept and can be fractionated into, eg, impulsive action, impulsive choice, response inhibition, reversal learning, temporal discounting, and so forth. These different forms of executive functioning all contribute to understanding why a person may have less control over their behaviour – such as when taking substances – than others.[58] These different features of impulsivity can be measured through BCN-informed tests. Well-known tasks that are often included in forensic assessments are, for instance, stop-signal or go/no-go tasks, which aim to understand how well an individual is able to inhibit motor responses.[59]

[54] Meynen (n 51) 23.

[55] SJ Morse, 'Excusing the Crazy: The Insanity Defense Reconsidered' (1985) 58 *S California Law Review* 777, 817.

[56] S Penney, 'Impulse Control and Criminal Responsibility: Lessons from Neuroscience' (2012) 35 *International Journals of Law & Psychiatry* 99.

[57] For an excellent discussion on the issues with a volitional prong, see Meynen (n 51) ch 2.

[58] CA Winstanley, P Olausson, JR Taylor, JD Jentsch, 'Insight Into the Relationship Between Impulsivity and Substance Abuse from Studies Using Animal Models (2010) 34 *Alcoholism: Clinical and Experimental Research* 1306.

[59] MD Lezak and others, *Neuropsychological Assessment*, 5th edn (Oxford, Oxford University Press, 2012). For a more detailed discussion, see also ch 7 of this collection.

It is worth noting that, though there is overlap in their engagement of broader inhibitory control systems in the brain, these different forms of impulsivity can be differentiated at the level of specific neural mechanisms. Response inhibition has been linked to the right inferior frontal gyrus and the pre-supplementary motor area,[60] whereas choice impulsivity and temporal discounting are associated with the functioning of the ventral striatum, prefrontal cortex and limbic regions.[61] There is also a differing role of neurotransmitters in different forms of impulsivity.[62] In fact, the involvement of different brain regions coupled with the observation that different forms of impulsivity are substantively uncorrelated with one another has led some to argue that 'impulsivity' cannot be considered a unitary concept in any real sense and is rather a broad label for a collection of distinct mechanisms.[63]

Finally, to help understand the complexity of the behavioural equivalent of 'voluntariness', it is important to differentiate between diachronous and synchronous control. A common argument when discussing volitional impairment for addicts, especially in a prior fault discussion, is to refer to moments in which the defendant did not experience such a loss of control (yet) but is expected to anticipate such a lack. Indeed, if substance use may be considered involuntary due to an underlying addiction – admittedly mostly a theoretical argument – prior decisions in the development and continuation of the disorder are sometimes referenced to establish prior fault.[64] Effectively, what prior fault is addressing is a form of *diachronic* control. Despite control lacking at the time of the offence (*synchronous* control), for instance, due to acute intoxication, we may address the defendant's capacity for control in preventing this lack of control from happening. If that is also problematic, such as when the intoxication is fuelled by addiction, one may refer to an even older set of actions where the defendant was still in control of potential outcomes. Whether to coin it 'prior fault' from a legal perspective or 'diachronous control' from behavioural disciplines: both concepts capture the same essence, meaning that either the individual minimises the chances of such an 'uncontrolled' moment happening in the first place, or that he directly takes action against the feelings of diminished control.[65] An example of the first (minimising the loss of control) would be to avoid places where an addicted user may come across their substance of addiction, eg, by avoiding bars or drug-related paraphernalia. The second option, to take action against feelings of diminished control, could be the engagement in treatment to reduce cravings or remedy their addiction.

[60] AR Aron, TW Robbins and RA Poldrack, 'Inhibition and the Right Inferior Frontal Cortex' (2004) 8 *Trends in Cognitive Sciences* 170.

[61] SM Brown and others, 'Neural Basis of Individual Differences in Impulsivity: Contributions of Corticolimbic Circuits for Behavioral Arousal and Control' (2006) 6 *Emotion* 239.

[62] DM Eagle, A Bari and TW Robbins, 'The Neuropsychopharmacology of Action Inhibition: Cross-Species Translation of the Stop-Signal and Go/No-Go Tasks (2008) 199 *Psychopharmacology* 439.

[63] JL Evenden, 'Varieties of Impulsivity' (1999) 146 *Psychopharmacology* 348.

[64] Chapter 6 of this collection further explores this thought and highlights three scenarios in which culpability for addiction cannot straightforwardly be made out.

[65] J Kennett, NA Vincent and A Snoek, 'Drug Addiction and Criminal Responsibility' in L Neil and C Jens (eds), *Handbook on Neuroethics* (Dordrecht, Springer, 2014).

Directly relevant to prior fault, Morse has also stated before that addicted individuals experience 'lucid, rational intervals' between moments of intoxication, even if we would consider the direct usage to be involuntary.[66] However, as with synchronous control, diachronic control is not dichotomous either. The fact that there are, indeed, lucid intervals between usage, even for a severely addicted individual, does not automatically imply that there had been sufficient diachronic control – and by extension, that prior fault ought to apply. Various (in)capacities impact the ability to exercise diachronic control.[67] Some examples are the inability to foresee future consequences, ie, myopia for the future, poor physical health, or environmental constraints. Myopia for the future makes it more difficult to foresee, and thus plan accordingly, a drug-free future. There is only a true capacity for choice when there is awareness of the consequences thereof. Poor physical health, additionally, distracts from making the 'right' decisions and also contributes to the monopolisation of attention already in place through the addiction. Diminished attention spans further complicate overseeing decisions and weighing alternatives. Finally, one may be able to exercise diachronic control and be expected to, eg, reach out to (mental) healthcare facilities, but environmental constraints may severely limit the options available. All in all, although the individual may theoretically have been able to exercise diachronic control, they may practically be seriously impaired in doing so.

Thus, this section aimed to show how dichotomous legal concepts that play a fundamental role in understanding prior fault, such as the concept of voluntariness, have very different scientific equivalent meanings. Although there are valid reasons why legal criteria are dichotomous in nature, and we do not wish to change that necessarily,[68] it does demonstrate how the law dilutes a complex behavioural construct into overly simplistic notions of voluntary and involuntary acts. This highlights the discrepancy between the legal notion of prior fault and the outlook from BCN disciplines. Moreover, it may ultimately invite legal structures to reconsider their dichotomous approach. For that to be a possibility, however, we would first need to address the broader challenge presented in allowing empirical findings to change normative structures. The next section explores the integration of empiricism with norms, as an example of the is-ought divide.

[66] SJ Morse, 'Addiction and Criminal Responsibility' in J Poland and G Graham (eds), *Addiction and Responsibility* (Cambridge, MIT Press, 2011) 191.

[67] J Kennett, *Agency and Responsibility: A Common-sense Moral Psychology* (Oxford, Clarendon Press, 2001).

[68] Although, it can be an argument to allow for an in-between alternative. Eg, in Dutch and German criminal law, the insanity defence equivalence is a dichotomous concept, as it is in many other jurisdictions, and differentiates between responsible and non-responsible. However, a generalised diminished insanity defence also exists, which allows for defendants to be held diminished responsible whenever their behaviour was impacted by a disorder but in which case the defendant still remained somewhat rational or somewhat in control. The general acceptance of this concept is also the result of the unsatisfactory black-or-white approach which does not reflect the different shades of grey that human nature can represent.

V. Connecting Empiricism to the Law

So far, we have shown that other disciplines may be relevant – or even fundamental – in evaluating prior fault. Now that we have established the role of other disciplines, it is important to discuss how such information can help (national) doctrine move forward. We believe that incorporating other disciplines in the discussion of prior fault would be part of a circular process. Legal research has identified lacunas in the conceptualisation and application of prior fault rules, which – when not immediately solvable through further legal research – call for the addition of other disciplines. In turn, such external insights can aid the development of said law. However, when the nature of the research conducted is distinctly different, it is necessary to be careful when integrating the two. We argue that doctrinal and normative questions are not immediately compatible with the nature of empirical data, and vice versa. As such, it is our viewpoint that two moments of translation, so to speak, are required in the process of interdisciplinary legal research.

The first is to identify which other disciplines can aid the legal problem, and perhaps more importantly, how. Effectively, this involves research conducted by non-legal disciplines to provide information on the problem. Later, the opposite process ought to take place, and these findings from such other disciplines need to be translated back into normative legal recommendations. As an example of the first process, consider the legal problem of not sufficiently differentiating between various situations of prior fault, such as a defendant using substances recreationally or one who used them pathologically to self-medicate a mental disorder. Other disciplines can provide support: maybe psychological research can offer insights into volitional impairments that may be more pronounced in the latter. Then, as an example of the second process, the differences in impairments between the two types of offenders need to be translated back into legal guidelines or criteria that consider such differences, such as prior fault criteria. Simply including this information into a prior fault assessment framework is impossible without considering the broader legal structure in which the problem was situated to begin with, as well as certain normative deliberations (eg, would the inclusion of such differences not be unduly time-consuming or be in conflict with certain legal principles?).

To be concrete, we assert that it is fairly straightforward to conclude that bias and stigma surrounding substance use impact prior fault conclusions and potentially result in overcriminalisation or legal inequality. Moreover, we can argue that the seemingly behavioural underpinnings of prior fault, such as voluntariness, do not reflect the breadth of the concept when addressing it from a BCN perspective. It is quite the jump, however, to then provide normative regulations on how the law ought to regulate such potential disparities (eg, that prior fault rules should not apply in cases of severe addiction). This can be informed, but not dictated, by empirical evidence.

This is not a discussion unique to this current collection or distinct for this topic. The compatibility of empiricism and normativity is a matter rooted in the same discussion as the so-called 'is-ought divide'. A concept coined by Hume, it essentially states that there can be factual statements and value-based statements, and that these two classes are logically distinct. Or rather, as Searle suggests, the is-ought distinction declares that descriptive insights cannot result in evaluative conclusions without at least one additional (evaluative) premise.[69] This additional premise is our mentioned moments of translation. Believing otherwise, ie, that statements of fact and value are readily compatible, has been coined the naturalistic fallacy by Moore.[70] Fast-forward to present-day discussions, and we see that the problem is still very much debated and by now has also caught on in the context of empirical research on legal topics. So-called 'gap studies' aim to understand the dynamics between doctrinal legal research ('law in books') and empirical-legal studies ('law in action').[71] The existence of this research area illustrates that there can be considered a divide between the nature of empirical information and the application thereof to the law. Importantly, if, as we attest, this gap between empirical legal and doctrinal or normative legal research indeed exists and needs to be bridged, then it is even more important to carefully consider the divide between non-legal empirical information and doctrinal and/or normative research. After all, in the case of this collection, the empirical information is not always legal in nature (such as the studies discussed in chapter seven of this collection), although they have legal consequences.

We do not intend to engage in the fundamental philosophical discussion but simply mean to illustrate that the currently highlighted problem, that being the way in which we can incorporate findings from BCN sciences into prior fault rules, is neither new nor unique at its core. Rather, we invite a discussion on how to practically navigate the nature of empirical research in relation to normative matters in the context of prior fault. The previous sections highlighted the relevance of insights into control and legal decision-making in understanding the problems that arise with the current prior fault rules. How can we, practically, draw from these findings and incorporate them into legal practice?

One solution is to employ a clear legal assessment framework for prior fault and create a corresponding behavioural framework alongside. For instance, let us consider what would happen if foreseeability (ie, whether the defendant would foresee the negative consequences of the prior fault behaviour – in this case, the use of substances) were a consistent and established requirement for the application of prior fault rules.[72] With foreseeability as a requirement for prior fault, there is a potential for a behavioural expert to advise the court on the capacities of the defendant in being able to foresee the negative consequences of substance

[69] JR Searle, 'How to Derive "Ought" From "Is" (1964) 73 *The Philosophical Review* 43.

[70] GE Moore, *Principia Ethica* (London, Cambridge University Press, 1903).

[71] See, eg, JB Gould and S Barclay 'Mind the Gap: The Place of Gap Studies in Sociolegal Scholarship (2012) 8 *Annual Review of Law and Social Science* 323.

[72] As also discussed in ch 2 of this collection. See also the discussion on foreseeability as a requirement in Goldberg and others (n 3) and in Goldberg (n 40).

use.[73] This allows for the incorporation of insights from BCN-sciences, channelled through expert witness advice to the courts, leaving judges or juries to ultimately decide on prior fault. However, clear and consistent requirements for the application of prior fault rules are crucial for this approach to work. In the Netherlands at least, these frameworks are inconsistent at best and contradictory at worst.[74] In English law, these frameworks are no more straightforward, in significant part owing to their piecemeal development through case law in the face of complicated questions around the nature of human behaviour. A single, coherent interpretation is challenged by variation in foresight requirements according to context,[75] uncertainty over interactions with types of defence,[76] and ambiguous delineation between types of intent.[77] A first step would be, therefore, to establish clearer assessment criteria to understand if and how prior fault rules are applied. Afterward, an equivalent behavioural framework may be created to inform the judge on these criteria.

A similar construct can be found when deciding on the non-accountability offence (the insanity defence equivalence) in the Netherlands. This is a legal concept decided upon by the judge, yet the role of the expert witness, ie, usually a forensic psychologist or psychiatrist, is crucial in this process. They advise the judge on the presence and nature of the mental disorder, the role it played in the defendant's behaviour at the time of the offence, and whether the offence can therefore be accounted to them.[78] If the defendant is considered (at least partially) accountable, he can consequently be held (diminished) responsible for the harm. It is not by accident that these behavioural questions mirror the legal questions that the judge needs to answer in order to motivate their decision for a non-accountability defence.[79] Due to this setup, the applicability of an excuse remains solely a legal

[73] Such a capacity would be reflexive of an *objective* foreseeability requirement, ie, whether the defendant was generally capable of foreseeing unintended effects. A *subjective* standard, on the other hand, would assess whether defendants had actually foreseen the consequences at the time of the prior fault activity or omission. Admittedly, an objective standard would benefit more easily from a behavioural assessment compared to a subject one: it will remain impossible to ascertain whether somebody actually did or did not believe something.

[74] See Goldberg and others (n 3); Goldberg (n 20); and J Bijlsma, 'Drank, Drugs en Culpa. Zelfintoxicatie en Culpa in Causa: Pleidooi voor een Voorzienbaarheidseis' [2010] *Delikt & Delinkwent* 654.

[75] Eg, foresight as to the specific consequences of their actions, or merely foresight as to the general risk of their actions causing harm.

[76] Eg, intoxicated self-defence, or where intoxication overlaps with mental illness.

[77] Per *DPP v Majewski* [1976] UKHL 2, voluntary intoxication cannot establish a defence to crimes of basic intent, but may challenge mens rea with respect to crimes of specific intent. The common law distinction between crimes of basic and specific intent is beyond the scope of this discussion, suffice to say that the US Model Penal Code describes it as 'an abiding source of confusion and ambiguity in the penal law' (§ 2.02 cmt. at 231 n 3) and its utility in English law was characterised by Lord Salmon in *Majewski* as follows: 'The answer is that in strict logic this view cannot be justified. But this is the view that has been adopted by the common law of England, which is founded on common sense and experience rather than strict logic' (at 482E).

[78] See Meynen (n 51).

[79] The legal requirements for this defence constitute: (1) the presence of a mental disorder; (2) a causal connection between the disorder and the offence at hand; and (3) the decision, based on the

decision, but aspects of the mental disorder are clarified by a behavioural expert, who advises on the matter. In practice, a browse through case law suggests that most judges will follow the advice given, but it is possible – and happened, for instance, in the Supreme Court case of footnote 7 – that the judge deviates.[80]

We envisage a similar approach towards prior fault.[81] This does justice to the legal and normative nature of the concept whilst acknowledging that certain aspects thereof may be best explained by experts from BCN-disciplines.

VI. Conclusion

This collection offers a multidisciplinary and (legal) comparative approach towards prior fault, intoxication and addiction. In order to understand the necessity of such an approach, this chapter set out to discuss the different ways in which non-legal disciplines may inform the law: in general and specifically related to the concept of prior fault. We show that not only are these other disciplines relevant, but that they are even necessary to adequately evaluate the approach towards intoxication and addiction. The importance of a multi-disciplinary outlook is rooted in three main arguments. First is that – despite strong normative roots to the existence of prior fault rules, as evidenced by the historical background – human agents apply these rules and have to assess cases of intoxicated and/or addicted defendants in courts. Knowing that bias and stigma are prevalent with regard to mental disorders, and substance use disorders in particular, it is evident that legal professionals can be impacted in their decision-making. Interdisciplinary research is necessary to uncover such effects and to help explain *how* and *why* cases of addicted defendants are judged the way they are.

Second, one of the main premises of prior fault is that substance use and subsequent intoxication is voluntary. Despite the behavioural association of this term, the law seems to employ a rather dichotomous approach towards voluntariness: either the substance use is voluntary, or it is not. This stands in stark contrast with the BCN-meaning of voluntariness, which is represented as a scale. Moreover, as volitional aspects in legal concepts are notoriously difficult to measure, we discussed various behavioural components which may help assess the amount of control an agent has, such as impulsivity and inhibition, which may serve as an empirical equivalent to the normative notion of voluntariness.

Lastly, we highlight how the use of other disciplines in evaluating norms can lead to fundamental translation problems. Others have argued that empirical insights could never (automatically) have meaningful consequences for norms: what *is*

disorder and the causal connection, to consider the defendant non-accountable. See: Supreme Court of the Netherlands, 17-10-2023 ECLI:NL:HR:2023:1295 (*Thijs H.*).

[80] This matter is also discussed in ch 2 of this collection under III.B.

[81] This has also been suggested before, see Goldberg (n 20).

does not dictate what *ought*. Our view is that creating empirical frameworks which match the normative principles of the legal concepts is useful in two ways. On the one hand, it clarifies the role of behavioural experts, as this approach allows them to steer clear of drawing normative (legal) conclusions and stick to their expertise. On the other hand, BCN-information presented in clear frameworks provides legal professionals with the necessary building blocks to adequately assess the behavioural aspects of a defendant's responsibility. We used the example of Dutch behavioural expert reports in the assessment of the insanity defence to illustrate how these two frameworks, empirical and normative, can co-exist and inform one another.

All in all, our chapter provides an overview of the use of BCN-sciences to understand and evaluate prior fault rules. Our ambition is that it guides the reader through the remaining chapters in this collection, by bridging the legal challenges associated with prior fault with the various non-legal insights provided in the upcoming chapters.

5

When Addiction Matters to the Criminal Law: Some Thoughts on the Voluntariness in Voluntary Intoxication

HANS S CROMBAG AND REINOUT W WIERS

I. The Intersection of Substance Use Disorders and Criminal Justice

People who meet the diagnostic criteria for substance use disorders[1] (ie, addiction) or are otherwise alcohol or drug-involved, frequently appear in criminal court as defendants (Ds).[2] For instance, a recent survey of 3,320 Ds in South London showed that some 25 per cent had been diagnosed as substance-addicted,[3] whilst among male prisoners in England frequent alcohol use and dependency were estimated to range between 18 and 30 per cent, and between 10 and 48 per cent when other drugs of abuse were included.[4] Additionally, 2007 Department of Justice figures of perceptions of victims of violent offences in the United States (US) showed that 26 per cent reported their offender to have been under the influence of drugs or alcohol at the time of the assault,[5] and similar estimates for 2013–14 in England & Wales (E&W) were even higher, with victim-perceived offender intoxication rates reaching a staggering 51 per cent.[6]

[1] Based on the American Psychiatric Association's Diagnostic Statistical Manual (DSM-5), alongside the World-Health Organization's (WHO) International Classification of Diseases (ICD-11), the most frequently used and referenced diagnostic handbook. Note that throughout we use 'addicted' or 'addiction' to refer to 'people meeting criteria for substance use disorder or pathological gambling'.

[2] P Brown and others, 'Prevalence of Mental Disorders in Defendants at Criminal Court' (2022) 8 *BJPsych Open* e92.

[3] ibid.

[4] In female prisoners as high as 30 to 60%; S Fazel, P Bains and H Doll, 'Substance Abuse and Dependence in Prisoners: A Systematic Review' (2006) 101 *Addiction* 181.

[5] AJ Beck, SA Kline and LA Greenfield, 'Survey of Youth in Custody' (Bureau of Justice Statistics, 1987); AJ Beck and others, 'Survey of State Prison Inmates' (Bureau of Justice Statistics, 1991); C Wolf Harlow, 'Drugs and Jail Inmates' (Bureau of Justice Statistics tr, US Department of Justice, 1989).

[6] Home Office, 'Drug Misuse: Findings from the 2013/14 Crime Survey for England and Wales' (2014).

Data such as these reinforce a public understanding and perception of substance involvement and addiction on the one hand and criminal offending on the other, closely interlocking; even if the reasons for this relationship are intricate and moderated by a range of factors, including type of drug (eg, alcohol vs stimulants vs opioids), the nature of the offence (eg, violent or non-violent), and so forth. And the relationship becomes more robust in the presence of other, comorbid mental health conditions (ie, dual diagnosis). To this point, 74 per cent of convicted US state prisoners diagnosed with a mental health disorder (versus 56 per cent without) were found to also abuse or be dependent on alcohol or drugs. A similar analysis among prisoners diagnosed with any mental health disorder showed 51 to 62 per cent used or were dependent on drugs of abuse or alcohol, with more than a third admitting that they were intoxicated by drugs and/or alcohol at the time of their offence.[7] We come back to the issue of comorbidity between substance use disorders and (other) mental health disorders when we consider the unique legal challenges that such individuals and the courts they appear in face.

The over-representation of individuals with addiction or substance involvement among criminal Ds raises the question of whether such Ds should be treated differently under the law, particularly given the high prevalence of comorbid mental health conditions.[8] And in several jurisdictions, including in the UK and US, special ('problem-solving' or 'recovery') drug courts have been established with this aim, to divert addicted or substance-involved Ds away from punishment and towards treatment and rehabilitation.[9] Additionally, with growing evidence of long-lasting neurobiological changes resulting from and contributing to addictive drug use,[10] and recognition of substance abuse disorders as mental health conditions properly so-called in clinical diagnostic manuals such as DSM-5 and ICD-11, should we not consider addiction on par with other recognised mental health conditions, including as a basis for exempting or mitigating the criminal responsibility of addicted Ds?

This (admittedly broadly framed) question about whether and how addiction and otherwise problematic substance use impact (if at all) decisions about criminal (or moral) responsibility has generated significant amounts of research and debate. From neuroscientists and psychologists studying to better understand the acute and long-term cognitive consequences associated with drug or alcohol's actions on the brain – including how impulse/inhibitory control mechanisms

[7] Versus 26% when not suffering a mental health problem; DJ James, LG Beatty and BJS Statisticians, 'Mental Health Problems of Prison and Jail Inmates' (2006) *Bureau of Justice Statistics Special Report*.

[8] S Fazel and others, 'The Mental Health of Prisoners: A Review of Prevalence, Adverse Outcomes and Interventions' (2016) 3 *The Lancet Psychiatry* 871.

[9] J Collins, W Agnew-Pauley and A Soderholm (eds), *Rethinking Drug Courts: International Experiences of a US Policy Export* (London, London Publishing Partnership, 2019).

[10] Described by some as drugs 'usurping systems in the brain'; GF Koob and ND Volkow, 'Neurocircuitry of Addiction' (2010) 35 *Neuropsychopharmacology* 217; S Sinha and others, 'Heroin Addiction Explained: How Opioids Hijack the Brain' *The New York Times* (19 December 2018), www.nytimes.com/interactive/2018/us/addiction-heroin-opioids.html accessed 19 August 2024.

and decision-making[11] are linked to structural and functional changes in frontal-striatal circuitries[12] – to legal scholars debating whether such changes undermine cognitive, volitional and/or rational capacities in ways relevant to the criminal law. We will not spend a great deal of time or space here rehearsing such evidence and debates, mostly directing the reader to the original sources and only briefly outlining the principal reasons why, for the most part, in Anglo-American law (and most other jurisdictions), the legal position of addiction and substance abuse is at best uncertain and mostly limited to the sentencing stage of trials.[13] It is notable then that relatively little scholarship has been directed at sentencing, engaging more frequently with substantive law questions such as whether and how addiction-related cognitive/brain changes could undermine the legal requirements for criminal liability (eg, cause a lack of *mens rea* or volitional capacities) and/or provide a basis for a defence in law (eg, via duress or necessity defences).[14]

Our focus here is on a related but distinct legal doctrine, or set of rules, that in recent years have been a target of scholarly debate and critique, and (in E&W) of legal reform proposals, and where we argue that the position of addiction should be revisited. Specifically, in situations where D commits a criminal offence while acutely and severely intoxicated by alcohol and/or drugs, to such an extent that they are not (as a matter of law) liable because they lacked requisite *mens rea* (or potentially but less likely, because of a lack of voluntariness) at the time of the offence. In such cases the legal rules in E&W (and similar rules exist elsewhere) enable courts to hold D responsible anyway (ie, as if *mens rea* were present) by blaming her for becoming intoxicated with a dangerous drug at an earlier point in time; the notable exception is if D's intoxication was deemed involuntary.[15]

Our aim here is to examine whether the rules also provide a unique instance when considering the relevance of addiction; where blaming D's choice to become intoxicated might reasonably be questioned as being voluntary in the clinical context of an ongoing substance use disorder; especially if that addiction is comorbid with other mental health conditions, which, as we demonstrate, is often the case.

[11] Or even, specifically moral decision making; RM Sapolsky, 'The Frontal Cortex and the Criminal Justice System.' (2004) 359 *Philosophical Transactions of the Royal Society B: Biological Sciences* 1787.

[12] FT Crews and CA Boettiger, 'Impulsivity, Frontal Lobes and Risk for Addiction' (2009) 93 *Pharmacology Biochemistry and Behavior* 237; RZ Goldstein and ND Volkow, 'Dysfunction of the Prefrontal Cortex in Addiction: Neuroimaging Findings and Clinical Implications' (2011) 12 *Nature reviews Neuroscience* 652.

[13] In ch 3 of this collection, the author engages further with issues related to prior fault during sentencing.

[14] RJ Bonnie, 'Responsibility for Addiction' (2002) 30 *The Journal of the American Academy of Psychiatry and the Law* 405; S Morse, 'A Good Enough Reason: Addiction, Agency and Criminal Responsibility' (2013) 56 *Inquiry: An Interdisciplinary Journal of Philosophy* 490; G Yaffe, 'Lowering the Bar for Addicts' in J Poland and G Graham (eds), *Addiction and Responsibility* (Cambridge, the MIT Press, 2011).

[15] *Majewski* [1977] AC 443.

II. Conceptualising Addiction as a Brain Disease

The argument that substance addiction matters to questions about criminal and moral responsibility goes something like this: In certain individuals, the use of certain drugs, under certain circumstances produces long-lasting, structural and functional changes to their brain. Specifically (though not exclusively), changes are seen in brain areas and processes responsible for 'normal' regulation of affective and motivational states (producing intense cravings for drugs) and/or for control and decision-making mechanisms (resulting in increasingly impulsive and myopic choice and action). Because these structural and functional changes are long-lasting, people with addiction 'lose' some of their normal capacities to decide what is right for them and/or to act accordingly, in ways that non-addicted individuals can; and in ways that they themselves could prior to developing their addiction.[16] In the words of the behavioural biologist Robert Sapolsky, impacting their ability to, 'when there is a choice between something harder and something easier, and the harder thing is the better thing to do, to do the harder thing'.[17] And if the harder and better thing means the lawful thing, then we might not want to blame addicted individuals in the same way as those non-addicted, on the basis that their normal capacities to do what's right and/or abstain from doing what's wrong have been compromised by pathological brain changes associated with their addiction.

The case has been made by many, including – importantly – by Alan Leshner and Nora Volkow, both of whom have served at different times as directors of the National Institute on Drug Abuse (NIDA, a subdivision of the National Institutes of Health), with the latter and current director saying:[18]

> To explain the devastating changes in behaviour of a person who is addicted, such that even the most severe threat of punishment is insufficient to keep them from taking drugs – where they are willing to give up everything they care for in order to take a drug – it is not enough to say that addiction is a chronic brain disease. What we mean by that is something very specific and profound: that because of drug use, a person's brain is no longer able to produce something needed for our functioning and that healthy people take for granted, free will.

[16] RZ Goldstein and ND Volkow, 'Drug Addiction and Its Underlying Neurobiological Basis: Neuroimaging Evidence for the Involvement of the Frontal Cortex' (2002) 159 *The American Journal of Psychiatry* 1642; A Verdejo-García, M Pérez-García and A Bechara, 'Emotion, Decision-Making and Substance Dependence: A Somatic-Marker Model of Addiction' (2006) 4 *Current Neuropharmacology* 17.

[17] For a recent examination of how substance-use related tendencies to act against one's better judgement ('Akrasia') might enable addiction, see RW Wiers, *A New Approach to Addiction and Choice: Akrasia and the Nature of Free Will* (Milton Park, Routledge, 2025).

[18] From a blog post titled 'Addiction is a Disease of Free Will' based on the inaugural lecture given as Director of NIDA on 12 June 2015. A similar (perhaps more cautious) point was made by (then NIDA director) Alan Leshner, in an influential editorial in Science magazine, writing that 'We need to face the fact that even if the condition initially comes about because of a voluntary behavior (drug use), an addict's brain is different from a nonaddict's brain, and the addicted individual must be dealt with as if he or she is in a different brain state.' AI Leshner, 'Addiction is a Brain Disease, and it Matters' (1997) 278(5335) *Science* 45.

Not without its critics,[19] the conception of addiction as a chronic brain disease (the 'Brain Disease Model of Addiction', or BDMA) has had tremendous impact, not only in convincing policymakers to steer large sums of tax money to fund scientific research into the clinical and biopsychological bases of addiction (arguably, a main reason for promoting BDMA). It has also penetrated debates beyond addiction neuroscience, including those around stigma and clinical treatment,[20] (moral) philosophy and ethics,[21] and the criminal law. And all that funding, research and debate have radically changed our understanding and perceptions of substance abuse and addiction and, more broadly how drugs, addiction, and other related external events and diseases impact brain function and dysfunction.

A scientific sea change in these efforts was undoubtedly the advent of *in vivo* human brain imaging (initially Positron Emission Tomography or PET, and then functional and structural Magnetic Resonance Imaging or MRI) for pure academic research reasons in the early 1990s. Before this, our understanding of the brain changes associated with drug exposure and addiction relied almost exclusively on studies using non-human animals (mostly rats). Early pioneering work by Volkow herself, Gene-Jack Wang and Joanna Fowler,[22] Chuck O'Brien and Anna-Rose Childress,[23] and numerous others,[24] showed structural and functional changes in the human addicted brain in areas like the prefrontal cortex and associated subdivisions of the striatum implicated in motivated action and decision-making. And whilst deep, cell-molecular level evidence and mechanistic, cause-and-effect understanding remain largely dependent on studies using non-human animals,

[19] The BDMA has drawn criticism from academics and clinicians (eg, reviews: N Heather and others, 'Challenging the Brain Disease Model of Addiction: European Launch of the Addiction Theory Network' (2018) 26 *Addiction Research & Theory* 249; N Heather and others, *Evaluating the Brain Disease Model of Addiction* (Milton Park, Routledge, 2022)).For several reasons, including that – different from other progressive brain disorders (eg, Alzheimer's or Parkinson's disease) – recovery is common with addiction and for ignoring social and environmental factors in its aetiology; eg, M Lewis, 'Addiction and the Brain: Development, Not Disease' (2017) 10 *Neuroethics* 7; GM Heyman, *Addiction: A Disorder of Choice* (Cambridge, Harvard University Press, 2010); CL Hart, 'Viewing Addiction as a Brain Disease Promotes Social Injustice' (2017) 1 *Nature Human Behaviour* 0055; but see, M Heilig and others, 'Addiction as a Brain Disease Revised: Why It Still Matters, and the Need for Consilience' (2021) 46 *Neuropsychopharmacology* 1715.

[20] CL Barry and others, 'Stigma, Discrimination, Treatment Effectiveness, and Policy: Public Views About Drug Addiction and Mental Illness' (2014) 65 *Psychiatric Services* 1269; AC Tsai and others, 'Stigma as a Fundamental Hindrance to the United States Opioid Overdose Crisis Response' (2019) 16 *PLOS Medicine* e1002969.

[21] Editorial, 'Animal Farm' (2015) 506 *Nature* 5.

[22] ND Volkow, JS Fowler and G Wang, 'The Addicted Human Brain: Insights from Imaging Studies' (2003) 111 *Journal of Clinical Investigation* 1444.

[23] AR Childress and others, 'Limbic Activation during Cue-Induced Cocaine Craving' (1999) 156 *The American Journal of Psychiatry 11*.

[24] HC Breiter and others, 'Acute Effects of Cocaine on Human Brain Activity and Emotion' (1997) 19 *Neuron* 591; Goldstein and Volkow (n 12); JM Stapleton and others, 'Cerebral Glucose Utilization in Polysubstance Abuse' (1995) 13 *Neuropsychopharmacology* 21; JK Zubieta and others, 'Increased Mu Opioid Receptor Binding Detected by PET in Cocaine-Dependent Men Is Associated with Cocaine Craving' (1996) 2 *Nature Medicine* 1225; A Pfefferbaum and others, 'Reorganization of Frontal Systems Used by Alcoholics for Spatial Working Memory: An fMRI Study' (2001) 14 *NeuroImage* 7.

in vivo structural and functional human brain imaging has provided important evidence of translational validity.

An important corollary of BDMA relates to research on relapse and remission rates – important not just because of treatment implications but because evidence from clinical outcome studies of high relapse rates has often been cited as evidence that the addicts' brains have changed persistently and, in the words of Leshner, 'is distinctly different from a nonaddict brain'.[25] How else could we explain a person who has recovered from addiction and has been successfully 'clean' for months or years suddenly relapsing and doing so repeatedly?[26] And doing so whilst saying that, above all else, they wish to remain 'clean' and stop using drugs, unless we deduce that something has persistently changed in their brain? It is an understanding repeated by many addiction and/or alcoholism recovery and treatment programs, including (and famously so) Alcoholics Anonymous (AA), whose central theme reads 'Once an alcoholic, always an alcoholic.' As we discuss in greater detail below, while clinical outcome studies have indeed described how most people treated for their addiction relapse, there is now a wealth of epidemiological evidence showing quite a different and more complex pattern, with recovery (partial or full) being the most frequent outcome.[27]

Additionally, and as others have pointed out, the mere fact that some event, experience, agent, or drug changes the brain says little about whether those changes are indicative of a persistent, pathological disorder or disease; let alone whether they might be relevant to questions about mental capacity and responsibility.[28] Many things change the brain, and persistent changes in behaviour or psychology, for instance, due to development, maturation or learning, are assumed to be caused by changes in brain structure and function, even if evidencing this experimentally may (yet) be difficult. But equally, there are 'normal range' changes, and then there are 'abnormal range' or pathological changes. Few would argue that the changes caused by viral encephalitis to Clive Wearing's brain,[29] resulting in

[25] Leshner (n 18) 46.

[26] Estimates of remission/relapse events vary dramatically for different drugs, and depend on several variables (eg, treatment, psychiatric co-morbidity), but especially for drugs such a cigarettes and alcohol, multiple remission/relapse instances are common (eg, JF Kelly and others, 'How Many Recovery Attempts Does It Take to Successfully Resolve an Alcohol or Drug Problem? Estimates and Correlates From a National Study of Recovering U.S. Adults' (2019) 43 *Alcohol, Clinical and Experimental Research* 1533. While clinical outcome studies have emphasised frequent relapse, epidemiological studies paint a different picture, with recovery as the modal response (eg, Heyman (n 19).

[27] Alcoholics Anonymous, *Alcoholics Anonymous Big Book* (New York, Alcoholics Anonymous World Services, 2002) 33.

[28] T Fenton and RW Wiers, 'Free Will, Black Swans and Addiction' (2016) 10 *Neuroethics* 157; AE Goldberg, 'The (in)Significance of the Addiction Debate' (2019) 13 *Neuroethics* 311; Heyman (n 19); Morse (n 14).

[29] Clive Wearing (born 1938) was an accomplished composer and musician when, in 1985 at the height of his career, he contracted a type of HSV encephalitis that produced widespread and profound brain damage, including bilaterally to his temporal lobes and hippocampus. Consequently, Wearing has suffered a near complete loss of his ability to form new memories (ie, anterograde amnesia) as well as not recalling aspects from his past (retrograde amnesia). Wearing describes the experience as feeling that he has only recently awoken from a comatose state.

near complete anterograde and retrograde amnesia, or the progressive memory degradation associated with Alzheimer's dementia, are on the same quantitative or qualitative level as brain changes that underlie day-to-day, or 'normal', age-related forgetting. It is entirely standard practice for physicians to draw such lines between 'normal' and pathological, even when – in cases of mental health and disorder where diagnostic criteria are vague and biomarkers are absent – it is complex (and often problematic) to know *where* that line should be drawn, especially in individual cases. But also thinking about aetiology, drugs, and the routes by which they are consumed (eg, by intravenous injection or inhalation) are (when used recreationally) far from normal, tapping into evolutionarily old brain regions in ways to produce extraordinary effects and changes more likely to be maladaptive. Not because drugs produce novel effects by novel mechanisms, but because the magnitude and nature of their effects are unlikely to be reproduced by events, stimuli, or circumstances present in the niche in which organisms have adapted through evolution.[30]

Before considering the legal implications, one last point: Discussions around addiction, mental health, the brain, and criminal/moral responsibility do not infrequently stray into first-principal debates about free will and determinism. Some argue that neuroscience shows us that neural 'decisions' to act can occur well before the time of the conscious decision that we presumed causes them, questioning whether any act can be considered free or non-determined.[31] Immensely clever studies and findings like these provide compelling food for thought for philosophers and scientists – and the correct interpretation of the so-called 'Libet-paradox' continues to be researched and debated[32] – but they matter little to the law, which is much less ambitious when debating the necessary and sufficient conditions for criminal responsibility and blame. The law requires understanding of an ability to recognise and choose between alternatives (rationality) and to act or refrain from acting (volition) in line with prevailing common-sense beliefs and understanding that humans have about themselves and (the average) others; or what Stephen Morse calls 'folk-psychological' beliefs.[33] And insofar as it entertains questions about first principal determinism or free will, the law assumes a default that such common-sense free will exists (independent of the question to what extent it is based on a deterministic system or not), unless there are reasons (ie, evidence) in individual cases to question this, eg, in cases of severe mental impairment. Debates about free will and biological determinism are interesting, but from a legal perspective, they are distractions

[30] RM Nesse and KC Berridge, 'Psychoactive Drug Use in Evolutionary Perspective' (1997) 278 *Science* 63.

[31] B Libet and others, 'Time of Conscious Intention to Act in Relation to Onset of Cerebral Activity (Readiness-Potential): The Unconscious Initiation of a Freely Voluntary Act' (1983) 106 *Brain* 623.

[32] A Schurger, JD Sitt and S Dehaene, 'An Accumulator Model for Spontaneous Neural Activity Prior to Self-Initiated Movement' (2012) 109 *Proceedings of the National Academy of Sciences* E2904.

[33] S Morse, 'Culpability and Control' (1994) 142 *University of Pennsylvania Law Review* 1587; Morse (n 14).

from what are concrete and practical questions that *try to* objectively, and we will see narrowly, define mental and volitional capacities required by the law for criminal responsibility.

III. The Law's Response to Acute and Prior Intoxication(s)

A foundational principle of criminal law is that individuals are only criminally responsible if they had the requisite *mens rea* (guilty mind) and/or volitional capacity at the time of the offence. It is a principle with deep and old roots in criminal law theory and moral philosophy, and that has been subject to extensive legal scholarship over centuries, including by the likes of HLA Hart, captured by '… those whom we punish should have had, when they acted, the normal capacities, physical and mental, for doing what the law requires and abstaining from what it forbids, and a fair opportunity to exercise these capacities'.[34]

It is on this general principle that we do not blame or criminalise acts committed by children under the age of criminal responsibility or by persons with profound developmental disabilities and/or mental disorders (eg, by satisfying the M'Naghten insanity defence)[35] or acts committed whilst sleepwalking or caused by epileptic seizures. And more generally, when, for whatever reason, a person at the time of the alleged offence lacked requisite *mens rea* ('guilty mind') for the offence.[36] Likewise, if acute intoxication by alcohol or drug use, or the cumulative effects of past intoxications leading to addiction, results in a lack of *mens rea* or impairs volitional control, this could in theory provide a basis for denying criminal liability. However, in practice and across jurisdictions, the viability of such a 'defence of intoxication'[37] is highly constrained.

First and foremost, because the law typically requires only a very low level of awareness and control to satisfy the requirements for *mens rea* and voluntary action. This means that even a minimal degree of awareness or self-control will be enough to find D liable criminally. To be clear, this low threshold for rational or

[34] HLA Hart, *Punishment and Responsibility: Essays in the Philosophy of Law* (Oxford, Clarendon Press, 1968) 152.

[35] The M'Naghten standard as originally formulated by the UK House of Lords excludes from criminal prosecution any person who 'at the time of the committing of the act, … was labouring under such a defect of reason, from disease of the mind, as not to know the nature and quality of the act he was doing; or, if he did know it, that he did not know he was doing what was wrong'. *M'Naghten* [1843] 10 Cl & Fin 200.

[36] Simple mistakes fall into the category, eg, someone mistakenly taking an umbrella incorrectly thinking it was their own, the law would not normally blame them for such an honest mistake.

[37] Our use of the term 'defence' here is not strictly accurate, as the absence of *mens rea* and/or volitional capacity means that one or both elements of the offence are not present, meaning no offence has been committed. Legal challenges on this basis are therefore more accurately understood as denials of liability. AP Simester 'Intoxication is Never a Defence' (2009) 1 *Crim LR* 3.

volitional capacity (or, depending on how you want to look at it, high threshold for incapacity) is not specific to cases involving intoxication or addiction. Rather, it applies universally to any legal challenge of D's mental or volitional capacity. In this way, and from a rule of law perspective not unreasonably so, courts avoid having to deal with the complexities involved in assessing degrees of mental or volitional impairment, maintaining a clear and consistent (but low) requisite standard for criminal liability.[38]

But even in cases of severe intoxication or incapacitation caused by historic intoxication as in addiction, the courts have developed rules to ensure that liability can still be imposed; rules that operate on the principle that individuals' who become intoxicated to the point of near complete rational or volitional incapacitation voluntarily and/or who do so repeatedly, leading to brain changes and addiction, could still be held responsible for what the American legal scholar Paul Robinson called 'causing the conditions of their own defence'.[39] In essence, blaming their choice to become intoxicated.

IV. Prior Fault Rules Impute Blame and Responsibility Across the Law

The appeal of prior-fault intoxication rules lies in their ability to address complex moral and policy dilemmas, as illustrated by the case of Nadruku,[40] a rugby league player in Australia who became severely intoxicated and assaulted two women at a bar in Canberra. Charged with assault, the court found that his severe intoxication rendered him incapable of forming the necessary intent for the offence, leading to his acquittal. This decision (understandably) sparked significant public and political outrage, as many viewed it as a failure of the legal system to hold Nadruku accountable for what the court described as 'drunken thuggery'.

In cases like this, and one can imagine a range of similar scenarios involving intoxicated Ds,[41] where the usual analysis focusing on the time of the harmful act might lead to acquittal, prior-fault intoxication rules construct liability by looking back in time. The rules, in essence, allow the absence of *mens rea* or voluntariness at the time of the offence to be supplanted by D's prior fault in becoming voluntarily intoxicated at an earlier time. As a result, Ds like Nadruku are found responsible

[38] U Maoz and G Yaffe, 'What Does Recent Neuroscience Tell Us about Criminal Responsibility?' (2015) 3 *Journal of Law and the Biosciences* 120.

[39] PH Robinson, 'Causing the Conditions of One's Own Defense: A Study in the Limits of Theory in Criminal Law Doctrine' (1985) 71 *Virginia Law Review* 1.

[40] *Nadruku SC Small v Noa Kurimalawai* [1997] Australian Capital Territory Magistrates' Court Matter No CC97/01904.

[41] Consider, eg, scenarios where a D causes damage to another person's property but denies criminal liability by claiming that, due to intoxication, they did not foresee the risk of causing damage or mistakenly believed the property was their own. Or a D might harm another person by falling into them but argue that the harm was not voluntary due to a loss of control caused by intoxication.

and punished *as if* the necessary mental and volitional elements for the offence were present.

Notwithstanding their appeal on policy grounds (ie, ensuring accountability for dangerous drunks like Nadruku), the so-called 'prior fault' intoxication rules are problematic for a host of reasons as discussed elsewhere.[42] Not least because they blame action (becoming voluntarily intoxicated with a psychoactive substance) that in isolation would rarely be considered blameworthy (let alone criminally blameworthy). And as discussed throughout this volume, the rules (and/or the principals or logic that underlie them) operate in different ways across the criminal law to inculpate; eg, blocking defences otherwise available, including, as discussed by Child & Van der Wolf in chapter three, the partial defence of diminished responsibility due to an 'abnormality of mental functioning' caused by a 'recognised medical condition' in murder cases; and as one of us reported elsewhere, aggravating (or blocking mitigation) at sentencing on the basis of past intoxications leading to addiction.[43]

V. Defining 'Voluntary' in Voluntary Intoxication Through the Courts

Given their inculpating nature and wide applicability across the law, it will be clear that how courts define voluntary and involuntary intoxication is crucial, as the invocation of intoxication rules hinges on this distinction. And where broadly the position can be understood as voluntary intoxication occurring when D knowingly and willingly consumes an intoxicant, such as alcohol or drugs, aware of its nature and potential effects, in E&W, courts have attempted over the decades to clarify the distinction. In doing so they have generally taken a broad view of what constitutes voluntary intoxication, and (thus) a narrow view of what constitutes involuntary intoxication. It is worth briefly examining some of this case law to clarify how the distinction has evolved in law.

The concept of involuntary intoxication is perhaps least controversial in cases where D's drink is unknowingly adulterated or 'spiked', or where D was forced to consume an intoxicant under some form of duress. For example, in *Ross v HM*

[42] JJ Child, 'Prior fault: Blocking Defences or Constructing Crimes' in A Reed and M Bohlander (eds), *General Defences in Criminal Law* (Milton Park, Routledge, 2014); HS Crombag, JJ Child and GR Sullivan, 'Drunk, Dangerous and Celusional: How Legal Concept-creep Risks Overcriminalization' (2020) 115 *Addiction* 2200; S Dimock, 'What are Intoxicated Offenders Responsible For? The "Intoxication Defense" Re-examined' (2011) 5 *Criminal Law and Philosophy* 1; AE Goldberg and others, 'Prior-Fault Blame in England and Wales, Germany, and the Netherlands' (2021) *Journal of International and Comparative Law* 53; Simester (n 37).

[43] N Sinclair-House, JJ Child and HS Crombag, 'Addiction Is a Brain Disease, and It Doesn't Matter: Prior Choice in Drug Use Blocks Leniency in Criminal Punishment' (2020) 26 *Psychology, Public Policy, and Law* 36.

Advocate[44] D's drink was spiked with multiple drugs, including LSD, leading him to hallucinate and injure several people with a knife. Although D was initially convicted of attempted murder, his conviction was overturned on appeal due to his lack of *mens rea*, clarifying that his intoxication was *involuntary* (and so the prior-fault intoxication rule did not apply) because he was not and could not have been aware that his drink had been spiked.

In *R v Allen*,[45] D was understood to have voluntarily consumed homemade wine but claimed the wine ended up being much stronger than he expected, leading him to, in a drunken and confused state, commit sexual assault. The court was asked to consider whether Allen's intoxication was involuntary since he did not knowingly place himself in the condition of severe intoxication (as the wine was much stronger than expected). The court, however, held that Allen's drinking had been a voluntary act and that, whereas Ross was truly unaware of having ingested any drugs, mere ignorance as to the strength of the alcohol being consumed was no defence. As he had chosen to drink (homemade) alcohol, a dangerous intoxicating substance, and should have known or ought to have known the risks of consumption. The other issue to note here then is that the mere fact that, different than, eg, LSD, alcohol is a legal drug, bears no relevance to the legal status of alcohol as a dangerous drug.

A seemingly clear exception exists for prescription medications, as held in *R v Hardie*.[46] In this case, D was charged with arson and criminal damage after consuming a large amount of Valium® and setting fire to a wardrobe. Although initially found liable, on appeal his conviction was overturned because the court determined that D could not have anticipated the risks associated with his action, and there was no evidence that he knew the drug would likely render him aggressive or incapable of appreciating the risks to others. The critical distinction between *Hardie* and our homemade wine drinker in *Allen* lies in the context of the substance consumed – *Hardie* involving a medicinal, prescribed drug where adverse effects on mental incapacity or risk of aggression would not have been foreseen. However, courts have also held that if D consumes a substance for medicinal purposes, it may still be considered voluntary if taken without proper medical guidance and/or in a manner (and amount) not prescribed by a medical professional. The medicinal exemption seems to rely therefore on an appeal to professional (medical) authority – rather than on any intrinsic quality of the nature of the drug itself (ie, medicinal versus non-medicinal). Indeed, with the notable exception of alcohol and somewhat dependent on jurisdiction, nearly all existing recreationally consumed psychoactive drugs are and/or have in the past been used and prescribed for medicinal purposes.

What we see then is courts trying to define not just whether the act of becoming intoxicated at T1 was voluntary in a strict sensory-motor sense or even in

[44] *Ross v HM Advocate* [1991] JC 210 (High Court of Judiciary).
[45] *R v Allen* [1988] Crim LR 698.
[46] *R v Hardie* [1985] 1 WLR 64.

a manner that hinges on an intellectual or rational capacity to choose between multiple options, including the option to not drink; but rather (or additionally) whether there is something particularly risky or dangerous, and therefore blameworthy, about that choice in terms of (at least implicitly) having been able to have predicted or foreseen a potential or risk of (any) harmful consequence.

It is perhaps salient then that, against this quite nuanced understanding that has in E&W developed through the case law, looking to clarify what is blameworthy about voluntary intoxication based on some type of foresight, knowledge, and/or understanding of D when becoming intoxicated, recent proposals for reform of the rules have excluded any form of intoxication. Even if D's intoxication resulted from consuming an intoxicant in the context of a clinical addiction, it still counts as voluntary for purposes of triggering the prior-fault intoxication rules.[47]

We turn next to the question of whether the law's rigid approach to understanding and defining voluntary intoxication – understandable as it may be from an evidence and rule of law perspective to avoid scientific and clinical vagaries around gradations in voluntariness – by excluding addiction from consideration, might be challenged by improved understanding that not all addictions are the same. Indeed, where the BDMA (or any 'unified' general theory or model of addiction or other mental health condition) becomes counterproductive to its own aim to promote the idea that those suffering from addiction should be treated differently, on the point that the 'addict's brain is different from a nonaddict's brain',[48] is that it treats addicted brains as the same (in a word, diseased). In doing so, the model lacks the individual-level nuance that the law seeks to decide who should or should not be held liable and punished; and in a way, provides a sort of 'get out of jail free card' to substance-involved or addicted Ds that, given the frequency with which they appear in the criminal court, would neither be practically nor politically viable. More critically and as increasingly recognised, and as we have known for some time based on a large sample of epidemiological studies looking into remission and relapse rates, whereas most diagnosed as addicted seem to retain a clear level of control and capacity to spontaneously and voluntarily choose to not take drugs (ie, to go into remission), a (small) minority seem to persistently lack this volitional capacity over their drug use.

VI. Addiction Severity and Relapse Rates

On its face, it seems uncontroversial that among individuals diagnosed with a substance use disorder, there are some that are clinically more severely disordered than others. Even though formal diagnostic staging is mostly limited to the field of cancer medicine, physicians use terms like minor, moderate, major, severe,

[47] The Law Commission, 'Intoxication and Criminal Liability'; The Law Commission, 'Intoxication and Criminal Liability', www.lawcom.gov.uk/project/intoxication-and-criminal-liability-2009.

[48] Leshner (n 18).

(a symptomatic, aggressive, progressive, benign, refractory, acute, chronic, and so forth to describe different levels of disease or symptom severity, treatability and/or prognosis, and so forth; and there are good clinical and non-clinical reasons to do so. We may be prescribed opioid-based painkillers (analgesics) for severe, debilitating back pain, but not so much for moderate to mild backaches, where a non-opioid analgesic (eg, NSAIDs) would suffice. And while experiencing the symptoms of a *minor* flu might make us decide to work from home for the day, a *major* flu will have us calling in sick to spend a couple of guilt-free days in bed.

But it was not until the most recent, fifth edition of the Diagnostic Statistical Manual (DSM-5) that Substance Use Disorders (SUDs) have been clinically 'staged' by severity, principally based on the number (from two to eleven) of diagnostic criteria met; with two or three symptoms indicating a mild; four or five, a moderate; and six or more symptoms, a severe SUD.[49] Greeted as a significant improvement over its previous versions, it remains relatively uncommon (at least outside of clinical medicine) to hear references to persons suffering a mild or moderate SUD versus someone described as being severely addicted. Rather, depending on some ill-defined threshold, you either are or are not addicted or alcoholic and/or suffering from a substance abuse disorder; one might say, a rather lawyerly way of looking at it.

But for some time, the evidence has pointed to an understanding of addiction as not a one-size-fits-all condition; rather, addiction varies widely in severity and impact. As we discuss below, data on relapse rates show that while most individuals with SUDs eventually recover, a small but significant portion face prolonged struggles with recovery. This variance often correlates with the presence of co-occurring other mental health disorders, which can make overcoming addiction more difficult. Some of the initial evidence for this came from studies in the 1970s by Lee Robins, commissioned by the US government to study opioid (and other drug) use and addiction rates among soldiers during and after the Vietnam War.

VII. Lee Robins' Studies on Drug-use and Addiction Rates Among US Military Personnel During the Vietnam War

During the Vietnam War, recreational use of substances like marijuana and heroin was rife among US soldiers. Understandably, there were significant concerns about the long-term impact of this drug use on soldiers once they returned home, with

[49] The rationale for this approach was described in a subsequent paper by the DSM-5-working-group for Substance Abuse Disorders, clarifying that 'Many severity indicators are possible (eg, levels of use, impairment, or comorbidity), and the Substance-Related Disorders Work Group sought a simple, parsimonious approach. A count of the criteria themselves serves this purpose well, since as the count increases so does the likelihood of substance use disorder risk factors and consequences' in DS Hasin and others, 'DSM-5 Criteria for Substance Use Disorders: Recommendations and Rationale' (2013) 170 *The American Journal of Psychiatry* 834.

many fearing that a wave of heroin abuse and addiction would sweep through the US. In response, then US President Richard Nixon declared heroin addiction the nation's 'No. 1 Public Health problem' and established the Special Action Office on Drug Abuse Prevention (SAODAP), managed out of the White House and headed by Jerome Jaffe, a medical doctor and Professor of Clinical Psychiatry. Among Jaffe's first actions was to invite Lee Robins, a leading epidemiologist and Professor in the Department of Psychiatry at Washington University in St. Louis, to undertake a series of studies to ascertain the severity of the problem and to better understand the long-term effects of heroin use among army veterans.[50] Over a period of approximately three years, Robins' research team conducted interviews with over 1,400 veterans, collecting data on their drug use before, during and after their Vietnam military service, as well as their social and psychological adjustment to post-war life.

For academics and clinicians interested in better understanding substance abuse, addiction and the variables and circumstances that contribute to relapse/remission rates among those addicted, Robins' studies are essential reading, revealing several interesting and unexpected outcomes: First, the data confirmed that, as feared, nearly half (45 per cent) of the soldiers had tried narcotic drugs while in Vietnam between 1970–71 (34 per cent tried heroin and 38 per cent opium),[51] and nearly 20 per cent were diagnosed as addicted to opioids at the moment they left Vietnam.[52] Contrast this with the currently ongoing and seemingly intractable opioid epidemic in the US, with estimates between two and four per cent of US residents dependent on opioids, driven in significant part by overprescription of opioid painkillers.[53] It is clear then that problematic opioid and other drug use among active service personnel in Vietnam was exceptionally high, no doubt driven by the extraordinarily stressful combat circumstances plus the easy availability of high-grade opioid (and cannabinoid) drugs in southeast Asia.

Second, and contrary to fears of importing a nationwide opioid addiction epidemic, Robins' report revealed that most veterans diagnosed as addicted to heroin or opium in Vietnam stopped using the drug shortly after returning to the US. Even three years out, most veterans who had been diagnosed as addicted

[50] LN Robins, 'Vietnam Veterans' Rapid Recovery from Heroin Addiction: A Fluke or Normal Expectation?' (1993) 88 *Addiction* 1041; LN Robins, DH Davis and DW Goodwin, 'Drug Use by U.S. Army Enlisted Men in Vietnam: A Follow-up on Their Return Home' (1974) 99 *American Journal of Epidemiology* 235.

[51] Estimates for regular marijuana use were close to 80%.

[52] This 20% number was based on self-reports by soldiers 'claiming' that while in Vietnam they had felt strung out or addicted to narcotics, and follow-up reports of frequency and length of use, and withdrawal symptoms.

[53] DH Epstein, M Heilig and Y Shaham, 'Science-Based Actions Can Help Address the Opioid Crisis' (2018) 39 *Trends in Pharmacological Sciences* 911; DA Fishbain and others, 'What Percentage of Chronic Nonmalignant Pain Patients Exposed to Chronic Opioid Analgesic Therapy Develop Abuse/Addiction and/or Aberrant Drug-Related Behaviors? A Structured Evidence-Based Review' (2008) 9 *Pain Medicine* 444.

during their military service maintained their sobriety. Robins summarised her findings as follows:[54]

> In the first year after return, only 5% of those who had been addicted in Vietnam were addicted in the US. This finding was totally unlike the outcomes of young men treated in Lexington, the Federal Narcotics Hospital at the time. When those young men were followed 6 months later, two-thirds were found to already be re-addicted (Stephens & Cottrell, 1972). Even veterans still on narcotics at departure from Vietnam were doing very well 8–12 months after return. The curve showing the likelihood of any use, heavy use, and addiction for veterans was the mirror image of that for treated civilians. When we followed veterans at 3 years, only 12% of those addicted in Vietnam had been addicted at any time in the 3 years since return, and for those re-addicted, the addiction had usually been very brief.

Importantly, as Robins goes on to clarify, the 'remarkable' recovery rates were not attributable to recovery treatment, as only a small percentage (between two and 14 per cent) of soldiers identified as addicted sought drug abuse treatment upon their return, and the vast majority 'recovered' and remained abstinent on their own. In fact, and paradoxically, as Robins elaborates, the opposite appeared to be the case; those soldiers who did receive treatment experienced relapse rates comparable to those of young civilian men in the previously mentioned Lexington studies,[55] of whom two-thirds had relapsed by the time they conducted the interviews.

Robins' Vietnam Veteran studies remain a cornerstone in the field of addiction studies, demonstrating the complexities of substance abuse and the importance of considering the broader social and environmental contexts in which drug use occurs. We discuss it here because it also is one of the first longitudinal studies – using a large, diverse sample of young persons (but mostly male) with free availability to high-grade narcotics – to demonstrate what might be obvious to some but is too rarely considered: that there are differences between addicted individuals and that where most might easily 'kick' their addiction, others, even if a small minority, do not. But if it is not differences in availability (access) or actual use or differences in other environmental risk factors such as exposure to extreme stressors, then what explains the differences in remission or relapse rates?

VIII. How to Make Sense of Both High and Low Relapse Rates

It will be clear that Robins' findings documenting that most veterans who were addicted to heroin in Vietnam recovered upon returning to the US challenge the brain disease model of addiction (BDMA) or at least the prevailing view then and

[54] Robins (n 50) 1045.

[55] R Stephens and E Cottrell, 'A Follow-up Study of 200 Narcotic Addicts Committed for Treatment under the Narcotic Addict Rehabilitation Act (NARA)' (1972) 67 *The British Journal of Addiction to Alcohol and Other Drugs* 45.

now that addiction is a permanent and intractable brain and clinical condition, indicating addicts' inability to choose abstinence over drug use. If addiction is a disease properly so-called, then like other diseases, high remission rates should have been unlikely, or at least unlikely without some form of treatment. Sceptics at the time in and outside academia raised several objections to Robins' conclusions by noting potential methodological flaws and design weaknesses by relying on self-reports that overestimated recovery rates; the unique nature of the study population involving combat soldiers in extraordinary circumstances so unlikely to represent the 'typical' addiction patterns; and even accusations of scientific misconduct or bias. Robins addresses these criticisms in her 1993 retrospective review, defending the study's methodology and findings.[56]

Still, Robins' findings remain controversial, or in her words, '… still not entirely incorporated into public and scientific views';[57] and/or the findings are often taken to show the phenomenon of context-dependency of drug craving and relapse.[58] But this does not undermine the fundamental conclusion that, contrary to what the BDMA predicts and clinical outcome studies fail to show,[59] remission from addiction may be much more common than expected.

It is the work by Gene Heyman[60] and others that has been critical in recent years in highlighting and clarifying the controversies in the remission/relapse findings. Indeed, many addiction clinic follow-up studies report that treatment fails to secure long-term abstinence is the rule, and when addicted patients do manage to stop using, the cessation is frequently reported to be temporary.[61] However, as Heyman points out, it is important to consider that, like Robins reported in her studies, even when available, the majority of people with addiction do not seek treatment, and so a valid question is to what extent clinic-based samples are representative of the wider population of addicted individuals. Indeed, those who do enter treatment are significantly more likely to suffer from co-occurring psychiatric and medical conditions compared to those who do not seek treatment.[62]

The first issue then is that clinic-based studies risk a biased sample of more complex clinical presentations and provide a distorted picture of addiction in the wider community. As Heyman points out, reliance solely on hospital data

[56] Robins (n 50).

[57] ibid 1041.

[58] HS Crombag and others, 'Context-Induced Relapse to Drug Seeking: A Review' (2008) 363 *Philosophical Transactions of the Royal Society of London, Series B, Biological Sciences* 3233; NE Zinberg, *Drug, Set and Setting: Basis for Controlled Intoxicant Use* (New Haven, Yale University Press, 1986).

[59] EM Brecher, *Licit and Illicit Drugs. The Consumers Union Report on Narcotics, Stimulants, Depressants, Inhalants, Hallucinogens, and Marijuana – Including Caffeine, Nicotine, and Alcohol.* (Boston, Little Brown and Company, 1972); MJ Fleury and others, 'Remission from Substance Use Disorders: A Systematic Review and Meta-Analysis' (2016) 168 *Drug and Alcohol Dependence* 293.

[60] Heyman (n 19).

[61] M Gossop and others, 'The National Treatment Outcome Research Study (NTORS): 4–5 Year Follow-up Results' (2003) 98 *Addiction* 291; DA Wasserman and others, 'Factors Associated with Lapses to Heroin Use during Methadone Maintenance' (1998) 52 *Drug and Alcohol Dependence* 183.

[62] DA Regier and others, 'Comorbidity of Mental Disorders with Alcohol and Other Drug Abuse. Results from the Epidemiologic Catchment Area (ECA) Study' (1990) 264 *JAMA* 2511.

for understanding conditions such as influenza would fail to capture the broader trajectory of the illness. Similarly, addiction clinic data may miss critical insights into recovery patterns among individuals who do not seek or receive treatment.

Concerns such as these about overreliance on treatment-based samples in informing understanding about population-level addiction and mental health epidemiology led the US federal health institutes to launch a series of large-scale, population-based surveys to examine the prevalence and correlates of psychiatric disorders in the general US population. Surveys that included individuals regardless of treatment history (but also including individuals seeking and receiving treatment), creating a representative sample of the general population. Consequently, they are believed to offer a more accurate and representative depiction of the natural course of addiction and/or other mental health conditions.

IX. Findings from Large Sample Epidemiological Surveys of the Wider US Population

Three major US psychiatric surveys that distinguished between drug dependence and abuse revealed striking results.[63] Across these studies, which collectively assessed tens of thousands of participants, approximately 2,700 individuals met DSM criteria for lifetime addiction to illicit drugs. The key finding from these studies was much in line with Robins' findings: most of these individuals no longer met the criteria for dependence at least one year prior to the diagnostic interview. With an average participant age of about 42, the findings showed that drug dependence typically ended in the late twenties or early thirties.

Similarly, a 2011 re-analysis by Lopez-Quintero et al of the 2001–2002 National Epidemiological Survey of Alcohol and Related Conditions (NESARC), which surveyed a representative sample of 43,093 US adults, underscored these patterns.[64] Lifetime cumulative probability estimates of dependence remission were 83.7 per cent for nicotine, 90.6 per cent for alcohol, 97.2 per cent for cannabis and 99.2 per cent for cocaine. Half of these cases of nicotine, alcohol, cannabis and cocaine dependence remitted approximately 26, 14, six and five years after dependence onset, respectively. So, while, depending on the drug and moderated by

[63] KP Conway and others, 'Lifetime Comorbidity of DSM-IV Mood and Anxiety Disorders and Specific Drug Use Disorders: Results from the National Epidemiologic Survey on Alcohol and Related Conditions' (2006) 67 *The Journal of Clinical Psychiatry* 247; FS Stinson and others, 'Comorbidity between DSM-IV Alcohol and Specific Drug Use Disorders in the United States: Results from the National Epidemiologic Survey on Alcohol and Related Conditions' (2005) 80 *Drug and Alcohol Dependence* 105; LA Warner and others, 'Prevalence and Correlates of Drug Use and Dependence in the United States: Results From the National Comorbidity Survey' (1995) 52 *Archives of General Psychiatry* 219.

[64] C Lopez-Quintero and others, 'Probability and Predictors of Transition from First Use to Dependence on Nicotine, Alcohol, Cannabis, and Cocaine: Results of the National Epidemiologic Survey on Alcohol and Related Conditions (NESARC)' (2011) 115 *Drug and Alcohol Dependence* 120.

several sociodemographic variables, time to successful remission varied dramatically and, in the case of legal and/or (more) readily available drugs, was long, most of those initially diagnosed as addicted eventually recovered. Remarkably, but again in line with Robins' findings with heroin users, the cumulative probability of recovery exceeded 90 per cent for most substances; again suggesting that for most individuals meeting DSM diagnostic criteria for addiction, recovery is the eventual expected outcome.

On a brief aside, as said, the variability in recovery rates appears to reflect (in part) differences in drug availability rather than, eg, inherent pharmacological properties. In the analysis just mentioned, for alcohol (licit and readily available), half took 26 years to quit; for cannabis (illicit but in many places readily available), six years; and for cocaine (illicit and less readily available), five years. We repeat this here because discussions around legalisation, decriminalisation or depenalisation often include arguments that legalisation has minor effects, if any on population-wide usage levels, and data seem to support this in some instances.[65] But data such as that by Lopez-Quintero and colleagues suggest that for those already using and addicted to drugs, removing barriers to obtaining these can have a significant negative impact on the longer-term trajectory of their addiction and efforts to abstain successfully; in a way, making addiction more 'disease-like' than otherwise would have been the case.[66] The point being, there may be many good reasons to legalise, decriminalise, or depenalise drugs like heroin, cocaine, and especially cannabis, but the idea that this would not negatively impact established, problematic 'addicted' drug use (and therefore drug use more widely) is not one of them.

The high remission rates observed in national surveys starkly contrast with the much lower success rates reported in treatment settings. Part of the explanation for these differences lies in the characteristics of the populations being studied. Going beyond the clinic and looking at the risk factors of relapse more widely based on simple correlation analyses, Heyman and others point to several: these include being single/not married, lower socio-economic settings and lower school attainment (ie, grades), fewer absences from school, fewer hours worked per week, poor social life, and so forth; or what Heyman and others have described as 'alternative reinforcers'.[67] Grifell and Hart[68] – both outspoken critics of the BDMA view – also point to the importance of these alternative, nondrug options to decrease problematic drug-taking, citing evidence that alternative reinforcers can

[65] M Melchior and others, 'Does Liberalisation of Cannabis Policy Influence Levels of Use in Adolescents and Young Adults? A Systematic Review and Meta-Analysis' (2019) 9 *BMJ Open* e025880; J Connolly, 'Reports Examine Effects of Decriminalisation of Drugs in Portugal' (2009) 30 *Drugnet Ireland* 22.

[66] Lopez-Quintero and others (n 64).

[67] JG Bachman, LD Johnston and PM O'Malley, 'Smoking, Drinking, and Drug Use among American High School Students: Correlates and Trends, 1975-1979' (1981) 71 *American Journal of Public Health* 59.

[68] M Grifell and CL Hart, 'Is Drug Addiction a Brain Disease?' (2018) *American Scientist*, www.americanscientist.org/article/is-drug-addiction-a-brain-disease accessed 23 January 2025.

be used effectively to treat substance-use disorders using so-called contingency management.[69] Defining personally relevant alternative reinforcers is also part of other recent treatment approaches such as cognitive training approaches that supplement other treatments.[70]

But more critical for the present discussion about the voluntary nature of drug use in some individuals, it has been well understood for some time that treatment-seeking addicted individuals are more likely to exhibit higher levels of comorbidity, including and especially co-occurring psychiatric disorders, which complicate both the course of addiction and the likelihood of sustained recovery.

X. On the Issue of Mental Health Co-morbidity and Addiction

Definitionally, comorbid mental health conditions encompass a spectrum of psychiatric disorders that frequently co-occur with SUD. Common examples include major depressive disorder, anxiety disorders, post-traumatic stress disorder (PTSD), schizophrenia, bipolar disorder, attention-deficit/hyperactivity disorder (ADHD), and personality disorders.

Especially critical in our understanding of addiction and mental health co-morbidity have been US-based National Institute of Mental Health Epidemiological Catchment Area (ECA) survey studies – a program of research initiated in response to the 1977 report of the President's Commission on Mental Health with the purpose to create the largest data set on the prevalence and incidence of mental disorders in the US. One of these analyses by Regier and colleagues of 20,291 ECA respondents reported prevalence rates of 22.5 per cent for non-substance mental disorders, 13.5 per cent for alcohol dependence-abuse, and 6.1 per cent for other drug dependence-abuse.[71] People with mental disorders showed 2.7 times higher odds of developing an addictive disorder, with 29 per cent lifetime prevalence, including 22 per cent overlap with alcohol and 15 per cent with other drug disorders. In turn, those with SUDs showed increased comorbidity risks: specifically, individuals with SUDs were seven times more likely to develop another type of addiction. Mental disorder comorbidity was present in 37 per cent of those with alcohol disorders and 53 per cent of those with other drug disorders (ie, an odds ratio of 4.5). Comorbidity rates were notably higher in speciality treatment settings, with the highest rates found in prisons, particularly involving antisocial personality, schizophrenia, and bipolar disorders.

[69] NM Petry, 'Contingency Management: What It Is and Why Psychiatrists Should Want to Use It' (2011) 35 *The Psychiatrist 161*.

[70] RW Wiers and others, 'Approach-Bias Retraining and Other Training Interventions as Add-On in the Treatment of AUD Patients' [2023] *Current Topics in Behavioral Neurosciences* 1.

[71] Regier and others (n 62).

Likewise, in an analysis of a clinically assessed, multiethnic sample consisting of 9,142 individuals with the diagnosis of schizophrenia, bipolar disorder with psychotic features, or schizoaffective disorder (and 10,195 control individuals), Hartz and colleagues reported similar findings;[72] individuals with severe psychotic disorders had much greater risks (odds ratios between 3.5 and 4.6) for smoking, heavy alcohol use, heavy cannabis use, and (other) recreational drug use. These heightened risks were seen across races or ethnicities and both males and females had elevated risks for smoking and alcohol use, marijuana, and drug use. Moreover, and more directly to the point of remission and abstaining from drug use, public health efforts that successfully decreased smoking among younger individuals had little impact on individuals with severe psychotic illness.[73]

Data like these are abundant and, as Heyman argues, provide an important explanation of what in the field of epidemiology is known as the 'Berkson effect': describing how, where medical convenience samples of individuals who have been in some type of treatment are used, the associations found in studies of these samples are often incorrectly presumed to apply to all patients. But beyond this, they describe a clinical profile of a subset of addicted individuals for whom their addiction is more severe or intractable than the wider population of substance involved and diagnosed as addicted that appear more capable of, to return to the phraseology of Sapolsky, 'choose to do the hard but better thing', or what one of us has recently described in the Akrasia model of addiction, the tendency to not act against one's better judgement.[74]

XI. Conclusions

The relationships between addiction, mental health disorders, and criminal responsibility present complex challenges that resist simplistic solutions in both clinical practice and legal doctrine. While the brain disease model of addiction has been criticised (convincingly in our view) as overly reductive and misleading for the general population of substance users, it may retain relevance for a subset of individuals with severe addiction, especially those with co-morbid mental health conditions. This subset, small on a wider population level but over-represented in clinical settings, demonstrates more intractable patterns of use and poorer treatment outcomes, suggesting reduced capacity for voluntary control of their drug

[72] SM Hartz and others, 'Comorbidity of Severe Psychotic Disorders with Measures of Substance Use' (2014) 71 *JAMA Psychiatry* 248.

[73] ibid.

[74] Wiers (n 17). See also N Heather and G Segal, 'Is Addiction a Myth? Donald Davidson's Solution to the Problem of Akrasia Says Not' (2015) 4 *International Journal of Alcohol and Drug Research* 77; as well as RW Wiers, S van Gaal and ME Le Pelley, 'Akrasia and Addiction: Neurophilosophy and Psychological Mechanisms' in J Harbecke and C Herrmann-Pillath (eds), *Social Neuroeconomics: Mechanistic Integration of the Neurosciences and the Social Sciences* (Milton Park, Routledge, 2020).

or alcohol use, and that we feel should be considered legally significant. The high prevalence of co-morbidity between substance use disorders and other mental health conditions calls for a more nuanced (read: cautious) approach to legally relevant questions around voluntariness of consumption and intoxication, especially relevant when it comes to deciding whether the (already problematic) prior fault intoxication rules and/or principles should be invoked in instances where acute intoxication at the time of the offence undermines requisite *mens rea* and/or voluntariness. To be clear, cases such as these – where the level of intoxication is such that *mens rea* and/or volition is undermined in a legally relevant manner – are rare; but where the threshold is met, we think addiction or substance involvement is a relevant consideration for some individuals.

Moreover, the interplay between SUDs and other comorbid mental health conditions creates evidential conundrums for courts attempting to apply traditional doctrines of prior fault and voluntary intoxication. As we and others have discussed,[75] cases like *R v Taj* illustrate these challenges when needing to distinguish between the effects of acute intoxication, withdrawal from intoxication, ongoing addiction, and/or (other) underlying mental health conditions – distinctions that are crucial for legal outcomes (with voluntary intoxication triggering the application of the prior fault rules) but that can be nearly impossible to make with any level of certainty (and therefore consistency) in practice. Again, a more nuanced approach may be needed when dealing with Ds who present with such complex co-morbidities. Rather than treating severe addiction as a potential reason for invoking prior fault mechanisms (based on past, historic intoxications), courts might better conceptualise it as a potential symptom or manifestation of underlying mental health conditions that could have exculpatory (or at least, *not* trigger inculpatory rules and practices) or mitigating relevance.[76]

Indeed, in the context of the prior-fault intoxication rules, recognising severe addiction as a potential indicator of underlying mental health issues raises additional complexity when attempting to establish causality between drug use and mental health conditions. In cases where drug use appears to have induced or exacerbated mental health issues, traditional prior fault principles may still maintain relevance, as the initial decision to consume substances could be viewed as a voluntary act preceding the subsequent mental health complications and therefore a basis for backwards-looking blame.[77] The situation becomes more challenging when mental health conditions precede and potentially contribute to the development of addiction. In such scenarios, applying prior fault principles becomes problematic, as the drug use may be more accurately understood as a symptom of the underlying mental health condition rather than a purely voluntary act. The

[75] *Taj* [2018] EWCA (Crim) 1743; Crombag, Child and Sullivan (n 42); JJ Child, HS Crombag and R Sullivan, 'Defending the Delusional, the Irrational, and the Dangerous' (2020) 4 *Crim LR* 306.

[76] The next chapter of this collection (ch 6) continues discussing situations in which addiction may not be straightforwardly blameworthy.

[77] But for *Beard* [1920] AC AC 479.

current legal framework as well as recent proposals for reform fail to recognise, let alone accommodate, these complexities. In doing so, they fail to engage with well-established scientific and clinical epidemiological understandings of the varied ways in which mental health conditions and substance use disorders interact, and risk over-criminalising vulnerable Ds suffering from co-morbid mental health conditions and addictions.

6

Criminal Responsibility in Addiction Pathways

JAMES BROWNING AND ANNA GOLDBERG

I. Introduction

The degree to which an addicted agent should be considered incapacitated is a popular question within the disciplines of neuroscience and philosophy, though whether addicted intoxication is best characterised as a choice or a compulsion is a debate which is unlikely to be resolved soon.[1] This chapter seeks to highlight a more discrete issue of relevance to criminal law theorists which has to date received limited attention: how addicted intoxication fits within the evaluative exercise of blaming or excusing conduct.

It is trite to note that consumption of psychoactive substances plays a causal role in harmful acts and outcomes. Much has been said about the blameworthiness of somebody who violates the criminal law while so inebriated he may not have had the required capacities to be held responsible. It is somewhat puzzling then that comparatively little has been said specifically about the addicted harm-doer, whose behaviour in becoming intoxicated appears to be less obviously culpable in light of the volitional impairment addiction can cause.[2] There is good reason to relieve the topic from its relative absence of scholarship, not least because addiction explains a great deal of criminally prohibited behaviour.[3] Both acquisitive crimes and under-the-influence offending are motivated in whole or in part by the need to feed an addiction or occur as a direct result of addicted intoxication. The causal link between

[1] See, eg, N Levy (ed), *Addiction and Self-Control: Perspectives from Philosophy, Psychology, and Neuroscience* (Oxford, Oxford University Press, 2013).

[2] Some have of course already attempted to address this issue, see, eg, D Husak, 'Addiction and Criminal Liability' (1999) 18 *Law and Philosophy* 655; PH Robinson, 'A Brief Summary and Critique of Criminal Liability Rules for Intoxicated Conduct' (2018) 82 *The Journal of Criminal Law* 381. From an interdisciplinary and socio-scientific lens, the problem of the addicted defendant and their criminal responsibility has received more attention comparatively. For an excellent overview, see J Kennett, NA Vincent and A Snoek, 'Drug Addiction and Criminal Responsibility' in L Neil and C Jens (eds), *Handbook on Neuroethics* (Dordrecht, Springer, 2014).

[3] MG Vaughn, CP Salas-Wright and JM Reingle-Gonzalez, 'Addiction and Crime: The Importance of Asymmetry in Offending and the Life-Course' (2016) 35 *Journal of Addictive Diseases* 213.

addiction and offending is, in these instances, clearly made out; and it is plausible that, absent a defendant's addiction, many of these harms would be avoided.

Addiction raises unique challenges to the arguments legitimising prior fault intoxication rules, notably by labelling addicted intoxication as voluntary and/or reckless. Part of our objective is to explore this issue in greater detail. Furthermore, while some may be satisfied that there is culpability to be found in addiction (ie, the onset of addiction is fuelled by blameworthy acts), we will show that in many instances such a generalisation stretches credibility. Given that intoxication rules impute blame to any one instance of intoxication, but an addicted defendant may – unlike his recreationally intoxicated counterpart – reasonably assert that he was acting *less* (if at all) voluntarily or recklessly due to cravings or withdrawal, a doctrine of prior fault therefore necessarily relies on normative conclusions on a defendant's addiction pathway.

This chapter's first task, after this introduction, is to flesh out this hypothesis, strengthening our claim that an application of prior fault to any instance of addicted intoxication can only be sound if it is to incorporate blame for a defendant's behaviour in becoming addicted.[4] Given the scope of the collection within which this chapter is based, we do not intend to devote much ink to issues beyond addiction in the application of prior fault doctrines. Instead, our account of the rules in section II will focus on areas specifically relevant to addiction, and it is worth noting that while we refer frequently to English law, we do not intend our analysis to be applicable to only one jurisdiction but to any that attributes blame to intoxication in order to circumvent legal orthodoxy. Consequently, comparative remarks to other jurisdictions may be employed to illustrate a more generalised application of our arguments. Upon completion of this task, we move to section III to explain the underlying rationale found in the general part of the criminal law for holding people responsible and for excusing them. After surveying the literature on what makes an agent responsible (be it the freeness of his choices, or his choices as they reflect upon him),[5] we demonstrate that there is a theoretical account of blame within a prior fault doctrine which can be attributed to the addicted defendant. Having made out the relationship between addiction and liability in both specific and general terms, we will be well primed to demonstrate that the reasoning required to legitimise addicted intoxication as an instrument of inculpation struggles to survive real-world application.

To upend the logic we spent sections II and III constructing, we advance three case studies. In section IV, we look at addiction rooted in pre- and early adolescent

[4] At present, addiction is afforded no explicit relevance in placing blame under a prior fault intoxication framework. This cannot mean that addiction *is* irrelevant, as any sensible analysis of causation in addicted T1 intoxication would show. Our view that this requires finding fault in the condition of addiction is explored in s II of this chapter.

[5] Choice and capacity theories of responsibility have some distinct contours, as can be evidenced from the nuances between the arguments of, say Moore and Hart. In the spirit of efficiency, and due to confines of space, we have opted to combine these accounts of responsibility into one. This is the subject of s III of this chapter.

drug use, concluding that dominant theories of responsibility do not convincingly validate the censure which currently follows from prior fault rules. Iatrogenic addiction (incidental addiction arising from medical treatment) is the subject of section V, where we again conclude that the onset of volitional impairment with respect to drug taking is not in any meaningful way attributable to the choices or character of the addict. Section VI, our final case study, is dedicated to an examination of a comorbid addicted defendant, where we question whether addicted drug users with additional psychiatric conditions can be said to be acting culpably.

II. Blaming the Addicted Defendant

Our first important task, from which all others stem, is to prove that addiction is not simply relevant to explaining causation for a criminally prohibited act or outcome, but is in fact an ingredient in establishing liability.[6] While not universally accepted,[7] the view that a doctrine of prior fault enables convictions for some intoxicated harm-doers might be seen as the prevailing view amongst scholars of criminal law. In brief, if an agent (D) consumes an intoxicant at one point (the T1 intoxication) and later goes on to conduct himself in some way prohibited by criminal law, though without the typical fault element required for a conviction (the T2 act), he will not escape liability for causing that harm,[8] often subject to varying jurisdictional caveats.[9]

Prior fault rules cannot be said to command widespread popularity. For one, it has been reasonably argued that the doctrine fundamentally mislabels a defendant's wrongdoing, thereby inappropriately exercising the powerful stigmatising effect of criminal sanction. These fair labelling worries run concurrently with concerns over the appropriateness of criminalising defendants based on their

[6] For the avoidance of doubt, the cases under review here are limited to those which may be subject to a prior fault construction of liability, ie, where a defendant's acute intoxication renders him unable to form *mens rea*.

[7] See, eg, AP Simester, 'Intoxication Is Never a Defence' [2009] *Crim LR* 3.

[8] *DPP v Majewski* [1977] AC 443. Note intoxication has been explicitly linked with recklessness as understood in English law, but our use of the phrase in this chapter should be interpreted more broadly, in line with our objective not to limit our analysis to any one jurisdiction.

[9] In English law, intoxication is only relevant to a defendant's liability when he lacks the necessary fault element (*mens rea*) for any subsequent offence due to his intoxication. Furthermore, inculpation is only possible for an offence requiring basic, rather than specific, intent. If a defendant commits a harm requiring specific intent, such as murder, there will usually be an underlying basic intent offence, such as manslaughter, for which he can still be convicted. In civil law systems such as the Netherlands or Germany, prior fault rules often prevent the exculpatory effects of an excuse, commonly insanity defence equivalents. In such situations, questions may arise addressing the (normative) equivalence between the T1 act of intoxication and the lack of blameworthiness at T2. For a comparative overview of the challenges associated with prior fault, see: AE Goldberg and others, 'Prior-Fault Blame In England And Wales, Germany And The Netherlands' (2021) 8 *Journal of International and Comparative Law* 53.

fault in becoming intoxicated, rather than insisting on finding the fault ordinarily necessary for conviction of any given offence, ie, equivalence concerns.

A prosaic hypothetical highlighting both worries can be easily made. Consider Thelma, an ostensible law-abiding member of her local community who enjoys recreational drinking with friends at the weekend. There have been previous instances of her drinking what she considers 'too much', but the only harm which has ever come from it is a bad headache and a worrying outflow of cash from her current account to the local pub. One weekend, though, in a state of heightened intoxication, she seriously injures another, though she can reliably claim she had no intention of doing so and nor was she aware that her conduct was at all risky. While we believe Thelma when she says she drank so much that she was neither aware nor in control of her bodily movements, it does her no good in law. Even if the court agrees that it appears highly probable that she acted without intention or subjective recklessness at T1, a conviction is possible. Her fault in excessive drinking is not in dispute, as that occurred at a point in time when she was able to engage with and direct her conscious will towards some action. Her intoxication relieves the prosecution of proving any internal fault element at T2.[10] Her criminal blameworthiness can be located in a non-criminal act, yet her liability is not for reckless drinking but for some other offence she went on to cause later.

There is, of course, an intuitive appeal here, which is worth pausing to reflect upon. Intoxication rules are engaged in large part in doctrines endorsing both retributivism and deterrence. Concerns raised by English judges indicate a fear that without the rules, intoxicated offending would go unpunished.[11] We do not seek to settle the debate as to their overall efficacy or legitimacy, though we do point out that if proving fault at T2 is exceedingly difficult (or indeed impossible), then we should question whether it is appropriate to label an acutely intoxicated defendant's wrong as anything other than dangerous intoxication.[12] Moreover, prior fault intoxication rules are notably absent in a number of countries, and these jurisdictions are not lining up with giddy anticipation to replicate the approach outlined above.[13]

So, evidentially, Thelma's T1 intoxication, presupposed as a free act, provides the court with enough proof of her wrongdoing to relieve Crown counsel of convincing a jury she acted culpably at T2: the T1 prior fault stands in. The prosecution's case now becomes very easy. Causation plus intoxication equals guilt, so

[10] *DPP v Majewski* (n 8) 474–475. The dichotomous relationship between offences of basic and specific intent have been complicated by the judgment of *R v Heard* [2007] 1 Cr App R 37. It now appears to be the case that certain elements of offences can themselves be subdivided into basic and specific intent.

[11] Similar arguments are also found in Dutch jurisprudence: see annotation by 't Hart in Supreme Court, 28-6-1983, *NJ* 1983 53 annot. AC 't Hart, ECLI:NL:HR:1983:AC8052.

[12] This is largely the approach taken by German courts. For an introduction and comparative overview thereof, see Goldberg and others (n 9).

[13] See, eg, the rejection of *Majewski* in Australia in the case of *O'Connor* [1980] HCA 17, and the continuing application of *Kamipeli* [1975] 2 NZLR 610 in New Zealand.

on a balance of probabilities, we can be confident that Thelma will be convicted. She might do well to say to the court that she thinks she was very foolish in getting as drunk as she did and that she should have and could have drunk responsibly.

Let us move our focus to Thelma's good friend Louise, who is drowning her sorrows while her erstwhile drinking companion serves her custodial sentence. Louise too ends up so intoxicated that she loses control of herself and causes some criminally prohibited harm. The prosecution can argue that, much like Thelma, Louise made a choice to get dangerously intoxicated and deserves punishment for it. What, then, when Louise turns around and says that she is in fact addicted to alcohol, has been unable to control her drinking for years, and every time she tries to restrain it, she invariably suffers from powerful cravings and debilitating withdrawal symptoms? Unfortunately for Louise, no matter how dangerous her withdrawal symptoms[14] and how overpowering her cravings, her intoxication will not satisfy the legal definition of involuntary intoxication. But it remains that Louise cannot convincingly be expected to self-censure like Thelma and say she should and could have controlled herself at T1. Thus, despite the circumstances being materially different from that of her friend Thelma, she is as much to blame for her intoxication.

Traditional critiques of prior fault intoxication rules have considered whether or not it is defensible to construct liability from voluntary intoxication. Our issue with the rules is necessarily more fundamental: the difference between Thelma and Louise tells us that we have good reason to challenge addicted T1 intoxication as equally voluntary as non-addicted T1 intoxication. A great deal continues to be said about the volitional impairment of addicts in relation to their drug use. We need not resolve that here, instead pointing out that those who consider addicted drug taking a choice certainly consider it an impaired one.[15] While it is almost certainly true that a number of those who meet the diagnostic criteria for addiction might reasonably be deemed able to exercise self-control at T1, such a designation cannot be universal. Indeed, even those who argue that addicted persons behave dysfunctionally (though short of behaving compulsively) sometimes caveat this account by pointing to those on the extreme end of the spectrum of addiction, where cognitive impairment may be so great as to render imputations of choice inappropriate.[16]

We should be satisfied for purposes here that Louise is a serious alcoholic. Whereas prior fault rules usually substitute incapacity at T2 for voluntary fault at T1, the law appears unconcerned that Louise might lack any realistic notion of capacity at *both* T1 and T2, so it is open to us to inquire what exactly she is to be

[14] Note that withdrawal symptoms can indeed become dangerous to the point of life-threatening. See: LA Trevisan and others, 'Complications of Alcohol Withdrawal: Pathophysiological Insights' (1998) 22 *Alcohol Health and Research World* 1 61.

[15] GM Heyman, *Addiction: A Disorder of Choice* (Cambridge, Harvard University Press, 2009).

[16] O Flanagan, 'Willing Addicts? Drinkers, Dandies, Druggies, and Other Dionysians' in N Heather and G Segal (eds), *Addiction and Choice: Rethinking the Relationship* (Oxford, Oxford University Press, 2016) 79.

blamed for. If we are convinced that she was so intoxicated at T2 to not know what she was doing, then it cannot be the T2 act. If she was the type of drug user whose abstinence resulted in serious physiological pressures, then it would be unreasonable to say she acted voluntarily at T1 in the same way that Thelma did. Addiction requires us to consider T1 in a way that traditional accounts of prior fault intoxication do not. Typically, T1 is considered a distinct temporal event, capable of being carved out and examined against an agent's thoughts, desires and actions. For the addicted agent, though, this is not the case. T1 addicted intoxication is capable of being driven by not just desire but desire coupled with at least a subjective necessity. It is intimately linked to the drug consumption that occurred in the weeks, months and years prior to harm-doing behaviour. As such, the intoxication which occurred immediately antecedent to any criminally prohibited behaviour cannot be rationally severed from the overall development of tolerance and cravings, and the potentially fatal threat of withdrawal.

Despite this, addicted T1 intoxication is labelled voluntary and reckless in the same way recreational intoxication is, though, as we have shown, that cannot be because both are soundly considered free choices. If addiction and its panoply of physiological pressures are an ingredient of prior fault, then we should be satisfied in concluding that addiction is considered a blameworthy condition. As we will show in section III, a defendant is not typically censured where he lacks any control over a situation. It is realistic, then, to conclude that addicted intoxication is treated as culpable despite the volitional impairment, because the volitional impairment was self-induced by a defendant's historic acts in becoming addicted. Such a reading may not appear immediately charitable, though it is a necessary inference if we think that criminal law only ascribes responsibility for serious offences where it considers there to be blame. Its plausibility is further strengthened by the principle of *actio liberia in causa*, where a defendant will not be considered unfree in his choices if he is responsible for his own incapacity.

The case for responsibility in addiction need not rest on a conscious choice to become addicted. When today's chronic alcoholic took his first, second and third drink, he is unlikely to have done so thinking it would result in dependency years later. Yet while many addicted individuals will no doubt have begun experimenting with a substance without a subjective belief that they would become addicted, it does not necessarily need to follow that we conclude they are not responsible for it. Some elucidation on what the law considers involuntary intoxication reinforces this point. It is only where a defendant is unknowingly spiked by another, or where he takes prescription medication as prescribed and suffers an unforeseen reaction, that criminal law considers intoxication involuntary.[17] These routes to T1 intoxication are in part excusable because the defendant could not fairly be expected to guard against them.

[17] D Ormerod, K Laird and M Gibson, *Smith, Hogan, and Ormerod's Criminal Law* (Oxford, Oxford University Press, 2024) ch 9.4.2.

The patient who takes his pain medication as prescribed and suffers violent hallucinations has not acted recklessly, nor has the drinker who incompetently injures another after their drink was laced by some sinister actor. It is not that either outcome was unforeseeable – prescription drugs carry warning signs, and the fact that drinks can get spiked is well-known – but that there was no operative fault attributable to the agent. As English law currently stands, he who takes a serious amount of drink or drugs *should* have given greater regard to the danger he may pose later. It is therefore open to us to conclude that, in the context of addiction, English law imposes a standard of objective risk-taking in drink and drug use which leaves an addicted defendant liable for their intoxication.

To assess whether a defendant is responsible for his addiction may not require asking whether he chose addiction, and not even whether the agent thought he was likely or possibly going to become addicted. Instead, the first question could simply be whether the addicted agent embarked upon his experimentation phase with knowledge that psychoactive substances are dangerous. If he answers in the affirmative, he cannot later throw up his hands and say, 'I had no idea this would happen.' If he did not have an informed appreciation of the risk, then we subsequently ask why he thought there was no harm from his consumption. This may be asked both subjectively, if he had given thought to it and proceeded anyway, or objectively, with regards to his circumstances as we can evaluate them. More on this will come later, but it does establish the basis of blameless addiction. If we cannot be satisfied that an addicted individual knew or should reasonably have known that he was taking a risk, then it stands to reason that his addiction is blameless, thus so is his T1 intoxication.[18]

There is undoubtedly a challenge in deciding at which point in the addiction pathway we should investigate an agent's responsibility. We argue that the most logical point is at first use, and before the onset of addiction, ie, from feelings of *liking* but before feelings of *needing*.[19] These are the circumstances within which an agent first found themselves experimenting with the relevant substance.[20] Addiction theorists agree that agency over consumption is strongest in the pre- and early-experimentation stage,[21] so assessing responsibility at this stage avoids the acrimonious debate over the nature of volition for the long-term, relapsing

[18] Note that the mere fact that an underlying addiction would be blameless does not automatically imply that the subsequent intoxication would also be blameless: this will always be dependent on the actual capacities of the defendant at the time of the defence. This chapter is primarily concerned with the subset of addicted persons where we have good reason to doubt that their addicted intoxication should be characterised as voluntary.

[19] For the reward effects of various different substances, see: PM Duncan, *Substance Use Disorders: A Biopsychosocial Perspective* (Cambridge, Cambridge University Press, 2021) pt IV.

[20] An exception to this is iatrogenic addiction, where there is no 'experimentation' phase, as will be discussed in s IV.

[21] This is sometimes done implicitly, as the disease model of addiction relies upon evidence that neural changes from repeated drug use encourages continued use. Ie, the longer an agent uses, the more difficult it will be to refrain. On reward learning, see: JC Horvitz and BL Jacobs, *Principles of Behavioural Neuroscience* (Cambridge, Cambridge University Press, 2023) ch 11.

addict. This approach also has practical benefits: identification of any other period where we might examine responsibility would be necessarily arbitrary ('before adulthood'), or entirely vague ('before addiction') and inapplicable in reality.[22]

Some may argue that a tracing exercise to find blame over such a wide temporal scope cannot possibly be accommodated within the exercise of ascribing criminal responsibility. On this point we disagree. While it is often cited that prior fault rules leverage T1 intoxication to construct blame for a T2 act, what act 'T1 intoxication' refers to will seldom be entirely clear. By design, the intoxication rules are agnostic to whether it was a defendant's first or fifth act of consuming an intoxicant within any given period that caused acute intoxication sufficient to raise a reasonable doubt over T2 *mens rea*. Scholars have tended to focus on the instance of intoxication immediately antecedent to the prohibited conduct, but it is important to recognise that a state of acute intoxication may be the result of a number of acts over a significant temporal scope rather than a single one, with each act contributing, but not directly causing, acute intoxication. Here we must reiterate the point that it is very difficult (if at all possible) to dismember individual instances of addicted intoxication from the onset and maintenance of the addiction itself.

If we return to Louise, the addicted long-time friend of Thelma, we remember that she was drinking away her sorrows when she became incapacitated and caused some harm. When was her T1 intoxication? For Thelma it is somewhat clearer. We might struggle to identify the exact point Thelma shifted from intoxication to *acute* intoxication, but we know she was sober when she went to the pub the day she caused harm. Louise, by contrast, might have woken up the day she caused harm drunk from her consumption the night before. She might have been in a heightened state of inebriation for days, weeks or longer. To identify Louise's blameworthy *act* is evidently exceedingly difficult.

It is here that we think most confusion is possible with regard to doctrinal interpretations of intoxication rules and addiction. The sympathetic view for Louise tells us that if she could not control herself in drinking, or if such control came at a serious enough cost, then considering her intoxication a culpable failing might represent a gross mistake of the criminal law. Importantly, this view of addiction is open to challenge. Indeed, if we limit our analysis purely to the intoxication immediately antecedent to the harm-causing conduct (as orthodox accounts of prior fault do), then we must afford Louise some justification or excuse, as we would identify only her incapacity and not enquire as to the cause of such incapacity. The view that Louise is the architect of her own incapacity needs to be realistically considered; indeed, the way prior fault intoxication operates in the context of addiction demands that we examine whether Louise had set herself up for failure by the time she reached T1. The presence of addiction at T1 therefore

[22] If we were to say the duty to act was 'before his addiction sets in', one might counter with whether it is possible to demarcate the line between recreational use and addiction. Similarly, a test of 'when one recognises he has become addicted' falls victim to the same fate, while subject to the additional criticism that the addict is now subject to psychological and physical pressures to continue use.

need not demand that we jump to conclusions about volitional incapacity voiding responsibility, provided we are willing to examine the cause of the defect.

So far we have outlined the link between addiction and liability, proving that normative conclusions about the condition are a necessary part of any prior fault construction of liability. We have also started to lay the framework for a prescriptive account of blame in addicted intoxication by indicating that we need to examine whether or not the experimentation phase was reckless. Importantly, it follows that T1 incapacity is a starting point for further investigation rather than evidence of unprincipled convictions. Later in this chapter, we intend to show that the universal imputation of blame to addicted intoxication, rationalised on the logic outlined above, is capable of being fundamentally flawed. Before this, though, we must move to explain what it is in general terms to be a responsible agent.

III. Ascriptions of Criminal Responsibility

As we have seen, the hard edges required to determine guilt or innocence in specific terms can give rise to several problems. The high bar for involuntary intoxication, for example, might cause a perception of injustice on behalf of the severely addicted defendant. The undefined nature of T1 intoxication raises questions about the temporal scope of the criminal law's culpability analysis. Of course, liability necessarily rests upon these hard edges, though exposing their theoretical limitations requires patient consideration unavailable during a trial process.

Here, the general part of criminal law can step in to provide a better explanation of what is going on during a trial. Take the operational interpretation of causation. If a patron of a local pub is caught on CCTV punching the bartender, or a man clad all in black is caught fleeing with bags of money recently illicitly acquired from a local bank, liability is not yet made out – they may have had good reason to act as they did. Further interrogation into conduct is therefore required beyond the causal requirement. Agents are generally responsible for their actions, and society expects that patrons do not punch bartenders and citizens do not rob banks. That said, when certain types of extra information can be adduced as to why a defendant acted as he did, we might be persuaded to withhold disapproval. If, for instance, the bartender had created a belief that he presented a real and immediate risk to the life of the patron, or if we discovered the man clad in black had acted only on the basis that his family was being held hostage and the price demanded was obedience in the heist, our assessment of the conduct is fundamentally altered. They have caused an outcome, yes, but they are not necessarily to be censured for it.[23]

[23] For simplicity, we have restricted our terminology which may alter a responsibility to excuse. We are alert to the fact that some of the subsequent discussion may better be framed with reference to exemption or justification.

Let us translate this into the issue at hand. Imagine your neighbour two doors down who, having independently become blind drunk, inadvertently sets fire to his curtains, and the ensuing blaze injures your next-door neighbour. He may claim that he committed no crime because: a) he was so drunk he did not intend his actions; or b) he knew what he was doing but only did it because he was intoxicated. As we saw with Thelma and Louise, the first plea directs us to a conviction based on prior fault intoxication rules.[24] On the second plea, his intoxicated intent remains sufficient to establish liability.[25] On either account, courts conclude that he created the risk of some danger via his intoxication, and as such a danger was realised, he should be punished for any wrong that follows.

Specifically, he is held responsible for his intoxication and ensuing harm(s). But how is this explained in the general part of the criminal law? A shorthand answer is that he acted culpably. This chapter has already made a great many references to the largely analogous concepts of blame and responsibility, though we must say more about what it *is* to be culpable to come to comprehensive normative conclusions on the addicted defendant's blame. If the person is not addicted, his culpability is rooted in his recklessness in drinking at T1. If he is addicted, and his addiction is of a severity enough for us to question his ability to exercise self-control at T1, his culpability must be rooted in his recklessness in becoming addicted. The different standard here is certainly an issue worthy of greater investigation, but our task in this chapter must necessarily be confined to identifying the steps required to account for the current law. As we have demonstrated that addiction is a key component of liability in prior fault doctrines, we must embark on the task of providing a fuller account of what it means to be responsible and subsequently apply it to addiction. Some of this task has already been completed, such as in identifying the temporal scope under examination, as well as certain questions we will need to ask, such as whether a defendant realised there was a risk from substance (ab)use, and if he did not, why he did not.

Two theories of responsibility can be said to dominate criminal law scholarship. One account emphasises a defendant's capacity to make choices as central to his culpability. Excusable conduct in this theory is generally circumstantial: where the internal or external environmental pressure is such that choices are deemed unfree, a defendant need not be considered responsible for them.[26] By contrast, character theory is interested in conduct as it reflects upon an agent's internal dispositions.[27] On this account, motivating reasons for conduct indicate what somebody values, and deviating from social norms can mark an agent out as

[24] Note that many civil law jurisdictions do not require prior fault rules to establish intent in such cases, as evidence for intent may be obtained objectively through the defendant's actions, whereby mental incapacity becomes (largely) irrelevant.

[25] *R v Sheehan* [1994] 1 WLR 739.

[26] MS Moore, *Placing Blame: A Theory of the Criminal Law* (Oxford, Oxford University Press, 2010) ch 13.

[27] N Lacey, *In Search of Criminal Responsibility: Ideas, Interests, and Institutions* (Oxford, Oxford University Press, 2016) ch 2.

being of censurable character. If conduct is not reflective, ie, it is *out* of character, a defendant may be excused from his otherwise censurable behaviour. More must now necessarily be said about both theories.

For proponents of capacity reasoning, most notable among them being Hart,[28] a capacity to refrain from causing a criminal harm, qualified by a fair opportunity to do the right thing, is required to consider somebody a responsible agent. The assessment under this theory was explained by Michael Moore as first requiring an examination of a defendant's 'equipment' (his cognitive ability), after which, when combined with his circumstances, we can fairly assess whether somebody's behaviour is blameworthy.[29] Limitations on reasoning ability might modify our assessment of whether or not a defendant is properly thought to be responsible for his actions. Incapacity can take many forms, though for the purposes of the case studies we are exploring in sections four and six, we shall highlight psychiatric illness and age.[30]

The nature of liability in prior fault intoxication is compatible with capacity theory. Let us return to the neighbour two doors down. If he had no addiction and set out to get acutely intoxicated because he enjoyed it, we might conclude him to have acted in a blameworthy fashion. He lacked the capacity to refrain from setting his curtains alight at T2 because he was in a state of extreme inebriation, but he previously exercised his capacity in the causally relevant intoxication and had the opportunity to refrain. Here, the neighbour is a recreational drinker, and so he retained full agency not to become intoxicated; therefore our temporal lens need not extend far. As his inability to exercise capacity at T2 was contingent on his choice to become acutely intoxicated, he is afforded no excuse under this theory on the basis that he had both capacity and a fair opportunity during the antecedent intoxication.

Capacity theory also aligns with the logic of excusable intoxication. If we say the neighbour's causally relevant intoxication was the consumption of strong painkillers prescribed after a serious car accident, taken as instructed, our assessment is fundamentally altered. Strictly speaking, he had the capacity to choose not to take the painkillers. If, however, his doctor informed him that the risk of side effects was negligible and he had never had any issues with prescription medication before, it would be unreasonable to hold him responsible for the adverse side effects which caused the ensuing blame. Here, he had no fair opportunity to obey the law, even though his intoxication was, strictly speaking, a choice. His excuse is anchored in the fact that his harm-causing intoxication was neither a result of informed choice nor recklessness.

[28] HLA Hart, *Punishment and Responsibility: Essays in the Philosophy of Law* (Oxford, Clarendon Press, 1978).

[29] Moore (n 26) 554.

[30] Hart, while recognising the link between age and the ability to conform to legal norms, was critical of hard 'ages of responsibility', see Hart (n 28) 228–229; See also: N Lacey, *State Punishment* (Londen, Routledge, 1994) 62–65.

But what if the neighbour's causally relevant intoxication was an instance of addicted intoxication? Due to physiological pressures, he could plausibly raise that he was unable to exercise capacity and/or lacked a fair opportunity to avoid acute intoxication at T1. If the law was limited to examining the harm and the intoxication immediately antecedent to it, he must be afforded an excuse. However, as we have previously laid out, that need not necessarily be the whole story. Much like prior fault rules ignore T2 incapacity on previous faults, we are obliged to consider whether T1 incapacity is in fact excusable. Here, the experimentation phase is valuable evidence, and leads us to ask whether the agent had a chance of avoiding addiction. If we are satisfied that addiction is a result of free choices, and that there was a fair chance to avoid the state which caused T1 incapacity, the conduct can still be considered censurable under this reading.

Many scholars have suggested that choice and capacity are an incomplete part of the picture, and that further interrogation into a defendant's character is needed. It is not that choices do not matter here, but rather how they matter. Capacity theory focuses primarily on the relative freeness of a choice, asking whether or not a course of conduct is censurable given an agent's faculties and options. Character theory, on the other hand, is concerned with behaviour as it is suggestive of the nature of a person.[31] Theft offences are a neat example: he who steals is not just a thief, but he is also dishonest. The stigmatising effect of criminal law is central to this account of responsibility, whereby the choice to commit an offence results in lasting labels upon a defendant. Take homicide. After a guilty verdict for the most serious homicide offence in England, a citizen is not just regarded as having wrongfully killed another. He will widely be regarded as a murderer, and his status in society is fundamentally and permanently changed. Serious sexual offences, particularly those involving children, result in similarly stark and permanent consequences for any convict. For character theorists, this can be evidence that the criminal law is engaged not just in evaluating choices, but in evaluating people.[32]

We can apply character theory to the non-addicted neighbour who was acutely recreationally intoxicated. An account that considers his conduct in drunkenly causing a fire and injuring another is deserving of blame perhaps because of his propensity to engage in risky behaviour, evidence of which can be supplied by his dangerous intoxication. The act of becoming blind drunk might betray an unacceptable disregard for the safety of others, with the conclusion being that inculpation is justified. Here we can see that character theory does not examine behaviour in isolated snapshots, but instead asks what a defendant's choices say about them. It looks at the intrinsic nature of an agent (though it is not usually aligned with hard determinism).[33] Autonomy remains central to this account of responsibility in two respects. First, a defendant retains cognitive control over his choices. Feeling an urge to punch another during the heat of an argument is one thing, and doing it is another. Second, traits are not necessarily fixed nor static. Feeling the urge to

[31] Lacey (n 27).
[32] G Mousourakis, 'Character, Choice and Criminal Responsibility' (1998) 39 *Les Cahiers de Droit* 51.
[33] Lacey (n 27) 33–42.

punch people *all of the time* might suggest an unreasonable streak worth addressing. In addressing problematic character traits, an agent marks themselves out as being of good character. Ignoring dispositions which risk harm to one's self or others, such as a propensity for aggression or an inclination for acting dishonestly, does the opposite.

Under a character-centric account of criminal responsibility, excuses are typically predicated on acts which are out of character.[34] The defence of duress, for example, recognises that there can be significant pressure bearing down on a defendant to engage in otherwise prohibited conduct. This is in large part an extension of the 'unfree choice' logic of capacity theorists, though the conclusion is more comprehensive. Excuses, for character theorists, might also take the form of alienation, where an agent is excused on the basis that he is experiencing some extended aberration from his true self.[35] Additionally, as character is not ordinarily seen as fixed from birth, we must also enquire into whether a defendant's character has had the opportunity to develop fully at the time he commits any given harm. Much like the alternative theory based upon capacity, this theory is compatible with the structure of prior fault intoxication rules. If our pyromaniac neighbour had acted as a result of medical treatment at T1, we might conclude that his violent outburst was not reflective of his character. Instead, it was a moment of madness for which punishment would not be justified.

Placing responsibility in addicted intoxication is also possible in this theory, but again requires us to examine the early period of experimentation. The repeated voluntary acts required to pass the threshold of addiction may be perceived as demonstrative of short-term thinking at best, or grossly negligent risk-taking at worst (provided we are satisfied that a defendant knew, or was under some duty to have known, that his sustained experimentation with psychoactive substances carried some risk of addiction). Alienation, outlined above, might seem a readily available defence to the addict who acts contrary to social norms, but this will not necessarily be the case. If a seeming ineligibility for liability rests upon one's own previous actions, one is not actually ineligible at all. Therefore, the addicted defendant who may fairly raise alienation or out-of-character behaviour may still be liable if we can conclude his alienation or out-of-character behaviour was a result of previous acts for which he was responsible.

In this section, we have demonstrated that responsibility is made out either on the basis of an examination primarily on choices or on a reflective evaluation which identifies what an exercise of capacity says about a defendant's true nature. Both accounts may underpin attributions of responsibility to the addicted defendant, substantiating the characterisation of blameworthy addiction which we outlined in the previous section. Importantly, though, explaining responsibility

[34] This view is not universally accepted amongst those who endorse a character-centric account of criminal responsibility, see: V Tadros, *Criminal Responsibility* (Oxford, Oxford University Press, 2007) ch 2.

[35] ibid ch 1.

for addiction is rooted firmly in the experimentation phase, where we can be confident that there was freedom of choice before an agent's character might have become distorted by substance abuse. At this point, we have set out our introductory aims of linking addiction to liability and a possible theoretical basis for doing so. We now move to challenge that logic based on certain addiction pathways, which should provide a possible route to exculpation.

IV. Case Study I: Age of Onset

So, underlying liability is a finding that a defendant is being held responsible for some harm. In the context of addiction and prior fault rules, blame must necessarily be found with reference to a defendant's responsibility for becoming addicted. The first problem for criminal law is that this linkage presupposes that all addicted agents either had an informed choice at the point of experimentation, or that such information was available to them and disregarded. It is a familiar part of most criminal justice systems that there is an age before which we do not consider agents responsible for their actions. This is not the only concession the criminal law grants to the young. Between the age of criminal responsibility and the age of majority, we see defendants tried in different courts, receive special sentences and spend tariffs in alternative facilities. Theorists disagree over the purpose of this; for instance, Hart was critical of what he considered a blunt tool to determine incapacity, while Tadros has suggested age is linked to belief formation and thus the development of character. While the details differ, age is clearly relevant to our understanding of both responsibility and liability. As is currently the case, a defendant cannot escape liability on the basis of his addicted volitional impairment, indicating that he is responsible for it. If, however, his addiction can be traced back to a young age, such findings of responsibility are fundamentally challenged.

A comparative illustrative example is useful here. Consider the agent whose recreational drink and drug use begins in adulthood, perhaps in his mid-20s. By this age, the chances of him being exposed to public health campaigns which highlight the risks of alcohol or drug abuse are close to certain. Even if he had not been exposed to state-sponsored warnings (which, since the War on Drugs began in the 1970s, have been frequent), it is most likely he will have known somebody who has suffered from addiction or heard some cautionary tale. Provided he is endowed with typical cognitive capabilities, it is therefore difficult to imagine circumstances in which he was unaware that alcohol or drugs posed no risk to the agency of the user. Indeed, it is also common knowledge that the possession and distribution of many substances are punishable offences, and that many instances of offending are causally attributed to intoxication.[36] Thus, experimentation with addictive

[36] For a broader discussion, see: D Husak and P de Marneffe, *The Legalization of Drugs* (Cambridge, Cambridge University Press, 2005) ch 3.

substances during adulthood carries with it a clear risk to personal agency and, in cases of illicit substances, a presupposed association with criminal activity.

We have already set aside the point that today's addict was unlikely to have chosen his addiction. As there is no broad defence of an addiction, an excuse of a different sort is necessary. A capacity theorist who finds blame in addiction might argue that, by adulthood, an agent has the ability to exercise his capacity in accordance with societal norms, providing him both the internal ability to regulate his behaviour and the external knowledge of how he should do so. For character theorists, too, blame may be attributed to adult experimentation. By adulthood, an agent has become responsible for how he conducts himself in relation to his internal traits. Experimentation with addictive substances may, for the character theorist, indicate a propensity for risk-taking which has not been kept in check, or an undesirable prioritisation of the short-term pleasurable effects of a substance over responsible behaviour.

Conclusions such as these may be levelled against the adult, providing criminal law with shelter for its ignorance towards the difference between addicted and recreational intoxication. The logic is blunt but robust: adults are expected not to engage in risky behaviour and may be held responsible for the damage it may cause. It is less convincing, however, when applied to an infant. If an agent did not intend the outcome (as is improbable in the onset of addiction), then we must be satisfied that he had knowledge of some informed risk or should have. Crucial to this is the information available to the agent, his ability to rationalise it with regard to his own agency, and whether he has a developed understanding of social norms, all of which are not automatically presumed until a point of maturity. Acts of pre-maturity have a different responsibility assessment, and as we will presently demonstrate, there is good reason to avoid holding an agent responsible for his addiction if his substance use began prior to an age of legal responsibility or sufficient cognitive development.

Troublingly, empirical evidence on the topic indicates a need to take such an addiction pathway seriously. A 2013 study found more than 1 in 10 children in the US live with a parent who has a form of substance addiction, most of these young people being under five years old.[37] Households such as these are at higher risk of intra-household secrecy (where parents and children openly engage in deceiving one another), as well as violence and abuse.[38] This is subsequently linked to the intergenerational transmission of addiction: those who have grown up in a household where their immediate family engaged in substance abuse, particularly paternal alcoholism, are much more likely to become addicted themselves.[39] For

[37] L Lander, J Howsare and M Byrne, 'The Impact of Substance Use Disorders on Families and Children: From Theory to Practice' (2013) 28 *Social Work in Public Health* 194, 195.

[38] ibid.

[39] JI Zimić and V Jukić, 'Familial Risk Factors Favoring Drug Addiction Onset' (2012) 44 *Journal of Psychoactive Drugs* 173, 184.

children growing up in this environment, the effect of parental addiction has been noted as 'a primary cause of risky behaviour, drug addiction included'.[40]

This aligns not just with conventional wisdom on human behaviour (children learn about the world around them, including how to behave and act, from their primary carer),[41] but also with the underpinning rationale of theories of responsibility. If we think of an adult man raising his voice and threatening violence against a bank clerk, we will rightly consider him worthy of censure. The preteen doing the same to a parent is also worthy of censure, but surely of a very different type. This is in part because of the shifting view of agency as we age: the adult man should know better, the child perhaps not. Our view of the difference between the two is rooted not just in the conduct, but also in the relational dimension. We would not consider it the obligation of the bank clerk to modify and teach the adult man how to behave, as he is already responsible for his actions. But for the parent and the child, the censure should take the form not just of punishment but of teaching; the carer is responsible not just to rebuke but to modify.

Age is relevant to ascriptions of responsibility because, once the developmental process has advanced sufficiently, it is expected that agents understand there are sets of behaviours which are wrong and punishable. Of course this is not a never-ending excuse: the child who is taught that violence is acceptable will at some point be held responsible if he harms others. Attributing such responsibility for addiction is, however, far less straightforward, as the conduct of drinking or drug taking in childhood later gives rise to physiological pressures to continue use which ordinary criminally blameworthy conduct, such as violence or theft, does not.

So, for the adult experimenting, one might expect he will learn, or should have learnt, that drug and alcohol use carries the risk of addiction, and that dangerous intoxication may lead to some harm. But a younger person is not encumbered with the same expectation, particularly if his early-age drug use was normalised in his home by his authority figures. Our assessment of whether there is responsibility in intoxication or addiction must be fundamentally altered. By poisoning the developmental process, addiction with a young age of onset is not a condition for which an agent should clearly be held responsible. From a capacity theory perspective, his capacity has been stymied, and his opportunity to obey the law's requirements (in this context, avoiding addiction) is uncertain. From a character perspective, his character formation has been corrupted.

Inculpating on the basis of addicted intoxication must have a basis in imputing responsibility to the state of addiction. As we have shown, this requires satisfactory evidence that today's addict had the capacity and a fair opportunity to avoid later volitional impairment, or that his addiction is a result of character traits for which he is responsible (or could be expected to keep in check). Neither theory provides a convincing basis upon which to place responsibility in an addiction pathway with a young age of onset.

[40] ibid 184.
[41] Lander, Howsare and Byrne (n 38) 199.

V. Case Study II: Prescription Medication

Typically, addiction follows an experimentation phase with a substance.[42] An agent drinks regularly before realising he has drunk so often he cannot do without it, or that he has used so much of a drug that not using it gives rise to painful physical and psychological withdrawal symptoms. The arrival of these symptoms does not necessarily excuse. Consequently, the historical choice to use a substance with addictive properties, whether judged by capacity or character, is the one for which the addicted agent is held responsible.

'Experimentation', at its definitional core, requires two things. First, that a defendant is acting more or less independently (ie, he is acting via his own free will and without significant external pressure: he made 'a choice'). Second, there is some benefit derived from taking a substance (people take a drug and realise they like it, which typically becomes their reason to take it again – alcoholics would have been unlikely to become alcoholics if they did not, at one point, enjoy the effects of alcohol, etc).[43] These presuppositions are the basis upon which non-addicted intoxication is ordinarily seen as blameworthy: a defendant took the risk to prioritise his desire for a substance when he should have known better. In short, he acted recklessly.[44] Addiction is the consequence of experimentation run rampant. The high of a drug took priority too many times, or consumption occurred in too great a volume. The mind or body subsequently came to need, rather than like, the substance.[45]

Iatrogenic addiction, which is an addiction caused by medical examination or treatment, can be separated from these elements. As there is no experimentation phase, it is unclear how such an addiction pathway can be considered one for which an addict is responsible. It is worth providing an example of exactly what iatrogenic addiction could entail. An agent who approaches his general practitioner complaining of ongoing pain caused by, let us say, some non-blameworthy cause may be prescribed, at first instance or later, opiate-based painkillers. It may be clear to the patient that these medications are addictive substances, and as medical treatment is based upon consent, he is technically free to walk away. Most of us remain aware of the risks inherent in medical treatment, but we ordinarily place our trust in those with specialist training. In short, the doctor knows best. A choice to proceed with treatment is not an independent choice in the way that deciding to try cocaine or heroin is. A decision to follow medical advice is in a sense not really an ordinary choice at all – the weight of recommendations from an individual

[42] Naturally, this is only the case for a small subset of individuals. For many, experimentation will not lead to a dependency. See AE Goldberg, *Blaming the Addicted Brain: Building Bridges between Criminal Law and Neuroscientific Perspectives on Addiction* (The Hague, Eleven International Publishing, 2022) 33–36.

[43] Duncan (n 19) ch 1.

[44] *DPP v Majewski* (n 8) 475.

[45] F Mapua Filbey, *The Neuroscience of Addiction* (Cambridge, Cambridge University Press, 2019) ch 3.

endowed with professional authority and tasked with treating an ailment should not be understated. Furthermore, it is not a decision rooted in pleasure-seeking. There is a benefit to painkilling medication, of course, but it is a therapeutic one. A characterisation of this addiction pathway as reckless is a difficult sell.

The emergence of iatrogenic addiction as a serious public health concern has been covered most extensively in the US, where a crisis in opioid dependence has been fuelled in no small part by the intentional misrepresentation of the addictive qualities of the painkiller OxyContin. Once reserved for palliative and cancer care,[46] the opioid-based painkiller became widely prescribed due to misrepresentation of data by pharmaceutical giant Purdue Pharma, which pointed to the drug having a much lower risk of addiction than it actually did.[47] As a recent Stanford-Lancet study has highlighted, the high rates of opioid dependence were not just a consequence of a big pharma corporate conspiracy: a number of hospitals, pharmacies and individual clinicians derived significant financial benefit from encouraging the widespread prescription of addictive medication.[48]

It is estimated that around half of those who are classified as drug addicts in the US began their journey into dependence from using prescribed medication.[49] As the death toll linked to widespread opioid use in the US has rapidly mounted,[50] there has been a reversal of policy, but this was not before the approach was adopted in other jurisdictions such as the UK. A report published by the British Medical Association in 2015 concluded that doctors in the UK have been overprescribing addictive medication in both inappropriate cases and for much longer than recommended, often as a consequence of an absence of alternative treatments and the management of their own increasing workload.[51] A lack of clear, central guidance on how to handle patients who become iatrogenically addicted has resulted in further mistreatment, with clinicians negligently treating patients addicted to prescription medication as if they were addicted to alcohol or illicit drugs, quickly tapering them from their medication and causing severe withdrawal symptoms.[52]

Effective addiction treatment requires identification of why an addict in the first place became addicted. For drug addiction with a clear experimentation phase, it is ordinarily the case that a user's dysfunctional relationship with his drug is a form of escapism and/or a consequence of prioritising the psychoactive or inhibitory

[46] N Vadivelu and others, 'The Opioid Crisis: A Comprehensive Overview' (2018) 22 *Current Pain and Headache Reports* 16.

[47] Office of Public Affairs, US Department of Justice, 'Opioid Manufacturer Purdue Pharma Pleads Guilty to Fraud and Kickback Conspiracies' (24 November 2020) www.justice.gov/opa/pr/opioid-manufacturer-purdue-pharma-pleads-guilty-fraud-and-kickback-conspiracies accessed 1 June 2024.

[48] K Humphreys and others, 'Responding to the Opioid Crisis in North America and Beyond: Recommendations of the Stanford–Lancet Commission' (2022) 399 *The Lancet* 555, 566.

[49] Arthur Gale, 'Sacklers Sacked But Purdue Still Caused Opioid Epidemic' (2022) 119 *Missouri Medicine* 109, 109.

[50] Vadivelu and others (n 47) 16.

[51] BMA Board of Science, *Prescribed Drugs Associated with Dependence and Withdrawal* (British Medical Association, 2015) 11.

[52] ibid 13.

effects of a substance to the point of physiological dependence. This points to a psychological root cause, and so drug treatment programmes have developed to treat addiction as the offspring of a maladaptive brain and/or behaviour. For iatrogenic addiction, however, there is not necessarily an internal dysfunction that needs to be addressed, meaning he requires a different type of treatment – and access to such services is much more limited than the already scarce provision for addiction which began recreationally.[53]

Indeed, it is an indication of the unusual way prior fault rules currently operate that there is an excuse available to patients who have an iatrogenic adverse reaction to medical treatment, but an excuse is unavailable to the addicted defendant whose addiction onset is rooted entirely in prior medical treatment.[54] This is despite the fact that blame imputed to experimentation is rooted in the sum parts of recklessness, though no such conclusion is reached when we assess a patient who becomes addicted when following medical guidance (unless, for instance, the patient had a previous addiction he did not disclose – though this would be a case of deception and thus a different matter entirely).

We have already outlined the capacity and character case which might be made to attribute responsibility to the adult recreational user, but it is worth recapping with explicit reference to the experimentation period. For those more persuaded by a capacity account of responsibility, it might be said that the choice to exercise agency in taking a substance with known addictive qualities provides no automatic excuse for later volitional impairment: a defendant had the ability to act otherwise, but chose behaviour he knew or should have known to be risky. On a character account, his risk-taking may be the fundamental object of blame, and while he might lose his agency as he becomes alienated from his character, one might still wish to hold him responsible – perhaps in no minimal part because the nature of the experimentation phase is rooted in desire rather than necessity.

It is clear that iatrogenic addiction does not have the same inputs to the responsibility calculator. Whether or not a patient has a realistic appraisal of the addictive qualities of a drug he is prescribed, we have already pointed out that a choice to accept or disregard a medical professional's recommended treatment is not a choice in any ordinary sense, and certainly not a comparable one to substance experimentation. And as we discussed early on in this chapter, it is not a requirement of an excuse to have literally not had the ability to act differently, lest the agent whose drink is spiked be responsible on the basis that he should not have been in the bar or drunk the drink. In this instance, the intervention of another modifies our view of the situation. Of course, we are dealing here with antecedent addiction and not merely antecedent intoxication, but the same logic is applicable.

[53] ibid.

[54] Iatrogenic addiction has shown persuasive in diminishing culpability at sentencing, see: *R v Williams (Frank Joseph)* [2016] EWCA Crim 661. In terms of liability, continued use of a substance to which an agent is addicted would likely negative the prescription medication excuse on the basis of foresight of consequences, though we are unaware of a case which has addressed this explicitly to date.

The agent whose drink is spiked is excused because his intoxication was not an independent act, and responsibility is rooted in independent actions. The nature of the third-party interventions is different, yes, but nevertheless leads us to the same conclusion.[55]

VI. Case Study III: Comorbidity

Our final case study addresses addiction in the context of comorbidity, where an agent experiences the simultaneous presence of two or more disorders or conditions. Addiction frequently presents with other mental disorders.[56] For example, alcohol use disorder often co-occurs with bipolar disorders, schizophrenia, and antisocial personality disorder, as well as with various affective disorders (such as anxiety or depressive disorders).[57]

As this chapter sets out, the context of early experimentation is crucial to understanding the blameworthiness of addiction. We suggest there is a considerable difference between the adult agent who is of sound mind and begins experimenting with drugs in adulthood, and the agent who begins using drugs as a way of coping with an underlying mental disorder (ie, using substances as a form of self-medication). When determining the blameworthiness of addiction in the context of comorbidity, there are two important limbs to consider. First, where addiction is a corollary of another mental illness, the underlying mental illness may indicate that an agent is volitionally impaired at first use. In cases where a comorbid disorder gives us good reason to interrogate an agent's ability to reason effectively, it would be inappropriate to expect him to deploy the same balancing exercise when presented with the options of use and abstinence. It follows that we should be less ready to conclude that the comorbid agent could or should have recognised the risks inherent in psychoactive substance use. Second, the purpose of substance use ought to be considered. As we have demonstrated in the previous section, our assessment of blame must be different between drug use for recreational enjoyment, and drug use with a therapeutic benefit. Where there appears to be some sound medical ground to use a drug (whether licitly or not), the notion that such use is inherently reckless is less secure.

[55] Interestingly, research has empirically tested the notion that iatrogenic addiction (for instance through mismanagement of medication) ought to relieve prior fault applications. Their experiments found that when a defendant's addiction was iatrogenically caused, sentencing decisions were lowered compared to autogenic addictions. See: N Sinclair-House, JJ Child and HS Crombag, 'Addiction is a Brain Disease, and it Doesn't Matter: Prior Choice in Drug Use Blocks Leniency in Criminal Punishment' (2020) 26 *Psychology, Public Policy, and Law* 36.

[56] MA Schuckit 'Comorbidity Between Substance Use Disorders and Psychiatric Conditions (2006) 101 *Addiction* 76.

[57] American Psychiatric Association, *Diagnostic and Statistical Manual of Mental Disorders*, 5th edn. (Arlington, American Psychiatric Association, 2013) 496–497.

The presence of comorbid illness therefore raises questions about the nature of a defendant's agency at first use. If, as we have argued, prior fault logic suggests an addict is reasonably in control of whether or not he becomes addicted, and that his basis for first use must be blameworthy, this case study complicates automatic attributions of fault. Consider an adult without cognitive impairment who is offered a drug at a party and reacts positively. If he continues to take it because he associates its psychoactive qualities with feeling disinhibited and having a good time, it is one thing. One may consider him responsible for his addiction if, to begin with, he acted independently and only with the purpose of enjoyment. It is another thing for the agent with a serious comorbid disorder to experiment with drug use, first on the basis that we may not necessarily expect him to be as conscientious with regards to the risk of addiction as compared to his non-comorbid counterpart, but also because his drug use may be rooted not in enjoyment but in a feeling of desperation or necessity. Indeed, where first use proves substantial alleviation of another condition, it is very difficult to see how further drug use can be typified as reckless or blameworthy in the same way that drug use by an agent without cognitive impairment might be. Moreover, there are various conditions frequently comorbid with substance use disorders that present with impairments in executive functioning, such as impulse control.[58] As such, the defendant cannot be considered to be making equally informed choices or exercising self-control similarly to his non-comorbid peers in the use of substances.

Both theories of responsibility under examination in this work support our view that criminal responsibility derived from addiction is far from a foregone conclusion. Evidence suggests that a person with severe comorbidity has a heightened chance of becoming addicted compared to healthy peers.[59] This indicates that the comorbid agent is unable to choose freely in the same way a mentally healthy agent is. Consequently, the comorbid agent's impairment results in a different perspective towards his responsibility for any subsequent addiction, leading us to conclude that a capacity responsibility perspective of blame could, in certain cases, provide an agent with an excuse for his addiction.

Character responsibility also fails to provide a convincing account of how comorbid addiction and addiction rooted in recreational use are evidence of equal risk-taking. To satisfy attributions of blame under character theory, responsibility must be reflective of the character of a defendant. If a defendant has suffered from comorbidity from a young age, it is not clear he will ever reach the threshold of being

[58] For depression, see, eg, EW Leppink, K Lust and JE Grant, 'Depression in University Students: Associations with Impulse Control Disorders (2016) 20 *International Journal of Psychiatry in Clinical Practice* 3 146. For schizophrenia, see, eg, HC Tsuang and others, 'Impaired Impulse Control is Associated with a 5-HT2A Receptor Polymorphism in Schizophrenia (2013) 208 *Psychiatry Research* 2 105. For bipolar disorder, see, eg, P Najt and others, 'Impulsivity and Bipolar Disorder (2007) 17 *European Neuropsychopharmacology* 5 313.

[59] See, eg, G Baranyi and others, 'The Prevalence of Comorbid Serious Mental Illnesses and Substance Use Disorders in Prison Populations: A Systematic Review and Meta-Analysis' (2022) 7 *The Lancet Public Health* 6 e557.

eligible to be responsible at all, particularly if his comorbid disorder is one which has caused constant or near-constant mental impairment. In cases where comorbidity arises later in life, it may cause an agent to act in ways he never would have without it. Here, addiction is merely part of the tapestry of psychiatric illness and may explain harms caused but does not necessarily provide a basis of blame for them.

To be legitimate against theories of responsibility, liability contingent on addicted intoxication requires us to be satisfied that an agent could and should have acted differently. We argue that inculpation should be intimately linked with an assessment that the relevant facts on the risk of substance abuse were available, and that there was no good reason to disregard them. As empirical evidence makes plain that major mental illness is linked to initiating and continuing drug use,[60] it is unclear whether there is informed choice or recklessness on this pathway. It, therefore, cannot be presupposed that the comorbid addict is responsible for his addiction.

It is plausible that a comorbid agent has never had sufficient faculties of self-control to properly rationalise the underlying risk drug-taking carries. On these facts, there is a straightforward absence of blame on either capacity or character accounts of responsibility, as a defendant would never reach a level of development sufficient to hold him responsible for his behaviour. Where comorbidity develops later in life, after the point at which an agent has become accustomed to societal norms, desperation which arises from his other symptoms may give rise to an assessment that he was becoming immune to societal norms, and thus without the capacity or a fair opportunity to obey the law. It may also indicate extended alienation from his true character, rather than being reflective of censurable behaviour, especially where an agent's pain is so great that it distorts his view of society, and his place within it.

Comorbidity, much like addiction, is a complicated and varied spectrum. Some may make the challenge that mild to moderate comorbidity will not sufficiently detach an agent from his ability to make informed choices, and thus he should know not to take risks. It is worth addressing this challenge, as it provides a route to ascribing responsibility in spite of comorbidity. Even mild to moderate comorbidity which is resistant to treatment may eventually give rise to desperation, and thus the agent who is eligible for ascriptions of responsibility may no longer be if his capacity to make rational choices becomes so impaired by increasing feelings of hopelessness (indeed, it may provide evidence of character alienation in and of itself). Even in instances where incapacity is insufficient to vitiate responsibility under a strict capacity assessment, it may remain a challenge to the fair opportunity limb of capacity responsibility. That is to say, there may, strictly speaking, have been an active choice involved in the first use of drugs for the comorbid defendant, but the circumstances of his comorbidity may render that choice one for which we do not blame him.

[60] JC Titus, SH Godley and MK White, 'A Post-treatment Examination of Adolescents' Reasons for Starting, Quitting, and Continuing the use of Drugs and Alcohol' (2007) 16 *Journal of Child & Adolescent Substance Abuse* 31.

VII. Conclusion

This chapter had a number of objectives. To begin with, we made an effort to place addicted intoxication within the context of prior fault intoxication rules. The addict may fairly raise volitional impairment in relation to his substance use, and it is clear that some cases of addiction will make it impossible to delineate between any given instance of intoxication and the addiction itself. Yet as he is afforded no excuse, we conclude that prior fault rules must be specifically targeting the onset of addiction as a primary source of blame. To substantiate this finding, we attempted to construct the theoretical basis necessary to see addiction as blameworthy, underlying it with reference to competing theories of criminal responsibility.

We then tasked ourselves with arguing whether the outline of the potentially blameworthy addict is representative of a series of addiction pathways. By exploring analyses on the nature of excuses from the general part of criminal law, we applied the logic of the potentially blameworthy addicted defendant to three addiction pathways. Our case studies had two aims. First, we sought to make a convincing argument that these addiction pathways demand recognition on the basis of empirical evidence (ie, they are not fringe cases of addiction). Second, the application of theories of excuse to these case studies indicates that there is good reason to question whether volitional impairment can be attributed to acts for which we hold an agent responsible.

During the course of our analysis, we made a conscious choice to avoid contributing to the debate on whether an addicted defendant is responsible for his continued intoxication. Our focus has been confined to making the case that prior fault rules are already saying something about responsibility in the onset of addiction, and proceeding to interrogate these circumstances in a series of case studies. In focusing on intoxication rules and avoiding the debate on the choice to continue intoxication, we have left unaddressed a number of interesting and worthy questions.

First, as criminal law finds blame in addicted intoxication, we were required to construct a vision of blameworthy addiction. This allowed us to go for the 'low-hanging fruit', as it were, of clear cases where responsibility is absent. Of course, the very existence of a blameworthy addict has been and will continue to be disputed, but it has not been our purpose here to make that wider case. Second, we consider it possible that where we are satisfied that an addicted defendant had no responsibility for his addiction, and is later caught up in the criminal law but outside the ambit of prior fault rules, he may be entitled to a more widely applicable excuse for his conduct. This would, of course, challenge the notion of when (or whether) a drunken intent should be regarded in the same way as a sober intent. Third, we have shown that the case studies we presented do not neatly align with the scholarship in capacity or character accounts of criminal responsibility. While we have argued that these addiction pathways present convincing evidence for an excuse, there is not one presently available. The question which emerges from these findings is whether prior fault doctrines are in fact interested in the link between personal responsibility and blame at all.

7

Prior Fault and Alcohol Intoxication: A Cognitive Neuroscientific Perspective

PALOMA MANGUELE AND KYRIAKI NIKOLAOU

I. Introduction

Voluntary intoxication occupies a unique and often contentious space in criminal law. Under most legal systems – including in England & Wales and the Netherlands – when an individual voluntarily consumes a drug or an alcoholic drink at time point T1, they can be seen as bearing prior fault for subsequent unlawful acts at time point T2, even if they lacked the necessary *mens rea* or blameworthiness to be held responsible.[1] Thus, voluntary intoxication at T1 is seen as the origin of blame, replacing a lack of blame at T2 if they have offended whilst intoxicated.[2] However, the law's traditional approach towards the meaning of *voluntariness* in intoxication does not align well with the more nuanced portrait provided by research on the processes which lead to the initiation of drinking behaviour and alcohol's effects on the brain and behaviour. In this chapter, we use alcohol intoxication as a model to discuss the cognitive and (neuro)behavioural processes that might be relevant to prior fault discussions.

Alcohol is the most widely used psychoactive substance worldwide.[3] It is also legal and socially accepted in many cultures, making it uniquely important when discussing intoxication and responsibility.[4] Acute alcohol intoxication is frequently implicated in harmful behaviours and legal offences – indeed, nearly 40 per cent of violent crimes involve alcohol use.[5] Compared to other drugs, alcohol's pervasive

[1] AE Goldberg and others, 'Prior-Fault Blame in England and Wales, Germany and the Netherlands' (2021) 8 *Journal of International and Comparative Law* 53. T1 here refers to the action of taking the first drink, rather than to any decision-making process that leads to this, as we will explore later in this chapter.

[2] For in-depth discussions of blameworthiness, see chs 2 and 6 of this collection.

[3] World Health Organization, *Global status report on alcohol and health 2018* (Geneva, World Health Organization, 2019).

[4] R Room, T Babor and J Rehm, 'Alcohol and Public Health' (2005) 365 *Lancet* 519; TF Babor and others, *Alcohol: No Ordinary Commodity* (Oxford, Oxford University Press, 2010).

[5] LA Greenfeld, *Alcohol and crime: An analysis of national data on the prevalence of alcohol involvement in crime* (Washington, Bureau of Justice Statistics, 1998).

role in society and its well-studied effects on cognition and behaviour make it a model case for examining the concept of 'prior fault' in intoxication.[6] Because most individuals drink voluntarily, focusing on alcohol (especially in acute episodes) enables us to leverage an extensive scientific literature on how intoxication affects the brain and behaviour and to apply these insights to questions of voluntariness in discussions of legal responsibility.[7] Not only is alcohol use widespread, but it is also strongly linked to aggression, violence, and risky behaviour.[8] For example, alcohol is estimated to be involved in about 4 in 10 fatal motor vehicle accidents[9] and in a significant share of sexual assaults and domestic violence incidents.[10] Given this elevated risk profile, it is no surprise that legal systems pay special attention to alcohol intoxication. Unlike many illicit drugs, drinking alcohol is lawful and even socially encouraged in some settings, which complicates the legal evaluation of misconduct committed under intoxication.[11] We use alcohol as a focused case study throughout this chapter because it can serve to practically exemplify key issues relevant to prior fault – eg, widespread availability, legally sanctioned use, and strong empirical evidence linking it to cognitive impairment and harmful behaviours. However, many of the points we discuss (eg, the interplay between voluntary consumption and neurobiological and situational contexts) might also extend to other psychoactive substances and forms of acute and even chronic intoxication.

Although alcohol consumption is often and generally regarded as a conscious, voluntary action, considerable evidence indicates that both internal (eg, affective states, cognitive biases) and external (eg, social context, environmental cues) factors substantially shape an individual's motivation to initiate or continue drinking.[12]

[6] GF Koob and ND Volkow, 'Neurobiology of Addiction: A Neurocircuitry Analysis' (2016) 3 *The Lancet Psychiatry* 760.

[7] P Haggard, S Clark and J Kalogeras, 'Voluntary Action and Conscious Awareness' (2002) 5 *Nature Neuroscience* 382; CP Taggart, 'Retributivism, Agency, and the Voluntary Act Requirement' (2016) 36 *Pace Law Review* 645; JJ Child, 'Defense of a Basic Voluntary Act Requirement in Criminal Law from Philosophies of Action' (2020) 23 *New Criminal Law Review* 437.

[8] BJ Bushman and HM Cooper, 'Effects of Alcohol on Human Aggression: An Integrative Research Review' (1990) 107 *Psychological Bulletin* 341; ST Chermack and PR Giancola, 'The Relation between Alcohol and Aggression: An Integrated Biopsychosocial Conceptualization' (1997) 17 *Clinical Psychology Review* 621.

[9] HA Deery and AW Love, 'The Effect of a Moderate Dose of Alcohol on the Traffic Hazard Perception Profile of Young Drink-drivers' (1996) 91 *Addiction* 815; H Du and others, 'Effects of Alcohol and Fatigue on Driving Performance in Different Roadway Geometries' (2016) 2584 *Transportation Research Record: Journal of the Transportation Research Board* 88; NHTSA's National Center for Statistics and Analysis, *Traffic Safety Facts: Alcohol-impaired Driving* (Washington, US Department of Transportation, 2009).

[10] HM Foran and KD O'Leary, 'Alcohol and Intimate Partner Violence: A Meta-Analytic Review' (2008) 28 *Clinical Psychology Review* 1222; IM Wilson, K Graham and A Taft, 'Alcohol Interventions, Alcohol Policy and Intimate Partner Violence: A Systematic Review' (2014) 14 *BMC Public Health* 881; A Abbey, 'Alcohol's Role in Sexual Violence Perpetration: Theoretical Explanations, Existing Evidence and Future Directions' (2011) 30 *Drug and Alcohol Review* 481.

[11] Room, Babor and Rehm (n 4).

[12] IP Albery and D Frings, 'Contemplating the Micro and Macro of Alcohol Use and Misuse to Enable Meta-Understandings' in IP Albery and D Frings (eds), *The Handbook of Alcohol Use* (London, Elsevier, 2021); AL Howard and others, 'Planned and Unplanned Drinking to Get Drunk: A Registered Report

These influences can vary widely across situations and individuals, such that the action of consuming alcohol or taking subsequent drinks may not stem purely from a deliberate, fully informed choice in every instance.[13] Once drinking has begun, the impairing effects of alcohol on cognitive and behavioural processes do not necessarily scale in a simple, solely dose-dependent manner. Instead, they emerge in a complex interplay with factors such as personal tolerance levels, psychological stress, and the presence or absence of social facilitators or disinhibitors.[14] Many regular drinkers do not anticipate how quickly self-regulatory capacities – such as inhibitory control and risk assessment – can deteriorate, nor do they necessarily account for the ways that everyday factors (eg, fatigue, recent food intake, or fluctuating stress levels) contribute to variable outcomes in each drinking episode.[15]

These complexities are further amplified for individuals with an Alcohol Use Disorder (AUD), whose sense of volition may be compromised by neurobiological adaptations that potentiate craving and weaken executive control.[16] In these cases, the 'voluntariness' of alcohol consumption can be meaningfully constrained by changes in motivational circuits and stress-related pathways, making the decision to drink far less straightforward.[17] Consequently, even if one accepts that becoming intoxicated generally involves a chosen course of action and that some degree of cognitive or behavioural impairment is foreseeable, the empirical literature on the

Examining Willingness, Drinking Motives, and Protective Behavioral Strategies Using Ecological Momentary Assessment.' (2024) 38 *Psychology of Addictive Behaviors* 519; T Dominik and others, 'Libet's Legacy: A Primer to the Neuroscience of Volition' (2024) 157 *Neuroscience & Biobehavioral Reviews* 105503; Koob and Volkow (n 6); R Sinha, 'Chronic Stress, Drug Use, and Vulnerability to Addiction' (2008) 1141 *Annals of the New York Academy of Sciences* 105.

[13] M Field and others, 'Delay Discounting and the Alcohol Stroop in Heavy Drinking Adolescents' (2007) 102 *Addiction* 579; M Field and others, 'Acute Alcohol Effects on Inhibitory Control and Implicit Cognition: Implications for Loss of Control Over Drinking' (2010) 34 *Alcoholism: Clinical and Experimental Research* 1346; CE Wiers and others, 'Comparing Three Cognitive Biases for Alcohol Cues in Alcohol Dependence' (2016) 52 *Alcohol and Alcoholism* 242; CE Wiers and others, 'Effects of Cognitive Bias Modification Training on Neural Alcohol Cue Reactivity in Alcohol Dependence' (2015) 172 *American Journal of Psychiatry* 335.

[14] JJ Curtin and BA Fairchild, 'Alcohol and Cognitive Control: Implications for Regulation of Behavior during Response Conflict' (2003) 112 *Journal of Abnormal Psychology* 424; J Weafer and MT Fillmore, 'Alcohol-Related Stimuli Reduce Inhibitory Control of Behavior in Drinkers' (2012) 222 *Psychopharmacology* 489; LA Ray, J Mackillop and PM Monti, 'Subjective Responses to Alcohol Consumption as Endophenotypes: Advancing Behavioral Genetics in Etiological and Treatment Models of Alcoholism' (2010) 45 *Substance Use & Misuse* 1742.

[15] VA Ramchandani, PY Kwo and T Li, 'Effect of Food and Food Composition on Alcohol Elimination Rates in Healthy Men and Women' (2001) 41 *The Journal of Clinical Pharmacology* 1345; MR Yeomans, S Caton and MM Hetherington, 'Alcohol and Food Intake' (2003) 6 *Current Opinion in Clinical Nutrition and Metabolic Care* 639; Sinha (n 12); M Amlung and J MacKillop, 'Understanding the Effects of Stress and Alcohol Cues on Motivation for Alcohol via Behavioral Economics' (2014) 38 *Alcoholism: Clinical and Experimental Research* 1780; HC Becker, MF Lopez and TL Doremus-Fitzwater, 'Effects of Stress on Alcohol Drinking: A Review of Animal Studies' (2011) 218 *Psychopharmacology* 131; J Dora and others, 'How People Decide to Consume (More) Alcohol When Feeling Stressed' (forthcoming); Du and others (n 9).

[16] Koob and Volkow (n 6); J Dora and others, 'The Daily Association between Affect and Alcohol Use: A Meta-Analysis of Individual Participant Data' (2023) 149 *Psychological Bulletin* 1.

[17] D Seo and R Sinha, 'The Neurobiology of Alcohol Craving and Relapse' (2014) 125 *Handbook of Clinical Neurology* 355.

aetiology of problematic drinking – together with its neurobiological underpinnings – highlights the multifaceted nature of alcohol's effects. In particular, studies underscore how individual predispositions and contextual variables intersect with different doses of alcohol to produce heterogeneous behavioural outcomes.[18]

Meanwhile, it seems that legal systems often maintain relatively narrow frameworks for interpreting human behaviour in intoxication-related contexts, focusing on the assumption of personal responsibility without fully accounting for the neurobiological and situational complexities documented in scientific research.[19] In the case of prior fault, specifically, the law considers the moment of responsibility to be the act of consuming the drink rather than accounting for the decision-making process, for example. Such discrepancies between 'narrow' legal conceptions and 'broader' neuro-behavioural perspectives highlight the need for more nuanced approaches that integrate empirical findings into legal discussions.

In this chapter, we propose that the processes involved in alcohol intoxication do not unfold instantaneously nor in an entirely deliberate way. As we explained above, initial motivations and intentions to drink are shaped by the varied influences of cognitive, emotional, and social factors for different individuals. This suggests the importance of initiating the analysis before the act of drinking, followed by the moment of first consumption. Subsequently, alcohol's pharmacological effects on perception, cognition and the ability to control behaviour during intoxication vary based on several factors, including the amount consumed (dose; level of intoxication) and individual differences that relate to personality factors as well as on prior experiences using alcohol.[20] By situating alcohol use behaviour along a continuum, the chapter explores how shifting cognitive, emotional, and contextual factors influence individual choices. Together, this continuum relates to the doctrine of prior fault, particularly in debates over whether responsibility should attach when one takes the initial drink (T1), and it furthers discussion

[18] MT Fillmore and M Vogel-Sprott, 'Behavioral Impairment Under Alcohol: Cognitive and Pharmacokinetic Factors' (1998) 22 *Alcoholism: Clinical and Experimental Research* 1476; CA Marczinski and others, 'Alcohol-Induced Impairment of Behavioral Control: Differential Effects on Engaging vs. Disengaging Responses' (2005) 182 *Psychopharmacology* 452; RCME Engels and others, 'Drinking Motives, Alcohol Expectancies, Self-Efficacy, and Drinking Patterns' (2005) 35 *Journal of Drug Education* 147.

[19] AE Goldberg, 'Foreseeability and Prior Fault: Examining the Assessment Framework for Intoxication, Blame and Criminal Responsibility' (2024) 29 *Bialystok Legal Studies* 69; JJ Child, HS Crombag and R Fortson, 'Understanding the "Fault" in Prior-Fault Intoxication' in A Reed and M Bohlander (eds), *Fault in Criminal Law* (Milton Park, Routledge, 2022) 86; See N Sinclair-House, JJ Child and H Crombag, 'Addiction Is a Brain Disease, and It Doesn't Matter: Prior Choice in Drug Use Blocks Leniency in Criminal Punishment' (2019) 26 *Psychology, Public Policy, and Law* 36; OD Jones and FX Shen, 'Law and Neuroscience in the United States' in TM Spranger (ed), *International Neurolaw: A Comparative Perspective* (Heidelberg, Sprinter, 2012); S Morse, 'Avoiding Irrational NeuroLaw Exuberance: A Plea for Neuromodesty' (2011) 3 *Law, Innovation and Technology* 209.

[20] Deery and Love (n 9); M Kano and others, 'Low Doses of Alcohol Have a Selective Effect on the Recognition of Happy Facial Expressions' (2003) 18 *Human Psychopharmacology: Clinical and Experimental* 131; SK Kamboj and others, 'Processing of Facial Affect in Social Drinkers: A Dose–Response Study of Alcohol Using Dynamic Emotion Expressions' (2013) 227 *Psychopharmacology* 31; BN Sanov, L Kumar and KG Creswell, 'A Systematic Review of the Acute Effects of Alcohol on Emotion Recognition of Facial Expressions' (2023) 28 *Addiction Biology* e13345.

over whether the choice to become intoxicated constitutes a singular, discrete act. We argue that since the impairments surrounding alcohol consumption (and the decision to drink) can emerge sporadically and unevenly, grounding fault purely at the moment a person is said to have voluntarily initiated a drinking occasion may require that more nuanced appraisal.

We draw on empirical and theoretical perspectives from cognitive psychology and neuroscience to examine how scientific insights can clarify, challenge, or reinforce legal standards for attributing culpability to individuals whose intoxicated states lead to criminal harm. Because we are concerned with prior fault, we examine expressly *voluntary* intoxication. We aim not to advocate for a wholesale reconfiguration of legal doctrines or an overreliance on neuroscientific explanations that would overshadow practicality, normative considerations and established legal principles. Instead, we aim to cultivate conversation, emphasising how scientific data can deepen our understanding of human decision-making and the complexities of self-induced impairment.

We believe that law and neuroscience can find fruitful common ground despite differences in the meaning of terms. Thus, 'voluntariness' in the law may not necessarily imply any behavioural and/or empirical feature but is often interpreted as a normative assessment: after all, the dichotomous approach of the law towards voluntariness, ie, voluntary versus involuntary, does not reflect empirical realities.[21] Hence, even though science may provide insights into voluntariness and foreseeability, this does not necessarily mean that the law needs to be adjusted, as they may prefer their own normative, non-empirical definition. Still, these insights provide input for further discussion in the law, whereby by integrating empirical data, courts and policymakers can refine responsibility guidelines to better reflect actual real-life limitations.[22] Nevertheless, we also agree that caution is warranted. Overreliance on neuroscientific explanations could risk a brain-overclaim problem, where any mention of neural or psychological impairment is misconstrued as negating responsibility.[23] In reality, no single brain scan, cognitive test or paradigm can definitively prove that an offender 'could not help themselves'. Instead, the scientific data highlight general patterns – for example, that individuals with a history of heavy drinking are more prone to aggressive outbursts due to reduced prefrontal cortical functioning, for example[24] – while the law must still assess each defendant's personal culpability based on the circumstances.

Finally, it is important to note that the research studies presented here did not aim to answer questions surrounding the legal discussions on prior fault specifically; therefore, there are gaps in the scientific research when specifically trying to answer prior fault questions (namely, questions on the decision-making process and voluntariness of drinking), which shows even more the necessity of

[21] See ch 4 of this collection for further discussion.

[22] See also ch 3 of this collection, for thoughts about re-examining sentencing and diversion guidelines as well.

[23] Morse (n 19).

[24] Koob and Volkow (n 6).

interdisciplinary dialogue and collaboration, eg, between addiction or alcohol researchers and lawyers.

For the remainder of the chapter, we concentrate primarily on acute alcohol intoxication – the transient state of impairment during and immediately after a drinking episode – rather than long-term addiction per se. While AUD will at times be discussed as an important contextual factor, the chapter is not limited to AUD. Social drinkers and binge drinkers are included in our analysis since episodes of heavy drinking by non-dependent individuals can also lead to harmful outcomes and raise questions of responsibility. In fact, we begin in section II by briefly establishing the differences between these drinker profiles (particularly the hazardous drinkers: binge drinkers and individuals with AUD). From section III onwards, we start by reviewing the neurobiology of the cognitive processes that will be discussed (at the beginning of sections III and IV) before shifting to more cognitive and behavioural discussions. We adopt a chronological framework for elucidating the multifaceted ways in which alcohol consumption perturbs voluntary action and decision-making processes across the continuum of drinking behaviour. In the pre-drinking phase (section III), we explore factors that influence drinking behaviour *before* the first drink is consumed. Section IV examines the moment of initiating drinking, discussing how even a small 'priming' dose of alcohol can amplify the urge to continue drinking, and discusses early cognitive impairments that can be observed with low to moderate doses of alcohol. In section V we discuss some relevant cognitive and behavioural sequelae that occur during continued intoxication. With this chronological approach, we aim to elucidate that impairments are not linear, that they may occur much earlier in the timeline, and that the 'fault' (if any) may begin before intoxication, with decision-making and risk factors leading up to drinking, and after drinking initiation, pharmacological effects lead to impairments much faster than what is usually acknowledged.

However, we also acknowledge further nuance to this approach, as several cognitive factors, for example, metacognition, are repeatedly present at different time points along the continuum, albeit with qualitative changes.[25] In the concluding section, we present some future, still unanswered, questions that researchers could explore to inform debates on prior fault from a legal perspective.

II. Effects of AUD and Binge Drinking – Not All Drinkers are the Same

Prior to our chronological-based explorations that are the focus of this chapter, in this section, we briefly describe the different profiles of alcohol consumption that we encounter in binge drinkers and individuals with AUDs. We describe them

[25] For example, we discuss metacognitive alterations both in the pre-drinking phase and during intoxication.

because, although we are making a general argument, there will be points at which these profiles will have different effects on behaviour and cognition in comparison to a moderate social drinker.

While the acute effects of alcohol concern impairments during the drinking episode, chronic heavy drinking, as seen in individuals with an AUD, produces more extensive and enduring changes in the brain.[26] These long-term alterations can damage executive control functions, emotional regulation, and foresight well beyond any single episode of intoxication.[27] The risk here is that the legal doctrine treats repeated alcohol misuse as an ongoing series of voluntary acts. At the same time, neurological evidence suggests that chronic heavy use reshapes brain circuits in ways that complicate assumptions about free choice and the capacity to learn from previous alcohol-related harms.[28] This means that chronic use imposes a lasting footprint on neural circuitry rather than merely transient dysfunctions during acute intoxication.

Binge drinking is defined as a pattern of drinking characterised by shifts between periods of alcohol abstinence and binge episodes, which bring blood alcohol concentrations (BAC)[29] to 80mg/dl/0.08 per cent or higher. For a typical adult, this corresponds to consuming five or more drinks (male), or four or more drinks (female), in about two hours.[30] While binge episodes can produce immediate disruptions – slowed reaction times, impaired prefrontal cortex activity (PFC; critical for executive functioning of the brain),[31] and altered mood – these intense bouts of intoxication, followed by periods of no drinking, may still culminate in longer-term neural changes.[32] Although not as pronounced as the continuous damage observed in AUD, repeated cycles of high-dose exposure in binge drinkers have also been linked with compromised integrity in regions critical for executive functioning – including abilities to adapt to new rules, switch between tasks, and engage in verbal planning, etc.[33] And, as we will explore going forward, there

[26] Koob and Volkow (n 6).

[27] K Stavro, J Pelletier and S Potvin. 'Widespread and Sustained Cognitive Deficits in Alcoholism: A Meta-Analysis' (2013) 18 *Addiction Biology* 203.

[28] See ch 5 for a discussion on addiction and the meaning of voluntariness.

[29] This chapter primarily employs BAC as the reference point when discussing levels of acute intoxication because, although not the only metric available for quantifying, it is arguably the most widely used by researchers, practitioners, enforcement officials, and others; see: ER Aston and A Liguori. 'Self-estimation of Blood Alcohol Concentration: A Review' (2013) 38 *Addictive Behaviours* 1944. It is measured in grams of alcohol per decilitre of blood (g/dL). For example, in England & Wales, the legal limit for drink driving is 0.08 g/dL (80 mg of alcohol per 100 ml of blood) or 0.08% BAC, see: Road Traffic Act 1988, s 5 (England and Wales); Other jurisdictions, including Scotland, adopt lower legal thresholds, reflecting policy decisions aimed at reducing alcohol-related road accidents.

[30] National Institute on Alcohol Abuse and Alcoholism (NIAAA), 'Drinking Levels Defined' (2019) www.niaaa.nih.gov/alcohols-effects-health/alcohol-topics accessed Feb 2025.

[31] The prefrontal cortex (PFC) is central to executive functions, a set of cognitive processes that govern goal-directed behaviour, self-regulation, and adaptive decision-making.

[32] DN Stephens and T Duka, 'Cognitive and Emotional Consequences of Binge Drinking: Role of Amygdala and Prefrontal Cortex' (2008) 363 *Philosophical Transactions of the Royal Society B: Biological Sciences* 3169.

[33] M Fritz, AM Klawonn and NM Zahr, 'Neuroimaging in Alcohol Use Disorder: From Mouse to Man' (2022) 100 *Journal of Neuroscience Research* 1140; M Bühler and K Mann. 'Alcohol and the

are instances in which these different profiles will differently impact individuals across the chronological timeline from pre-drinking to full intoxication. We start the timeline with the pre-drinking stage below.

III. Factors Influencing the Action of Drinking: When Does 'Fault' Begin?

In this section, we will examine some of the processes that may influence drinking behaviour, including factors that affect the initiation of consumption at T1. Prior fault analyses of intoxicated misconduct often focus on the moment of intoxication.[34] However, by adopting a chronological approach, we aim to demonstrate that the chain of causation – and potentially the chain of responsibility – begins before the first drink is consumed. Even before any alcohol enters the bloodstream, cognitive processes are actively shaping the potential for subsequent drinking behaviour. They can bias decision-making and voluntary action, as anticipatory mechanisms and the activation of alcohol-related cognitions often characterise the pre-drinking phase.[35] In other words, an individual's mental state, expectations, motivations, and personal traits in the pre-drinking phase can critically influence whether they will drink and under what circumstances. By exploring these factors, we may gain a better understanding of when 'fault' might begin.

A. Neurobiological Dynamics in Pre-Drinking

As we will see in the forthcoming discussions, prior to drinking, anticipatory mechanisms (reward prediction, cue-reactivity, and intention formation) converge and set the stage, often tipping the balance in favour of initiating alcohol use unless strong counter-motivations and controls are in place. From a neurobiological perspective, chemical messengers in the brain play essential roles even before alcohol is consumed. Neurochemical signals substantially contribute to this stage, primarily through the actions of dopamine, opioids, GABA, and glutamate.[36]

Human Brain: A Systematic Review of Different Neuroimaging Methods' (2011) 35 *Alcoholism: Clinical and Experimental Research* 1771; M Oscar-Berman and K Marinkovic, 'Alcohol: Effects on Neurobehavioural Functions and the Brain' (2007) 17 *Neuropsychology Review* 239.

[34] Child, Crombag and Fortson (n 19).

[35] RR Reich and MS Goldman, 'Decision Making about Alcohol Use: The Case for Scientific Convergence' (2015) 44 *Addictive Behaviors* 23.

[36] P Christiansen and others, 'A Comparison of the Anticipated and Pharmacological Effects of Alcohol on Cognitive Bias, Executive Function, Craving and Ad-Lib Drinking' (2013) 27 *Journal of Psychopharmacology* 84; Koob and Volkow (n 6); C Fernando Valenzuela and S Zucca, 'Focus On: Neurotransmitter Systems' (2011) 34 *Alcohol Research & Health* 106.

Here we simplify the workings of these messengers, for the sake of upcoming pre-drinking phase discussions.[37]

Dopamine, the neurotransmitter linked to reward anticipation or 'wanting', surges when individuals anticipate rewarding stimuli such as alcohol. This effect generates the motivational state of 'I want a drink', eliciting feelings of desire or craving.[38] Dopamine acts prominently in deep areas of the brain linked to reward and motivation.[39] Concurrently, the opioid system governs the hedonic pleasurable sensations – the 'liking' of alcohol – based on previous experiences of pleasure or relief.[40] The opioid system works heavily in areas crucial for emotion and pleasure.[41]

Subtler influences stem from GABA and glutamate, neurotransmitters regulating baseline mood, stress, and cognitive control. GABA typically dampens neural excitability, promoting relaxation, whereas glutamate enhances alertness and cognitive function.[42] Alterations in these systems – whether transient or chronic – can heighten desires for alcohol by exacerbating negative moods, stress responses, or discomfort during sobriety.[43] Even in non-dependent drinkers, temporary increases in anxiety or stress hormones can rapidly translate intentions to abstain into the active pursuit of alcohol consumption. In habitual drinkers, imbalances in these systems create states of discomfort during sobriety, enhancing alcohol's appeal as a relief mechanism.[44] Even transient shifts in stress-related hormones can provoke a cognitive shift towards consumption, thus transitioning an intention to abstain into active drinking.[45] GABA and glutamate are prominently active in the prefrontal cortex (a region essential for cognitive control and decision-making).

Thus, pre-drinking neurochemical dynamics integrate with cognitive and behavioural factors to create the anticipatory state that influences subsequent drinking decisions. For the remainder of this section, we will examine the cognitive and situational factors that may influence the decision to drink.

[37] These chemical messengers play essential roles before alcohol is consumed, but as we will see in s IV, they are critically involved in the pharmacological impairments of acute intoxication, where we will present them relatively more expanded.

[38] TE Robinson and KC Berridge, 'The Incentive Sensitization Theory of Addiction: Some Current Issues' (2008) 363 *Philosophical Transactions of the Royal Society B: Biological Sciences* 3137; Christiansen and others (n 36); Seo and Sinha (n 17).

[39] Namely, the basal ganglia and ventral striatum.

[40] JM Wenzel and JF Cheer, 'Endocannabinoid Regulation of Reward and Reinforcement through Interaction with Dopamine and Endogenous Opioid Signaling' (2018) 43 *Neuropsychopharmacology* 103.

[41] Namely, the limbic system.

[42] G Riedel, 'Glutamate Receptor Function in Learning and Memory' (2003) 140 *Behavioural Brain Research* 1; Koob and Volkow (n 6).

[43] Koob and Volkow (n 6).

[44] GF Koob and ND Volkow, 'Neurocircuitry of Addiction' (2010) 35 *Neuropsychopharmacology* 217.

[45] Dora and others (n 15).

B. Intentions and Planning: (Un)Conscious Foreground of Drinking Decisions

In psychology, the Theory of Planned Behaviour (TPB) argues that conscious intentions are among the strongest predictors of behaviour.[46] In alcohol research, studies confirm that students or adults who state a clear aim to drink heavily often do so and experience negative outcomes such as blackouts.[47] However, forming an intention does not ensure consistent follow-through – a well-documented phenomenon known as the 'intention–behaviour gap' observed in health behaviours, including alcohol use.[48] People may plan to limit themselves to 'just one drink', only to exceed that limit due to social prompts, emotional stress, or the pharmacological effects of alcohol on self-control.[49] This can be seen in both planned and unplanned drinking. If the drinking is unplanned, by definition, one's prior intention was not to drink (or to drink less), so any consumption represents a failure to act on the initial goal – a lapse in goal-directed control.[50]

Despite TPB's popularity, critics argue that it can overemphasise conscious deliberation while underestimating contextual and habitual factors.[51] In the realm of alcohol use, especially in social settings, individuals often act spontaneously not through rational calculation at every turn. Additionally, TPB does not seem to comprehensively address how urges, cravings, or emotional states can rapidly shift one's intentions.[52] For instance, a person might start the day resolved to abstain, but encountering friends at a pub can trigger sudden desires, which can overshadow earlier goals. Interestingly, research also suggests that planned drinking (eg, intending a night out 'to let loose') can sometimes lead to higher total consumption than when drinking is unplanned. In such cases, people may

[46] I Ajzen, 'The Theory of Planned Behavior: Frequently Asked Questions' (2020) 2 *Human Behavior and Emerging Technologies* 314.

[47] SE Collins and KB Carey, 'The Theory of Planned Behavior as a Model of Heavy Episodic Drinking among College Students' (2007) *21 Psychology of Addictive Behaviors* 498.

[48] P Sheeran, 'Intention – Behavior Relations: A Conceptual and Empirical Review' (2002) 12 *European Review of Social Psychology* 1; BM Fennis and others, 'Bridging the Intention–Behavior Gap: Inducing Implementation Intentions through Persuasive Appeals' (2011) 21 *Journal of Consumer Psychology* 302; VG Morwitz and KP Munz, 'Intentions' (2021) 4 *Consumer Psychology Review* 26; B Mullan and others, 'The Role of Executive Function in Bridging the Intention-Behaviour Gap for Binge-Drinking in University Students' (2011) 36 *Addictive Behaviors* 1023.

[49] HR Hamilton, S Armeli and H Tennen, 'To Drink or Not to Drink: When Drinking Intentions Predict Alcohol Consumption and Consequences' (2022) 27 *British Journal of Health Psychology* 516; DW Foster, K Dukes and CE Sartor, 'The Road to Drink Is Paved with High Intentions: Expectancies, Refusal Self-Efficacy, and Intentions among Heavy Drinking College Students' (2016) 50 *Alcohol* 65.

[50] Hamilton, Armeli and Tennen (n 49); Foster, Dukes and Sartor (n 49).

[51] FF Sniehotta, J Presseau and V Araújo-Soares, 'Time to Retire the Theory of Planned Behaviour' (2014) 8 *Health Psychology Review* 1; but see I Ajzen, 'The Theory of Planned Behaviour Is Alive and Well, and Not Ready to Retire: A Commentary on Sniehotta, Presseau, and Araújo-Soares' (2015) 9 *Health Psychology Review* 131.

[52] Sniehotta, Presseau and Araújo-Soares (n 51).

mentally 'budget' a high intake as part of their plan, permitting themselves to exceed typical limits.[53]

Psychologically, the intention–behaviour gap highlights the difference between a more reflective mind, which sets intentions based on values and expectations, and a more impulsive or reactive system, which responds to cues and immediate desires.[54] If someone has not formed a strong, concrete implementation plan ('I will stick to soda, and if offered alcohol, I will say I'm driving'), their good intentions can be overridden by the pull of the moment. Studies tracking daily drinking behaviour confirm that even the best-laid plans can unravel under real-world conditions.[55] Spontaneous opportunities – like an unexpected invitation – often catch people unprepared to resist. Neuroscientists view this as a competition between top-down executive control, which is supported by areas of the brain that facilitate long-term intentions, such as the prefrontal cortex, and bottom-up impulses, which are triggered by areas of the brain that respond to habit and reward cues.[56]

In pioneering work in the 1980s, Libet and colleagues conducted classic experiments that demonstrated the brain initiates a readiness potential (RP), a buildup of neural activity, several hundred milliseconds before participants are consciously aware of deciding to move.[57] While these findings came from simple lab tasks (such as flexing a finger), they hint at the influence of 'unconscious' or preconscious processes in shaping behaviour.[58] Critics rightly note that real-life decisions, such as deciding to have a drink, are far more complex than a single finger twitch.[59] But the principle remains relevant: neural activity related to acting might begin before one fully realises or endorses that action.

Libet further proposed the idea of 'free won't', suggesting that although impulses may start preconsciously, people can still halt or veto a developing action if higher-level cognitive control is intact.[60] In alcohol contexts, this concept might translate

[53] M Wadolowski and others, 'Sipping, Drinking, and Early Adolescent Alcohol Consumption: A Cautionary Note' (2015) 39 *Alcoholism: Clinical and Experimental Research* 350.

[54] S Pieters and others, 'Impulsive and Reflective Processes Related to Alcohol Use in Young Adolescents' (2014) 5 *Frontiers in Psychiatry* 1; RW Wiers and others, 'Impulsivity, Impulsive and Reflective Processes and the Development of Alcohol Use and Misuse in Adolescents and Young Adults' (2010) 1 *Frontiers in Psychology* 1.

[55] Dora and others (n 16); Sheeran (n 48).

[56] Pieters and others (n 54); Wiers and others (n 54).

[57] CD Frith and P Haggard, 'Volition and the Brain – Revisiting a Classic Experimental Study' (2018) 41 *Trends in Neurosciences* 405; JF Christensen and others, 'Volition and Control in Law and in Brain Science: Neurolegal Translation of a Foundational Concept' (2024) 18 *Frontiers in Human Neuroscience* 1401895; Dominik and others (n 12); MN Braun, J Wessler and M Friese, 'A Meta-Analysis of Libet-Style Experiments' (2021) 128 *Neuroscience & Biobehavioral Reviews* 182.

[58] Frith and Haggard (n 57); Dominik and others (n 12); Braun, Wessler and Friese (n 57).

[59] U Maoz and others, 'Neural Precursors of Decisions That Matter – an ERP Study of Deliberate and Arbitrary Choice' (2019) 8 *eLife* e39787; suggesting that the RP reflects motor preparation for low-stakes, exploratory actions rather than meaningful goal-directed behaviour and that it may not extrapolate to complex, socially embedded choices.

[60] Dominik and others (n 12).

to resisting a growing urge[61] to drink – provided an individual's cognitive control systems are functioning well.

Where Libet emphasised a discrete motor readiness, another way to map this interplay between intentions and impulses could be the model of hierarchical cognitive control proposed by David Badre and colleagues.[62] This model proposes a broader view of how the prefrontal cortex orchestrates complex, goal-directed actions by suggesting that the PFC operates in layers of abstraction (ie, decision-making unfolds over time in nested stages):[63]

a) *High-Level Goals and Plans:* Representing abstract or longer-term goals – eg, 'I want to stay healthy', or 'I am reducing my alcohol intake'.[64]
b) *Intermediate Rules and Context:* With the brain weighing contextual factors – such as availability of alcohol, social norms, emotional states, or stress.[65]
c) *Motor Execution and Habits:* involving the motor system and habit loops handling well-practised routines, such as reaching for a glass or pouring a drink.[66]

This layered approach helps clarify how someone might 'decide' to drink. If higher-level goals like 'staying healthy' or 'limiting alcohol' remain prominent, they can inhibit or modify lower-level impulses. But if these goals fade – due to stress, social pressure, or diminished self-control – then lower-level processes (habit loops, reward cues) may prevail, culminating in that first sip.[67] Below, we discuss how alcohol-related expectancies and metacognitions (ie, beliefs about one's thoughts) further shape these decisions, and how core motives (eg, social bonding, coping, enhancement) can systematically tip the balance between intention and action.

C. Alcohol-Related Expectancies and Pre-Drinking Metacognitive Distortions

Before consuming alcohol, the intention to drink is influenced by alcohol outcome expectancies, ie, the beliefs and attitudes a person holds about the effects of drinking.[68] They represent metacognitive judgments about what alcohol will do

[61] Urges and cravings are discussed in the subsections below.

[62] D Badre, 'Brain Networks for Cognitive Control: Four Unresolved Questions' in PW Kalivas and MP Paulus (eds), *Intrusive Thinking: From Molecules to Free Will* (Cambridge, MIT Press, 2021); D Badre, *On Task: How Our Brain Gets Things Done* (Princeton, Princeton University Press, 2020).

[63] Badre 'Brain Networks' (n 62); Badre 'On Task' (n 62).

[64] In the anterior regions of the prefrontal cortex.

[65] At midlevels of the brain.

[66] At the more posterior (and often subcortical) regions of the motor system, and, for habit loops, the dorsal striatum.

[67] Badre 'Brain Networks' (n 62); Badre 'On Task' (n 62).

[68] Engels and others (n 18).

for them (or to them).[69] Expectancies can be positive (eg, anticipating pleasure, social confidence, relaxation) or negative (eg, expecting impairment or guilt). Research shows that, especially in youth, positive expectancies strongly predict drinking initiation and heavier use.[70] And expectancy theory in addiction suggests that such anticipated outcomes are significant proximal predictors of the decision to drink.[71] Expectancies thus have a metacognitive character because they are essentially predictions about one's own future mental and physical states under alcohol.[72] Someone with AUD might believe 'once I start, I won't be able to stop' (a negative expectancy about their own control). In contrast, a social drinker might believe 'a drink will help me loosen up and have fun' (a positive expectancy about social confidence). Notably, this predictive nature of expectations seems to imply a degree of foresight and planning in the pre-drinking phase, at least some deliberation about anticipated outcomes, peer context, and personal control.[73]

Alcohol-related expectancies are stored in long-term memory and can be primed by situational cues, influencing behaviour even in the absence of actual alcohol intake.[74] Thus, before drinking, a person's beliefs about alcohol can also shape their mindset and behaviour.[75] For example, some studies presented participants with the idea that alcohol increases sociability and found that participants who firmly held that expectancy, subsequently consumed more of a placebo beverage, as if the belief alone drove their drinking behaviour.[76] Moreover, pre-drinking expectancies can moderate actual impairment during intoxication: individuals who expect to become very impaired tend to show more significant performance decrements, whereas those who expect to stay in control show less impairment – even when everyone receives the same dose or only a placebo.[77] In short, what one anticipates alcohol will do can become a self-fulfilling prophecy affecting

[69] MM Spada, GB Moneta and A Wells, 'The Relative Contribution of Metacognitive Beliefs and Expectancies to Drinking Behaviour' (2007) 42 *Alcohol and Alcoholism* 567.

[70] M Pinquart and K Borgolte, 'Associations of Alcohol Outcome Expectancies with Alcohol Use in Adolescence and Emerging Adulthood: A Meta-Analysis' [2024] *International Journal of Mental Health and Addiction*.

[71] Foster, Dukes and Sartor (n 49).

[72] Spada, Moneta and Wells (n 69); F Gierski and others, 'Positive and Negative Metacognitions about Alcohol Use among University Students: Psychometric Properties of the PAMS and NAMS French Versions' (2015) 153 *Drug and Alcohol Dependence* 78.

[73] A Dijkstra, L Sweeney and W Gebhardt, 'Social Cognitive Determinants of Drinking in Young Adults: Beyond the Alcohol Expectancies Paradigm' (2001) 26 *Addictive Behaviors* 689; A Bulley, J Henry and T Suddendorf, 'Prospection and the Present Moment: The Role of Episodic Foresight in Intertemporal Choices between Immediate and Delayed Rewards' (2016) 20 *Review of General Psychology* 29.

[74] Foster, Dukes and Sartor (n 49).

[75] ibid.

[76] ibid; RF Leeman and others, 'Alcohol-Induced Disinhibition Expectancies and Impaired Control as Prospective Predictors of Problem Drinking in Undergraduates' (2009) 23 *Psychology of Addictive Behaviors* 553.

[77] P Christiansen and others, 'Bibi Ergo Sum: The Effects of a Placebo and Contextual Alcohol Cues on Motivation to Drink Alcohol' (2017) 234 *Psychopharmacology* 827.

behaviour before any alcohol is consumed and shaping one's subjective experience after drinking.

Besides expectancies, other metacognitive processes are also in play when individuals try to forecast their future drinking behaviour.[78] A common error is the 'hot-cold empathy gap': in a sober ('cold') state, one does not fully account for how the 'hot' state of being intoxicated will alter judgement or fuel disinhibition.[79] For instance, someone might assure themselves, 'I'll only have two drinks' without appreciating how alcohol's immediate effects could lead them to abandon that limit. This overconfidence is bolstered by the assumption 'I know my limits', yet evidence suggests that even experienced drinkers can misjudge how quickly or how strongly they will feel alcohol's impact.[80] Such flawed predictions about one's future self can reduce sound judgement before a single sip is taken. Moreover, these metacognitive distortions might be particularly acute for individuals with AUD, who may expect 'once I start, I won't be able to stop', or rely on drinking to self-medicate.[81] Conversely, social drinkers may hold positive expectancies, such as 'a drink will help me relax and fit in'.[82] In both cases, these beliefs function as proximal drivers of drinking decisions, influencing consumption even before the first drop of alcohol.

Together, alcohol-related expectancies and metacognitive distortions reveal how individuals' beliefs – both about alcohol's effects and their capacity to handle them – can set the stage for later outcomes. In the following sub-section we will explore drinking motives – how they arise from expectancies, metacognitive beliefs, and broader psychological needs – and discuss their role in shaping upcoming drinking behaviour. In section V, we will discuss metacognition once again, but from a pharmacological-effects perspective, once intoxicated.

D. Drinking Motives

Beyond broad intentions, the decision to drink, as posited by motivational models, is a result of an individual's evaluation of expected affective changes associated with consumption compared to abstinence.[83] Researchers probe the motives for

[78] Gierski and others (n 72); Spada, Moneta and Wells (n 69).

[79] G Helton and C Register, 'Hot-Cold Empathy Gaps and the Grounds of Authenticity' (2023) 202 *Synthese* 1; MA Sayette and others, 'Exploring the Cold-to-Hot Empathy Gap in Smokers' (2008) 19 *Psychological Science* 926; MM Spada and A Wells, 'A Metacognitive Model of Problem Drinking' (2009) 16 *Clinical Psychology & Psychotherapy* 383; G Caselli and others, 'Metacognitive Therapy for Alcohol Use Disorder: A Systematic Case Series' (2018) 9 *Frontiers in Psychology* 2619.

[80] Spada and Wells (n 79).

[81] ibid; Caselli and others (n 79).

[82] Spada, Moneta and Wells (n 69).

[83] WM Cox and E Klinger, 'A Motivational Model of Alcohol Use' (1988) 97 *Journal of Abnormal Psychology* 168. Cox and Klinger also explain how this value-based decision-making can be observed at the biochemical level. Interestingly, the authors explain that the processes are similar in both 'addictive' and 'nonaddictive' drinking and that often those decisions are 'nonconscious and automatised').

why people drink using questionnaires.[84] Yielding that several internal and external factors contribute to this value-based calculus. The most studied motives include: social (drinking to be sociable or celebrate), enhancement (to enhance positive mood or experience stimulation), coping (to relieve negative emotions), and conformity (to fit in or avoid rejection).[85] Motives tied to emotion regulation – enhancement and coping – are often linked to heavier consumption and adverse consequences.[86] For instance, one longitudinal study found that coping motives (drinking 'to forget worries' or alleviate distress) directly predicted a host of unique alcohol-related problems (eg, impaired self-control, risky behaviours, dependence symptoms), even after controlling for consumption levels.[87] In addition, during the COVID-19 pandemic, subjectively expressing high levels of stress, anxiety, depression, and drinking motives to cope, were related to increased alcohol consumption.[88] Enhancement motives (drinking 'because it's fun' or exciting) predicted problems indirectly by leading to greater alcohol intake.[89] In short, if someone's decision to drink is driven by a need to escape a negative emotional state or to achieve euphoria, they are more likely to drink to excess and suffer harm. However, a person with high coping motives might intend only to soothe their anxiety, yet their motive may predispose them to impaired judgment once drinking begins. We could argue that if one's motive to drink resulted from the need to self-medicate, one's decision to drink may not be an entirely 'voluntary' act as the law assumes.

E. The Influence of Urges or Craving, Situational Cues, and Attentional Bias

Craving represents a key proximal driver of drinking behaviour, also predicting initiation and continuation. It can be defined as an intense desire or urge to consume alcohol, often accompanied by intrusive thoughts (eg, 'I really want

[84] Engels and others (n 18); Cox and Klinger (n 83); Amlung and MacKillop (n 15).

[85] Cox and Klinger (n 83).

[86] SE Thomas and others, 'Coping Motives for Drinking Affect Stress Reactivity but Not Alcohol Consumption in a Clinical Laboratory Setting' (2014) 75 *Journal of Studies on Alcohol and Drugs* 115; WR Corbin, NM Farmer and S Nolen-Hoekesma, 'Relations among Stress, Coping Strategies, Coping Motives, Alcohol Consumption and Related Problems: A Mediated Moderation Model' (2013) 38 *Addictive Behaviors* 1912; M Rowicka, 'Differences and Similarities in Motives to Decrease Drinking, and to Drink in General Between Former and Current Heavy Drinkers – Implications for Changing Own Drinking Behaviour' (2022) 12 *Frontiers in Psychology* 734350; J Zaorska and others, 'Distress Tolerance and Emotional Regulation in Individuals with Alcohol Use Disorder' (2023) 14 *Frontiers in Psychiatry* 1175664.

[87] S Armeli and others, 'A Longitudinal Study of the Effects of Coping Motives, Negative Affect and Drinking Level on Drinking Problems among College Students' (2014) 27 *Anxiety, Stress, & Coping* 527.

[88] JD Wardell and others, 'Drinking to Cope During COVID-19 Pandemic: The Role of External and Internal Factors in Coping Motive Pathways to Alcohol Use, Solitary Drinking, and Alcohol Problems' (2020) 44 *Alcoholism: Clinical and Experimental Research* 2073.

[89] Engels and others (n 18); E Kuntsche and others, 'Why Do Young People Drink? A Review of Drinking Motives' (2005) 25 *Clinical Psychology Review* 841.

a beer') and a pull towards action ('I feel compelled to get a drink'). In clinical settings, craving is frequently measured before drinking onset to predict imminent consumption or potential relapse.[90] For instance, if someone rates their craving as 8/10 at 5 p.m., they are more likely to start drinking soon thereafter. Emotional states can heighten craving: negative affect often prompts coping-driven drinkers to seek relief, whereas positive affect may spur those who drink for enhancement.[91]

Craving is also tightly linked to situational and environmental factors. Studies using smartphone-based tracking show that individuals are significantly more likely to initiate drinking when in bars, at parties, or surrounded by peers who are drinking.[92] These 'in-the-moment' influences can easily override prior intentions to abstain or moderate.[93] In addition, perceived social norms can amplify urges – people who believe 'everyone else is drinking' are more inclined to join in themselves.[94] Interventions that correct overestimated peer norms have, in turn, been shown to reduce drinking, underscoring how social context shapes urge intensity.[95]

A further layer of complexity arises from alcohol-related cues, which can capture attention.[96] In psychology, this 'attentional bias' refers to the tendency to notice and focus on alcohol stimuli (eg, the sight of a bottle) more than neutral cues.[97] Heavy or dependent drinkers, in particular, exhibit marked attentional and approach biases, meaning they not only spot alcohol cues more quickly but also show a pull to move towards them.[98] Experiments using colour-naming tasks (Stroop paradigms) reveal that alcohol-related words slow performance because they attract cognitive resources, while joystick-based approach/avoidance tasks find that heavy drinkers pull alcohol images towards themselves faster than neutral images.[99] In essence, seeing alcohol can trigger a behavioural urge to seek alcohol and/or weaken the braking mechanism of self-control. These cue-induced tendencies make it harder to remain abstinent or moderate since the person's

[90] Dora and others (n 16); Christiansen and others (n 36); Seo and Sinha (n 17).

[91] D De Guglielmo and others, 'Voluntary and Forced Exposure to Ethanol Vapor Produces Similar Escalation of Alcohol Drinking but Differential Recruitment of Brain Regions Related to Stress, Habit, and Reward in Male Rats' (2023) 222 *Neuropharmacology* 109309; Christiansen and others (n 36).

[92] Collins and Carey (n 47); Dijkstra, Sweeney and Gebhardt (n 73).

[93] Howard and others (n 12); SA Griffin, LK Freeman and TJ Trull, 'Predictors of Unplanned Drinking in Daily Life: The Influence of Context, Impulsivity, and Craving in Those with Emotion Dysregulation' (2021) 118 *Addictive Behaviors* 106901.

[94] Dijkstra, Sweeney and Gebhardt (n 73).

[95] Babor and others (n 4); CM Lee and others, 'The Social Norms of Alcohol-Related Negative Consequences.' (2010) 24 *Psychology of Addictive Behaviors* 342.

[96] BA Anderson, PA Laurent and S Yantis, 'Value-Driven Attentional Capture' (2011) 108 *Proceedings of the National Academy of Sciences* 10367; CRH Brown, T Duka and S Forster, 'Attentional Capture by Alcohol-Related Stimuli May Be Activated Involuntarily by Top-down Search Goals' (2018) 235 *Psychopharmacology* 2087.

[97] M Field and W Cox, 'Attentional Bias in Addictive Behaviors: A Review of Its Development, Causes, and Consequences' (2008) 97 *Drug and Alcohol Dependence* 1; Anderson, Laurent and Yantis (n 96).

[98] Robinson and Berridge (n 38).

[99] Field and others, 'Delay Discounting' (n 13).

voluntary control is impaired by the environment before any consumption. At a neurobiological level, repeated pairings of alcohol cues with the alcohol reward can sensitise specific pathways in the brain, making these cues more salient and triggering a 'wanting' response that encourages drinking.[100]

Cravings and cue-reactivity differ in intensity across drinking profiles. Where social or moderate drinkers may experience mild, context-bound cravings that might not persist outside of specific cue-rich environments,[101] individuals with AUD may crave alcohol in a more pronounced and persistent manner, fuelled by withdrawal-related discomfort and deep-rooted habit loops.[102] Their baseline craving can be high even without explicit cues, and everyday triggers – like passing a familiar pub – can provoke relapse by activating 'wanting' at the brain level.[103]

Although such urges and cue-induced responses do not meet the legal threshold of 'involuntary intoxication', this body of evidence challenges potential views of 'voluntary' drinking as entirely rational. Furthermore, they seem to suggest varying degrees of volition.

F. Personality Traits and Decision-Making Deficits

Research consistently links impulsivity and sensation seeking, as well as heavier alcohol use and cognitive deficits in biased decision-making, to heavier alcohol use.[104] Individuals who exhibit high impulsivity might find the disinhibitory effects of alcohol particularly reinforcing, accelerating decisions to keep drinking despite apparent risks. Sensation-seekers, similarly, may experience heightened rewards from intoxication, increasing the likelihood of binge episodes. Over time, these personality-based vulnerabilities can feed into cycles of dependency or escalate the severity of alcohol-related harm. Laboratory tasks indicate that individuals who consume alcohol heavily tend to devalue future rewards – a phenomenon known as delayed discounting.[105] In other words, individuals prone to drinking

[100] Koob and Volkow (n 44).

[101] Dora and others (n 16); SC Moore and B Cusens, 'Delay Discounting Predicts Increase in Blood Alcohol Level in Social Drinkers' (2010) 179 *Psychiatry Research* 324; M Leganes-Fonteneau and others, 'Knowledge about the Predictive Value of Reward Conditioned Stimuli Modulates Their Interference with Cognitive Processes' (2019) 26 *Learning & Memory* 66.

[102] Koob and Volkow (n 44).

[103] Christiansen and others (n 36); Z Bollen and others, 'Craving Modulates Attentional Bias towards Alcohol in Severe Alcohol Use Disorder: An Eye-tracking Study' (2024) 119 *Addiction* 102.

[104] Eg: N Castellanos-Ryan and P Conrod 'Personality and Substance Misuse: Evidence for a Four-Factor Model of Vulnerability' in J Verster and others (eds), *Drug Abuse and Addiction in Medical Illness* (New York, Springer, 2012); L Mezquita, G Ortet and MI Ibáñez, 'Personality Traits and Alcohol Use and Misuse' in R Cooke and others (eds), *The Palgrave Handbook of Psychological Perspectives on Alcohol Consumption* (Cham, Palgrave Macmillan, 2021); A Tomassini and others, 'Decision Making, Impulsivity, and Personality Traits in Alcohol-Dependent Subjects' (2012) 21 *The American Journal on Addictions* 263.

[105] Field and others, 'Delay Discounting' (n 13); S Adams, AS Attwood and MR Munafò, 'Drinking Status but Not Acute Alcohol Consumption Influences Delay Discounting' (2017) 32 *Human*

heavily often have difficulty delaying gratification, which may tip their cost-benefit calculus in favour of a 'drink now, worry later' approach.

Risk-taking paradigms further illustrate decision-style differences between drinkers. In these tasks, participants are presented with choices that involve risk. For example, participants may be presented with four decks of cards (two 'good' with small rewards/penalties and two 'bad' with high rewards/losses). Optimal performance requires learning to prioritise long-term gains over short-term rewards.[106] In yet another task[107] participants pump a virtual balloon to earn money, with each pump increasing potential reward but also the risk of the balloon bursting (losing all accumulated gains). Research using these types of research paradigms suggests that riskier decisions and poor learning are associated with heavy drinking and impulsivity.[108] Yet, some studies of severely dependent individuals find lower risk-taking, possibly reflecting caution developed after repeated negative consequences or alcohol-induced cognitive deficits.[109]

Overall, these findings suggest that individuals who are impulsive or sensation-seeking struggle with the reflective thinking required by the 'reasonable person' standard in legal contexts. Their tendency to prioritise immediate rewards over broader outcomes can make them more prone to acting on the urge to drink, undermining efforts to remain abstinent or moderate. When such traits intersect with environmental cues or stressful situations, the inclination to drink often outweighs longer-term considerations.

All of these pre-drinking dynamics – ranging from intentions and expectancies to social cues and neurochemical signals – set the stage for whether someone moves on to actually consume alcohol. In the following two sections, we examine drinking initiation and continuation, beginning with the general neurobiology and including impairments for both stages (initiation and continuation).

Psychopharmacology: Clinical and Experimental e2617; Moore and Cusens (n 101); J MacKillop and others, 'Alcohol Demand, Delayed Reward Discounting, and Craving in Relation to Drinking and Alcohol Use Disorders' (2010) 119 *Journal of Abnormal Psychology* 106.

[106] Iowa Gambling Task (IGT). This task is widely applied in alcohol use disorder (AUD) and gambling disorder (GD) studies to quantify decision-making deficits. It tests the ability to resist immediate high rewards for sustained profitability. See D Barry and NM Petry, 'Predictors of Decision-Making on the Iowa Gambling Task: Independent Effects of Lifetime History of Substance Use Disorders and Performance on the Trail Making Test' (2008) 66 *Brain and Cognition* 243; I Kovacs and others, 'Decision Making Measured by the Iowa Gambling Task in Alcohol Use Disorder and Gambling Disorder: a Systematic Review and Meta-analysis' (2017) 181 *Drug and Alcohol Dependence* 152.

[107] Balloon Analogue Risk Task (BART). Measures real-time tolerance for escalating risk. This task is Sensitive to dose-dependent effects (eg, higher BAC levels increase risk-taking). See DA Harmon, AL Haas and A Peterkin, 'Experimental Tasks of Behavioral Risk Taking in Alcohol Administration Studies: A Systematic Review' (2021) 113 *Addictive Behaviors* 106678; TL Horn, JP Whelan and GT Weil, 'Does Acute Alcohol Consumption Increase Risk-Taking While Gambling? A Systematic Review and Meta-Analysis' (2022) 117 *Addiction* 2780.

[108] Kovacs and others (n 106); Horn and others (n 107).

[109] AD Ariesen and others, 'Risky Decision-Making in Adults with Alcohol Use Disorder – A Systematic and Meta-Analytic Review' (2023) 12 *Journal of Clinical Medicine* 2943.

IV. Initiation of Drinking (First Drink)

The neurochemical landscape set during pre-drinking is rapidly transformed upon initial alcohol consumption. To understand how voluntariness can be compromised by intoxication, we must first understand what alcohol does to the brain and behaviour. Alcohol's acute effects on the brain are not uniform. Several factors, including the dose consumed, the rate of drinking, food intake before or during drinking, and stress levels during drinking, as well as individual differences in body weight, sex, food metabolism, and genetic differences affecting alcohol metabolism, will affect the amount of alcohol ultimately measured in the blood (BAC), as well as the amount of time it will take for the effects of a BAC dose to subside, which in turn will mediate its effects on the brain and observed cognitive and behavioural functioning.[110]

In this section, we bridge from pre-drinking cognitive and neurobiological processes to the initiation of acute intoxication, providing a necessary foundation to fully comprehend alcohol's immediate reinforcing properties. We start by underscoring the neurobiological vulnerability underlying loss of control with alcohol consumption to set the stage for detailed exploration of initiation and continued drinking behaviours and the progressive cognitive and behavioural impairments observed during intoxication. We then explore the influence of alcohol priming effects and finish this section discussing inhibitory control impairments, which is arguably one of the earliest functions to be impaired even at low to moderate levels of alcohol.

A. Acute Neurobiological Effects of Alcohol Consumption

To fully comprehend how voluntary control over drinking may become compromised, a clear understanding of alcohol's acute neurobiological effects is essential. Acute intoxication involves multifaceted interactions across several neurotransmitter systems and brain regions, significantly influencing cognition and behaviour. Ethanol (C_2H_5OH), the psychoactive substance in alcoholic beverages, broadly impacts the central nervous system (CNS; comprised of the brain and the spinal cord).

Alcohol is considered a CNS depressant, a type of drug which reduces CNS activity.[111] However, it produces a dose-dependent biphasic pattern of

[110] For a detailed account of the factors which influence alcohol metabolism and the levels of BAC reached from a single dose of alcohol, the reader is directed to: H Thomasson, 'Gender Differences in Alcohol Metabolism: Physiological Responses to Ethanol' (2002) *Recent Developments in Alcoholism: Alcoholism and Women* 163; A Cederbaum, 'Alcohol Metabolism' (2012) 16 *Clinics in Liver Disease* 667. AW Jones, 'Alcohol, Its Absorption, Distribution, Metabolism, and Excretion in the Body and Pharmacokinetic Calculations' (2019) 1 *Wiley Interdisciplinary Reviews: Forensic Science* e1340.

[111] Wirral University Teaching Hospital, 'About Drugs' (nd), www.wuth.nhs.uk/our-departments/a-z-of-departments/substance-misuse-services/about-drugs/.

effects – ie, initial disinhibition followed by progressive neural inhibition.[112] Thus, under low levels of intoxication (BAC levels of 30–50mg/dl; 0.03–0.05 per cent), individuals experience mild euphoria, are more talkative and sociable, and feel less inhibited.[113] At higher doses (eg, at or above the legal drunk-driving limit, ie, 80–120mg/dl; 0.08–0.12 per cent), motor reactions become slower and less well coordinated, speech is slurred, and sedation and impairments in memory and attention are seen.[114] Amnesia, nausea, hypothermia and hypotension are observed at clinically significant doses of 200mg/dl/; 0.2 per cent, and at 300mg/dl; 0.3 per cent and above, an individual is unresponsive and has a significant risk of dying.[115] Alcohol exerts its acute effects by modulating key neurotransmitter systems, notably GABA (gamma-aminobutyric acid), glutamate, and dopamine, across critical brain regions.

GABA is the principal inhibitory neurotransmitter in the brain, as it slows down brain activity. Alcohol works through GABA systems to dampen cortical activity. This action underlies the sedative and anxiety-reducing effects of moderate drinking, often experienced as relaxation or lowered social inhibitions.[116] However, as alcohol-induced GABAergic signalling intensifies, higher-level cognitive functions – particularly those required for impulse control – are compromised.[117] This can explain why intoxicated individuals exhibit impulsive decision-making, risk-taking, and reduced capacity to self-regulate. In parallel with its GABAergic effects, alcohol inhibits excitatory neurotransmission by antagonising glutamate-related systems.[118] Glutamate is the primary excitatory neurotransmitter and plays a crucial role in learning and memory.[119] When glutamatergic-related activity is suppressed, the brain's ability to encode new information declines, sometimes manifesting in 'blackouts' or transient amnesia.[120] Cognitive slowing, delayed reaction times, and difficulties with complex problem-solving are further hallmarks of reduced glutamatergic signalling during acute intoxication.[121]

[112] CS Martin and others, 'Development and Validation of the Biphasic Alcohol Effects Scale' (1993) 17 *Alcoholism: Clinical and Experimental Research* 140.

[113] CF Valenzuela, 'Alcohol and Neurotransmitter Interactions' (1997) 21 *Alcohol Health & Research World* 144; Valenzuela and Zucca (n 36); KP Abrahao, AG Salinas and DM Lovinger, 'Alcohol and the Brain: Neuronal Molecular Targets, Synapses, and Circuits' (2017) 96 *Neuron* 1223.

[114] Valenzuela (n 113); Valenzuela and Zucca (n 36); Abrahao, Salinas and Lovinger (n 113).

[115] A Mirijello and others, 'Identification and Management of Acute Alcohol Intoxication' (2023) 108 *European Journal of Internal Medicine* 1.

[116] SJ Mihic and RA Harris, 'GABA and the GABAA Receptor' (1997) 21 *Alcohol Health & Research World* 127; Koob and Volkow (n 6).

[117] J Littleton, 'Neurochemical Mechanisms Underlying Alcohol Withdrawal' (1998) 33 *Alcohol* 7; FT Crews and CA Boettiger, 'Impulsivity, Frontal Lobes and Risk for Addiction' (2009) 93 *Pharmacology, Biochemistry & Behaviour* 237.

[118] In opposite to GABA, glutamate is the brain's main excitatory neurotransmitter.

[119] Riedel (n 42).

[120] R Chandrasekar, 'Alcohol and NMDA Receptor: Current Research and Future Direction' (2013) 6 *Frontiers in Molecular Neuroscience* 14; FT Crews and CA Boettiger (n 50).

[121] M Oscar-Berman and K Marinkovic, 'Alcohol: Effects on Neurobehavioural Functions and the Brain' (2007) 17 *Neuropsychology Review* 239.

Furthermore, a dopamine surge contributes to feelings of pleasure and reward that can reinforce continued drinking, occasionally escalating to binge patterns.[122] In other words, acute intoxication creates a transient state that reinforces alcohol consumption as a reward-seeking behaviour. As we discussed in section III, dopaminergic release is also linked to expectation-driven responses involving alcohol-related cues (eg, the sight or smell of drinks or environmental triggers such as social settings) occurring before alcohol consumption, mimicking placebo-induced anticipatory responses.[123] This is also related to tolerance, as chronic drinkers may experience conditioned dopamine spikes from alcohol-associated rituals (eg, glass clinking), sustaining consumption despite reduced pharmacological effects.[124] Additional neurotransmitter systems, including serotonin, norepinephrine, and endogenous opioids, significantly contribute to emotional dysregulation, impulsivity, and aggression under intoxication, alongside heightened euphoria and analgesic effects that potentiate continued consumption.[125]

Crucial brain regions affected include the prefrontal cortex, essential for executive functions such as working memory, cognitive flexibility, and inhibitory control, all significantly compromised under intoxication.[126] Limbic structures mediate emotional and memory disturbances, including heightened emotional reactivity or aggression and memory impairments.[127] The cerebellum's impairment manifests in motor control deficits, including slurred speech and coordination difficulties.[128] Collectively, alcohol's acute neurochemical effects significantly impair self-control, attentional processing, and memory encoding, even as motivational reinforcement to continue drinking persists.[129] Chronic or repeated acute effects establish long-term alterations in brain systems and regions, promoting sustained compulsive drinking patterns and perpetuating deficits in cognitive and behavioural control.[130] This forms the neurobiological basis for the cognitive and behavioural phenomena that manifest during the initiation (explored next and in the

[122] Koob and Volkow (n 6); MS Brodie, C Pesold and SB Appel, 'Ethanol Directly Excites Dopaminergic Ventral Tegmental Area Reward Neurons' (1999) 23 *Alcoholism: Clinical and Experimental Research* 1848. These papers highlight how alcohol enhances dopaminergic transmission within mesolimbic reward circuits, areas that have been linked to reinforcement and motivation, particularly in relation to reward, desire, and the placebo effect.

[123] Brodie, Pesold and Appel (n 122); F Benedetti, E Carlino and A Pollo, 'How Placebos Change the Patient's Brain' (2011) 36 *Neuropsychopharmacology* 339; KB Jensen, 'Placebo Effects beyond Dopamine' (2024) 22 *PLOS Biology* e3002812.

[124] AG Salinas and others, 'Long-Term Alcohol Consumption Alters Dorsal Striatal Dopamine Release and Regulation by D2 Dopamine Receptors in Rhesus Macaques' (2021) 46 *Neuropsychopharmacology* 1432.

[125] Effects on the neurotransmitter serotonin: S Da Cunha-Bang and G Moos Knudsen, 'The Modulatory Role of Serotonin on Human Impulsive Aggression' (2021) 90 *Biological Psychiatry* 447.

[126] Koob and Volkow (n 6); Abrahao, Salinas and Lovinger (n 113).

[127] Abrahao, Salinas and Lovinger (n 113).

[128] ibid.

[129] ibid.

[130] Koob and Volkow (n 6).

remainder of section IV) and the impairments derived from the further continuation of alcohol consumption (explored in section V), as both sections deal with the drug on board, with all its related pharmacological effects.

B. The Priming Effect: How Initial Alcohol Intake Drives Further Consumption

Understanding the priming effect is crucial for appreciating how alcohol consumption, initially perceived as voluntary (though often influenced by external cues and internal variables such as expectations, motivations, etc), can quickly become increasingly involuntary. We observed that even the decision to start drinking may not be fully voluntary, given the influence of those environmental and internal factors (see section III). After an initial small dose, alcohol consumption rapidly becomes even less voluntary, driven by strong physiological and psychological effects.[131] Importantly, this transition is not strictly linear; instead, it reflects complex interactions between biological responses to alcohol, learned associations from previous experiences, and situational cues, making subsequent drinking less well controlled.[132]

Empirical research consistently shows that even low doses of alcohol can elevate craving and subsequent drinking in both social and heavier drinkers.[133] For example, studies demonstrate that participants given a modest initial drink typically consume more in subsequent ad libitum drinking tests than those who received a placebo, even when the first dose is minimal and does not produce subjective intoxication.[134] This pattern has important implications: the initial voluntary choice to drink seems to quickly lead to biological and psychological processes beyond voluntary control.

Two main mechanisms explain why initial drinking often leads to increased alcohol consumption. First, consuming alcohol makes alcohol-related stimuli, such as the sight or smell of a drink, more appealing and attention-grabbing.[135] This heightened attention is linked to the brain's reward system, which normally helps individuals identify and pursue pleasurable activities. Even small amounts of alcohol can strengthen positive expectations about drinking, increasing cravings and the perceived attractiveness of further consumption.[136] Neuroimaging

[131] T Duka and JM Townshend, 'The Priming Effect of Alcohol Pre-Load on Attentional Bias to Alcohol-Related Stimuli' (2004) 176 *Psychopharmacology* 353.

[132] ibid; Fillmore and Vogel-Sprott (n 18).

[133] Duka and Townshend (n 131).

[134] ibid.

[135] ibid; KE Courtney, DG Ghahremani and LA Ray, 'The Effect of Alcohol Priming on Neural Markers of Alcohol Cue-Reactivity' (2015) 41 *The American Journal of Drug and Alcohol Abuse* 300; M Leganes-Fonteneau and others, 'An Interoceptive Basis for Alcohol Priming Effects' (2021) 238 *Psychopharmacology* 1621.

[136] Duka and Townshend (n 131).

studies have confirmed that alcohol cues significantly activate brain areas associated with reward processing, even in individuals who drink socially or those with more frequent alcohol use.[137] Consequently, even a minor initial dose makes additional drinks feel more desirable by increasing anticipation of pleasure.[138]

Second, even low doses of alcohol acutely impair inhibitory control processes, reducing the individual's ability to adhere to pre-established limits on consumption.[139] These inhibitory impairments are expanded next in this section. But, crucially, research by Fillmore and colleagues demonstrates that once alcohol-induced disinhibition occurs, it persists throughout the drinking episode without recovery within that session.[140] Miller and colleagues further clarify this effect, showing no tolerance development to alcohol's disinhibiting properties; heavy drinkers experience similar impulsivity after low doses as lighter drinkers, indicating repeated vulnerability.[141]

These combined effects – heightened cue reactivity and diminished inhibitory control – set up a self-reinforcing cycle. Alcohol intake rapidly escalates beyond initial intentions, creating an increasingly involuntary pattern of consumption.[142] Anecdotal expressions such as 'once I start, I can't stop' reflect this well-established pharmacological and psychological reality.[143]

People's expectations and beliefs about drinking, discussed earlier in section III, also influence how strongly they react to alcohol once they start drinking. However, with relevance for this stage: although expectations can significantly shape drinking behaviour, actual alcohol consumption has additional powerful effects – such as increasing attraction to alcohol-related cues and making self-control more complicated – that cannot be fully explained by beliefs alone.[144]

Recognising these priming effects challenges simplified legal and social perceptions of alcohol intoxication as merely a series of equally voluntary decisions. From our neurocognitive perspective, after consuming the initial drink, subsequent drinking decisions become progressively influenced by impaired cognitive and neural mechanisms, altering the individual's capacity for voluntary control in essential ways. Rather than a straightforward linear progression of voluntary acts, alcohol consumption represents a complex interplay of influences, raising

[137] Courtney, Ghahremani and Ray (n 135); L Baines and others, 'The Effect of Alcohol Cue Exposure and Acute Intoxication on Inhibitory Control Processes and Ad Libitum Alcohol Consumption' (2019) 236 *Psychopharmacology* 2187.

[138] MM Groefsema and others, 'Brain Responses to Anticipating and Receiving Beer: Comparing Light, At-Risk, and Dependent Alcohol Users' (2020) 25 *Addiction Biology* e12766.

[139] Fillmore and Vogel-Sprott (n 18); Weafer and Fillmore (n 14); Field and others, 'Acute Alcohol Effects' (n 13).

[140] Fillmore and Vogel-Sprott (n 18); Weafer and Fillmore (n 14).

[141] MA Miller, LR Hays and MT Fillmore, 'Lack of Tolerance to the Disinhibiting Effects of Alcohol in Heavy Drinkers' (2012) 224 *Psychopharmacology* 511.

[142] Duka and Townshend (n 131).

[143] Miller, Hays and Fillmore (n 141).

[144] Weafer and Fillmore (n 14).

important questions about accountability and decision-making capacity under intoxication, pharmacologically even from the very first drink.

Given the established connection between initial doses of alcohol and immediate impairments in inhibitory control, below we will specifically explore how this reduction in inhibitory control manifests cognitively and behaviourally, even at relatively low BAC levels. Understanding this initial impairment is critical for assessing responsibility and decision-making in intoxication scenarios.

C. Impaired Inhibitory Control and Selective Cognitive Impairments at Low BAC

Once intoxication is underway, even at modest blood alcohol levels, clear deficits in executive function emerge.[145] Chief among these is impaired inhibitory control – the ability to stop or withhold initiated, inappropriate or well-learned actions.[146] Laboratory tasks assessing this ability often ask participants to press a button in response to certain stimuli ('go') while refraining from pressing for others ('no-go'), or to stop an ongoing button press when a sudden 'stop' signal is presented. Under acute alcohol intoxication, participants consistently produce more false alarms (presses when they should not) and require longer to halt ongoing responses.[147] Practically, this explains why someone might appear conversationally sober after a few drinks yet begin to speak or act impulsively, failing to hold back comments or actions they would usually control. This slowdown can appear at BACs as low as 0.04–0.06 per cent, which many people reach after just two or three standard drinks consumed quickly.[148] Remarkably, these impairments are evident even when a person's simple reaction time (basic speed of responding) remains unaffected, indicating a targeted disruption of the brain's 'braking' system.[149]

This weakening of inhibitory control can lead to a cycle of continued drinking. As it becomes harder to hold back or self-regulate, saying 'no' to another drink becomes more difficult.[150] Indeed, research by Mark Fillmore and colleagues has linked acute alcohol-induced stop-signal impairments to increased self-administration of alcohol in the lab, suggesting that disinhibition plays a direct role in the inability to stop consuming once started.[151]

[145] See J Weafer and MT Fillmore. 'Low-Dose Alcohol Effects on Measures of Inhibitory Control, Delay Discounting, and Risk-Taking' (2016) 3 *Current Addiction Reports* 75.

[146] Field and others, 'Acute Alcohol Effects' (n 13).

[147] Weafer and Fillmore (n 14); W Bensmann and others, 'Acute Alcohol Effects on Response Inhibition Depend on Response Automatization, but Not on GABA or Glutamate Levels in the ACC and Striatum' (2020) 9 *Journal of Clinical Medicine* 481.

[148] Field and others, 'Acute Alcohol Effects' (n 13).

[149] CE Fairbairn, D Kang and KD Federmeier, 'Alcohol and Neural Dynamics: A Meta-Analysis of Acute Alcohol Effects on Event-Related Brain Potentials' (2021) 89 *Biological Psychiatry* 990.

[150] ibid.

[151] Field and others, 'Acute Alcohol Effects' (n 13).

Importantly, other aspects of cognition also suffer at relatively low BAC. Contrary to the common belief that one is 'totally fine' after a drink or two, evidence shows that certain cognitive domains are susceptible to even minimal doses of alcohol.[152] For instance, a meta-analysis of event-related potential (ERP) studies found that BACs as low as ~0.026 per cent – well below most legal limits – can significantly reduce the brain's P3b amplitude (an index of attentional resource allocation) and weaken error-related negativity (a marker of how the brain monitors mistakes).[153] Functionally, this means that even one or two drinks can impair a person's ability to attend to multiple cues and diminish their awareness of, or concern for, errors.[154] Divided attention – handling two tasks at once – can also deteriorate at BACs around 0.01–0.02 per cent, levels often reached after just one standard drink.[155]

Because alcohol initially depresses inhibitory mechanisms in the frontal regions of the brain, people may feel more outgoing and confident yet also become more impulsive.[156] That internal 'voice of caution' grows quieter, which is why someone who appears conversationally coherent might still act in ways they would not usually do. By the time BAC reaches ~0.04–0.06 per cent, these impairments become pronounced enough to compromise the ability to pause, weigh the consequences, and resist unwanted impulses. There is no absolute threshold below which cognition remains entirely intact: impairment can begin with the first drink.[157] As a result, even before obvious signs of intoxication emerge, the person's capacity to manage impulses and fully regulate their actions is already measurably diminished.

V. Further Impairments with Continued Alcohol Intoxication

With continued alcohol ingestion, its pharmacological effects cause widespread cognitive and behavioural impairments. These effects are usually graded – they worsen as blood alcohol concentration (BAC) rises – but do not necessarily happen all at once, they manifest across multiple functional domains. Here, we review evidence demonstrating impairments in some crucial cognitive modalities, including self-awareness and recognition of emotions.

[152] S Lannoy and others, 'Electrophysiological Correlates of Performance Monitoring in Binge Drinking: Impaired Error-Related but Preserved Feedback Processing' (2017) 128 *Clinical Neurophysiology* 2110.

[153] Fairbairn, Kang and Federmeier (n 149).

[154] ibid.

[155] J Weafer and MT Fillmore, 'Comparison of Alcohol Impairment of Behavioral and Attentional Inhibition' (2012) 126 *Drug and Alcohol Dependence* 176; Fillmore and Vogel-Sprott (n 18).

[156] Field and others, 'Acute Alcohol Effects' (n 13).

[157] Lannoy and others (n 152).

A. Alcohol Myopia: Narrowed Attention

Alcohol myopia is the phenomenon in which intoxication narrows the scope of attention and impairs foresight, causing people to focus on immediate cues and to neglect distant, peripheral, or abstract considerations.[158] This 'tunnel vision' effect helps, in part, explain many of the relevant impairments (such as risk-taking and aggression) within a unifying framework.[159] Under alcohol's influence, attention gravitates to what is right in front of the person (concrete cues or feelings) and away from what is subtle or future-oriented.[160] For example, a drunk driver might pay attention to staying in the lane immediately but not process the eventual possibility of an accident or police stop, or they may concentrate on steering and underestimate how fast they're going or how poorly they're gauging distance because the nuanced feedback from the environment is not fully registering.

The myopia effect implies a reduced ability to integrate multiple cues. Intoxicated individuals struggle to juggle complex information, especially when some require abstract reasoning or weighing future consequences.[161] Instead, the salient dominates (whether it be a tempting reward or a provoking insult), leading to simplified decision-making that often skews toward short-term gratification or reactive responses. Moreover, alcohol myopia is thought to be dose-dependent.[162] At very low BACs, a person might still consider longer-term factors reasonably well, but their mental horizon contracts as BAC increases.[163] High levels of intoxication can essentially create a state of moment-to-moment living, where only the present matters.[164] This might explain why severely intoxicated individuals often make bafflingly shortsighted choices (eg, starting a fight in front of a police officer or attempting to walk along a highway) – they are most likely not thinking beyond the here and now or noticing critical peripheral details.

[158] CM Steele and RA Josephs, 'Alcohol Myopia: Its Prized and Dangerous Effects' (1990) 45 *American Psychologist* 921.

[159] Chermack and Giancola (n 8); CM Steele and L Southwick, 'Alcohol and Social Behavior I: The Psychology of Drunken Excess' (1985) 48 *Journal of Personality and Social Psychology* 18.

[160] Chermack and Giancola (n 8); Steele and Southwick (n 159).

[161] KA Fleming and others, 'Effects of Alcohol on Sequential Information Processing: Evidence for Temporal Myopia' (2013) 27 *Psychology of Addictive Behaviors* 184; I Mocaiber and others, 'Alcohol, Emotion and Attention: Revisiting the Alcohol Myopia Theory' (2011) 24 *Psicologia: Reflexão e Crítica* 403.

[162] Fleming and others (n 161); AE Jaffe, CM Harris and D DiLillo, 'Observing Alcohol Myopia in the Context of a Trauma Film Paradigm: Differential Recall of Central and Peripheral Details' (2019) 43 *Alcoholism: Clinical and Experimental Research* 2203.

[163] Jaffe, Harris and DiLillo (n 162).

[164] ibid.

B. Metacognitive Awareness (or Lack Thereof) During Intoxication

Earlier, in section III we discussed some metacognitive impairments that could precede the initiation of intoxication. Here, we are back to metacognitive impairments, although after some degree of intoxication (as opposed to pre-drinking).[165] There seems to have been recent contention in the area,[166] but frequently research seems to suggest that intoxicated individuals often exhibit poor self-assessment of their abilities – essentially, they don't know that they don't know how impaired they are.[167] This is a metacognitive impairment: impairment in the ability to evaluate that one's own state is compromised. The result is often overconfidence in skills and judgment despite actual impairment.[168]

For instance, in a controlled trial, drivers at blood alcohol levels of 0.05–0.08 per cent (depending on jurisdiction, at the legal limit for driving) exhibited evident driving deficits. Still, they remained overly confident in their driving skills.[169] Empirical research with individuals who have a history of DUI (driving under the influence) illustrates this well. Van Dyke and Fillmore found that while alcohol-impaired driving performance was equal in DUI drivers and sober drivers, the DUI group was far more confident in their driving after drinking.[170] These drivers perceived themselves as fit to drive when they were not, which likely contributed to their decision to drink and drive. Overconfidence under alcohol extends beyond driving – intoxicated people may misjudge their coordination (leading to

[165] Also, one needs to be careful not to confuse self-awareness (being discussed here) with self-monitoring, discussed in s IV as one of the early impairments. Self-awareness involves metacognitive judgments about one's cognitive/emotional states (eg, 'Am I recognising emotions accurately?'). Self-monitoring focuses on tracking behaviours, for example, a food diary revealing discrepancies between perceived and actual eating habits. A key-difference is that self-awareness is metacognitive (internal judgment), while self-monitoring is behavioural (external tracking).

[166] See JR Evans and others, 'Alcohol Intoxication and Metamemory: Little Evidence That Moderate Intoxication Impairs Metacognitive Monitoring Processes' (2017) 31 *Applied Cognitive Psychology* 573; LA Monds and others, 'No Evidence That Alcohol Intoxication Impairs Judgments of Learning in Face Recognition' (2019) 33 *Applied Cognitive Psychology* 325.

[167] Eg, TO Nelson and others, 'Effect of Acute Alcohol Intoxication on Recall and on Judgments of Learning During the Acquisition of New Information' in TO Nelson and others (eds), *Metacognition and Cognitive Neuropsychology* (New York, Psychology Press, 2014); CA Honan and others, 'Alcohol Intoxication Impairs Recognition of Fear and Sadness in Others and Metacognitive Awareness of Emotion Recognition Ability' (2018) 18 *Emotion* 842; M Sauerland, NJ Broers and KIM van Oorsouw, 'Two Field Studies on the Effects of Alcohol on Eyewitness Identification, Confidence, and Decision Times' (2019) 33 *Applied Cognitive Psychology* 370.

[168] Monds and others (n 166).

[169] H Garrisson and others, 'Effects of Alcohol Intoxication on Driving Performance, Confidence in Driving Ability, and Psychomotor Function: A Randomized, Double-Blind, Placebo-Controlled Study' (2022) 239 *Psychopharmacology* 3893.

[170] N van Dyke and MT Fillmore, 'Alcohol Effects on Simulated Driving Performance and Self-Perceptions of Impairment in DUI Offenders' (2014) 22 *Experimental and Clinical Psychopharmacology* 484.

accidents), their social comportment (leading to inappropriate or criminal acts), their ability to handle conflict (leading them to start fights they cannot control), and, more recently, even their ability to recognise facial emotions.[171] In short, alcohol impairs self-monitoring, creating a gap between actual impairment and perceived impairment.

At the same time as alcohol diminishes one's ability to make subtle judgments, it also affects judgment confidence. There is preliminary evidence that moderate intoxication does not dramatically alter certain metacognitive judgments (eg, feeling-of-knowing) in straightforward tasks, suggesting that an individual might still report knowing they forgot something while under the influence.[172] However, overconfidence is common in more complex judgment domains (eg, social behaviour or driving skill), consistent with the phenomenon of 'alcohol myopia'.[173] For example, impairment in the ability to discriminate between correct and incorrect responses in emotion recognition has been observed, indicating reduced insight into one's own perceptual accuracy when intoxicated.[174]

We see this in social settings with the so-called 'beer goggles' effect: alcohol increases one's confidence in judgments of attractiveness or sexual interest, which can be viewed as a metacognitive distortion (overestimating one's chances or misreading signals while also being less aware of one's own inebriated state).[175] Similarly, an intoxicated person might be sure they are right in an argument due to inflated confidence, even when they are wrong.[176]

C. Alcohol's Effects on Social Cognition and Emotion Recognition

Alcohol doesn't just affect one's own internal control; it also affects how individuals perceive and interpret other people and social situations. This is important when considering crimes or harm that occur in social contexts (bar fights, domestic violence, sexual assault, etc) because misreading social cues or emotional signals

[171] AS Attwood and MR Munafò, 'Effects of Acute Alcohol Consumption and Processing of Emotion in Faces: Implications for Understanding Alcohol-Related Aggression' (2014) 28 *Journal of Psychopharmacology* 719.

[172] TO Nelson and others, 'Effects of Alcohol Intoxication on Metamemory and on Retrieval From Long-Term Memory' (1986) 115 *Journal of Experimental Psychology: General* 247.

[173] Mocaiber and others (n 161).

[174] CA Honan and others, 'Alcohol Intoxication Impairs Recognition of Fear and Sadness in Others and Metacognitive Awareness of Emotion Recognition Ability' (2018) 18 *Emotion* 842. This lack of awareness of impairment can have significant applied implications, hindering individuals' ability to adapt their behaviour in response to the environment, and without even realising that they are impaired.

[175] Attwood and Munafò (n 171).

[176] H Garrisson and others, 'Effects of Alcohol Intoxication on Driving Performance, Confidence in Driving Ability, and Psychomotor Function: A Randomized, Double-Blind, Placebo-Controlled Study' (2022) 239 *Psychopharmacology* 3893.

can contribute to those outcomes.[177] Alcohol can alter how we perceive and respond to other people, even at moderate intoxication levels.[178] Emotion recognition may become less accurate: some studies find that intoxicated individuals have trouble identifying certain facial expressions – for example, reduced ability to recognise fear or sadness in others' faces.[179] Although recent systematic reviews have shown that not all specific emotion recognition deficits are consistent across studies, misreading social cues becomes more likely at higher doses.[180]

Impairments in the theory of mind (ToM), which involves understanding others' perspectives and intentions, have also been documented. For instance, moderate alcohol exposure in a lab setting was shown to make people less adept at perspective-taking in a social task, especially when alcohol-related cues were present.[181] This suggests that intoxication (and even alcohol cues) can hinder one's ability to interpret what others know or intend, which could affect trust and empathy.[182] In terms of social trust and cooperation, alcohol's disinhibiting effect might cut both ways: on one hand, lowered inhibitions can increase sociability and willingness to trust strangers (someone mildly intoxicated might share more or be overly friendly);[183] on the other hand, misreading social signals or emotional cues could lead to misplaced trust or failing to detect untrustworthiness.[184]

Alcohol also affects social decision-making in moral or ethical contexts – as seen as part of social cognition. A large placebo-controlled study (0.6 g/kg alcohol, about ~.08 per cent BAC in many individuals) found that even a moderate dose selectively impaired moral reasoning: intoxicated participants shifted toward more utilitarian judgments, favouring outcomes over strict adherence to rules. In practical terms, they were more willing to make decisions that violated normative 'do no harm' rules if it achieved a perceived greater good, which indicates that alcohol can change the weighting of moral principles.[185] This dose also reduced altruistic

[177] Chermack and Giancola (n 8).

[178] Honan and others (n 174); AP Eastwood and others, 'Effects of Acute Alcohol Consumption on Emotion Recognition in High and Low Trait Aggressive Drinkers' (2020) 34 *Journal of Psychopharmacology* 1226; Sanov, Kumar and Creswell (n 20); JN Khouja and others, 'Effects of Acute Alcohol Consumption on Emotion Recognition in Social Alcohol Drinkers' (2019) 33 *Journal of Psychopharmacology* 326; Kano and others (n 20).

[179] Attwood and Munafò (n 171); Sanov, Kumar and Creswell (n 20).

[180] Sanov, Kumar and Creswell (n 20); Khouja and others (n 178).

[181] S Lannoy and others, 'Disentangling the Role of Social Cognition Processes at Early Steps of Alcohol Abuse: The Influence of Affective Theory of Mind' (2020) 102 *Addictive Behaviors* 106187; RL Monk and others, 'In People Who Drink More, Facets of Theory of Mind May Be Impaired by Alcohol Stimuli' (2023) 245 *Drug and Alcohol Dependence* 109811.

[182] Lannoy and others (n 181); Monk and others (n 181).

[183] J Dong, Q Zhao and Y Ren, 'Dark Side or Bright Side: The Impact of Alcohol Drinking on the Trust of Chinese Rural Residents' (2022) 19 *International Journal of Environmental Research and Public Health* 5924.

[184] ibid; AK Seid, 'Social Interactions, Trust and Risky Alcohol Consumption' (2016) 6 *Health Economics Review* 3.

[185] AA Duke and L Bègue, 'The Drunk Utilitarian: Blood Alcohol Concentration Predicts Utilitarian Responses in Moral Dilemmas' (2015) 134 *Cognition* 121; H Karlsson and others, 'Acute Effects of Alcohol on Social and Personal Decision Making (2022) 47 *Neuropsychopharmacology* 824.

behaviour in some measures, meaning that intoxication may make individuals more self-focused or shortsighted in social exchanges (eg, giving less to others or neglecting someone's discomfort).[186]

Interestingly, that same study noted little change in specific non-social risk tasks at 0.06 per cent, highlighting that social cognition might be uniquely sensitive to even moderate intoxication.[187] As intoxication increases, empathy and accurate social perception typically degrade further.[188] Extremely intoxicated individuals often miss subtle social cues (like someone's irritation or sadness), may respond inappropriately to others' emotions, and can become either overly trusting or inappropriately suspicious.[189] These impairments grow with higher intoxication, potentially contributing to social misperceptions or conflicts during drunken encounters.

D. Aggression & Hostility Biases

Finally and further to the above social-emotional impairments, alcohol also has a long-recognised connection to increased aggression. A significant proportion of violent crimes and assaults occur under the influence of alcohol.[190] The pharmacological effects of alcohol might contribute to this by lowering inhibitions (making existing aggressive impulses harder to suppress) and/or by altering cognitive appraisals of social situations.[191] One key cognitive change is a heightened hostile attribution bias when intoxicated – that is, perceiving ambiguous actions of others as hostile or provocative.[192] Research indicates that alcohol can lead to ambiguous social interactions being perceived as hostile.[193] For example, a drunk person might interpret an accidental bump as a deliberate shove or a neutral comment as an insult. Where a sober person might just ignore, this alcohol-related type of bias might trigger instead an aggressive response. Thus, alcohol might make benign cues feel threatening.[194] Relatedly, a recent series of studies in our lab showed that, compared to no-alcohol receiving subjects (placebo and controls), individuals in the high BAC group (0.08 per cent) avoided the stimuli perceived as hostile less,

[186] Duke and Bègue (n 185).
[187] ibid.
[188] Lannoy and others (n 181).
[189] Khouja and others (n 178); Sanov, Kumar and Creswell (n 20).
[190] Wilson, Graham and Taft (n 10).
[191] PR Giancola 'Executive Functioning: A Conceptual Framework for Alcohol-Related Aggression' (2000) 8 *Experimental and Clinical Psychopharmacology* 576.
[192] S Klein Tuente, S Bogaerts and W Veling, 'Hostile Attribution Bias and Aggression in Adults – a Systematic Review' (2019) 46 *Aggression and Violent Behavior* 66; CN DeWall and others, 'It's the Thought That Counts: The Role of Hostile Cognition in Shaping Aggressive Responses to Social Exclusion' (2009) 96 *Journal of Personality and Social Psychology* 45; A Pabst and others, 'Hostile Attributional Bias in Severe Alcohol Use Disorder' (2020) 129 *Journal of Psychiatric Research* 176.
[193] ibid.
[194] CS Sripada and others, 'Effects of Alcohol on Brain Responses to Social Signals of Threat in Humans' (2011) 55 *NeuroImage* 371.

and in a subsequent naturalistic study individuals who consumed very high doses (0.12 per cent), approached stimuli that they perceived as hostile more, suggesting a dose-dependent effect of behavioural decisions in the presence of perceived hostility.[195]

Aggression under alcohol might further be understood by the earlier noted inhibition conflict model of alcohol myopia.[196] In a provocative situation, there may be instigating cues (eg, someone's angry expression that encourages confrontation) and inhibitory cues (eg, fighting could result in arrest). When sober, a person in conflict can evaluate both, and often, restraint wins out. Alcohol, however, narrows attention to the most salient cues and impairs the processing of subtler inhibitory cues.[197] Suppose an intoxicated individual fixates on the immediate instigating cue (eg feeling disrespected) and fails to fully register the reasons to refrain (future consequences, empathy for the other person). In that case, an aggressive reaction becomes more likely. This is why alcohol-fuelled aggression often occurs, particularly in high-conflict situations – the person's focus locks onto the provocative aspect, and they effectively become blind to calming or restraining information.

Studies have confirmed that alcohol increases aggressive behaviour, especially in individuals prone to aggression or in situations that are provoking.[198] Not everyone becomes aggressive when drunk (personality and context matter greatly), but for those with aggressive tendencies, intoxication is a potent facilitator.[199] Furthermore, graded impairment is evident: at low intoxication, a person might just become more argumentative or irritable; at higher intoxication, they may become physically aggressive over minor provocations.[200] Their ability to foresee the consequences of aggression or to empathise with the victim wanes as intoxication deepens, contributing to more extreme acts of violence that sober they would never commit.[201]

Findings such as the latter may be among the most directly relevant to legal questions around intoxicated offenders, and the experiments that yielded them were designed for this reason. Specifically, if a defendant would not have believed that they were in danger but for their intoxication, the law does not seem to treat that belief as warranting mistaken self-defence.[202] The legal logic seems to be at odds with empirical evidence showing that alcohol reliably distorts threat perception and subsequent behavioural approach and avoidance choices to threat. And, once again, we must debate whether it is fair to expect laypeople to anticipate these cognitive distortions in advance of drinking.

[195] Publications under preparation.

[196] Mocaiber and others (n 161).

[197] ibid.

[198] Eg, PR Giancola and others, 'Alcohol, Violence, and the Alcohol Myopia Model: Preliminary Findings and Implications for Prevention' (2011) 36 *Addictive Behaviors* 1019.

[199] Attwood and Munafò (n 171); Eastwood and others (n 178).

[200] Chermack and Giancola (n 8).

[201] ibid.

[202] Child (n 7).

VI. Conclusions and Potential for Future Research

In this chapter, we reviewed the processes that can affect the initial decision to consume alcohol, the effects of alcohol priming on subsequent alcohol craving and consumption, and the impairments seen during acute alcohol intoxication. Our main argument is that: (1) the action of drinking; and (2) deciding to drink are not the same process from a neuroscientific point of view, and thus, we propose that discussions of responsibility and voluntariness should involve this nuance. Furthermore, we argue that even when considering the moment of action (T1), there may be room to consider that impairments begin very early and in a non-linear manner, which further complicates debates on voluntariness and control. We chose to focus on alcohol here precisely due to practical considerations: Alcohol is a legally available drug, and it frequently appears in offences involving aggression or negligence.[203] Many other controlled substances lack similarly extensive legal and regulatory frameworks, partly because they are less prevalent or give rise to different patterns of offending.[204] Despite its licit status, alcohol shares with other psychoactive drugs the capacity to impair judgment, reduce inhibition, and distort risk perception.[205] Yet one key difference is the predictable dose-response relationship many individuals learn through repeated alcohol use: most adult drinkers recognise that beyond a certain point, they become disinhibited or emotionally volatile.[206] By contrast, less socially normalised drugs may not carry the same cultural script – first-time or casual users may be ignorant of the potency or specific psychoactive effects. However, the structure of prior fault remains broadly similar: if you voluntarily ingest a mind-altering substance, you may be held responsible for any actions performed while impaired. Nevertheless, the processes involved in drinking behaviour outlined here, even though they apply to intoxication from other drugs, have quite different effects between drugs and depend heavily on several contextual factors.[207]

The concept of prior fault in law holds individuals accountable for choosing a state of impaired capacity.[208] Still, modern research complicates this narrative, revealing that a host of factors beyond black-and-white voluntariness mediate the choice to drink and the subsequent impairments. Indeed, the findings suggest that impairments are more nuanced, especially when one uses a chronological timeline

[203] D Nutt, LA King and LD Phillips, 'Drug Harms in the UK: A Multicriteria Decision Analysis' (2010) 376 *Lancet* 1558.

[204] SJ Morse, 'A Good Enough Reason: Addiction, Agency and Criminal Responsibility' (2013) 56 *Inquiry* 490.

[205] MS Mumenthaler and others, 'Psychoactive Drugs and Pilot Performance: A Comparison of Nicotine, Donepezil, and Alcohol Effects' (2003) 28 *Neuropsychopharmacology* 1366.

[206] M Benedek and L Zöhrer, 'Creativity on Tap 2: Investigating Dose Effects of Alcohol on Cognitive Control and Creative Cognition' (2020) 83 *Consciousness and Cognition* 102972.

[207] SH Ahmed and others, 'Non-Pharmacological Factors That Determine Drug Use and Addiction' (2020) 110 *Neuroscience & Biobehavioral Reviews* 3.

[208] Crombag, Child and Fortson (n 19).

to conceptually separate influencing factors and impairments. In this chapter we looked at three points, starting with the usually ignored moment before taking the first drink. As we observed, at the pre-drinking stage, factors like cues, cravings, stress, and mis-calibrated foresight play a significant role in why and how a person becomes intoxicated. During drinking, acute cognitive impairments and emotional distortions explain what the person does while drunk. The fact that the impairment can start very early, with priming effects that make the person prone to drinking a further glass, and with impairments in inhibitory control, makes us question whether there is such a thing as a non-risky amount of drinking.

Traditional legal analysis of intoxicated offences has tended to blur these phases, effectively treating the entire episode as one continuous course of conduct for which the initial decision is responsible.[209] We incorporate scientific insights for a more refined approach to emerge. For instance, before T1, one might ask, what was the individual's mental state and knowledge? Did they plan to get drunk? Did they have reason to expect they might commit a crime or lose control (eg, known propensity for violence when drunk), or were they overtaken by situational pressures or false confidence? Science can help identify which factors are foreseeable and which might not be, although legal discussions consequently need to address whether such findings ought to bear legal relevance. Our goal with such interdisciplinary dialogue is thus not to excuse wrongful acts, but to ensure that culpability is assigned in proportion to the actual capacities and faults of the accused, informed by the best available evidence.

Finally, while the evidence presented here on the factors influencing the decision to drink and how acute alcohol itself impacts ongoing motivation and behaviour during a drinking episode, the studies presented only looked at the effects of alcohol not mixed with energy drinks or caffeine. More research is needed in this area to fully understand the processes that motivate the decision to consume such mixed beverages and the exact effects they have on behaviour inhibition, error monitoring, self-awareness, and perceptions of emotion and hostility. Similarly, more research is needed to understand poly-substance intoxication effects.

[209] Sinclair-House, Child and Crombag (n 19); Child, Crombag and Fortson (n 19).

8

Addiction and Automatism

CLAIRE HOGG

I. Introduction

In England and Wales, defendants whose involuntary state was due to voluntary intoxication cannot be exculpated on grounds of automatism. But why is this the case? If the concept of legal automatism is founded on some version of the voluntary act requirement, then *ceteris paribus* the absence of voluntariness in these cases ought to preclude culpability. The question, then, is: which things are unequal in voluntary intoxication cases? The typical answer is prior fault. Since culpability cannot attach directly to involuntary action, it must derive from the operation of prior fault principles. Taking this framework as a given, then, the question concerning us is: can chemical addiction mitigate that 'prior fault' culpability in cases of voluntary intoxication and, if so, how?

The significance of this question is clear: if we believe that addiction is in *any* instance capable of mitigating a defendant's fault for (eg) taking a drink, then there are at least *some* cases of voluntary intoxication in which addiction may provide grounds to reject denials of automatism on a prior fault basis. Consequently, a blanket rule against the application of automatism rules in voluntary intoxication cases should be rejected. Of course, the degree to which addiction is capable of mitigating fault – and the nature of that mitigation – is far from clear. Naturally, this chapter does not purport to resolve the debate regarding addiction, voluntary intoxication, automatism, and culpability; what it does aim to do, however, is offer some clarification as to the relationships between these concepts. Over the course of this chapter, I will attempt to untangle some of the threads connecting automatism, voluntariness/the 'voluntary act requirement', prior fault rules, and addiction, to hopefully provide us with a clearer frame of reference for understanding how these concepts might work together. In the process, I will consider different models by which the relevance of addiction to prior fault culpability can be analysed and understood, including control/free will, theories of sufficient concern, and theories of reasonable or normative expectations. I will conclude, finally, with some general observations as to the preferable path forward.

II. On Legal Automatism

To begin, it may be helpful to differentiate two senses of the term 'automatism': the general sense and the strictly legal sense. Automatism, in the general sense, refers to a state in which a person's body moves without their conscious input – they move, in other words, as an automaton moves, independent of thought, deliberation, intention, or (potentially) even conscious awareness. The paradigmatic example here is the sleepwalker, whose body moves while his mind slumbers. It should be noted, however, that the key condition is not *un*consciousness per se, but lack of conscious, deliberative control;[1] as such, the term has been interpreted to apply to cases of psychomotor epilepsy,[2] as well as states of clouded consciousness in which the individual is technically awake but mentally 'absent'.[3] Accordingly, the Court of Appeal has described automatism as 'unconscious involuntary action [wherein] the mind *does not go with* what is being done'.[4]

Automatism in the strictly legal sense, meanwhile, refers on the most straightforward analysis to a particular legal defence for which general-sense automatism is the qualifying condition. It provides a defendant with a complete defence,[5] but is subject to certain requirements – first, that the lack of conscious control is complete;[6] second that the cause of the general-sense automatism does not fall within the scope of the status test for insanity;[7] and third that culpability cannot be

[1] See, eg, AP Simester and others, *Simester and Sullivan's Criminal Law: Theory and Doctrine* (Oxford, Hart Publishing, 2010) 112, cited in Law Commission, *Criminal Liability: Insanity and Automatism Discussion Paper* (2013) para 5.2: 'What counts is the inability to deliberatively control one's conduct – that one's movements are not responsive to a capacity to reason and deliberate about one's conduct. Obviously, where the defendant is altogether unconscious, her reasoning capacities will be inactive. But a defendant need not be unconscious before these capacities may be suppressed or inoperative.'

[2] *Bratty v Attorney-General for Northern Ireland* [1963] AC 386.

[3] See, eg, *R v T* [1990] Crim LR 256, in which a defence of automatism was granted to a defendant who had acted in a 'dream-like' or fugue state attributable to post-traumatic stress following a sexual assault.

[4] *Bratty* (n 2), emphasis mine. It may be interesting to contrast, however, the definition from the New Zealand Court of Appeal in *R v Cottle* [1958] NZLR 999, 1020 (cited in *Bratty* (n 2)), which is given as: 'action without any knowledge of acting, or action without any consciousness of what is being done'. Interestingly, this definition does seem to imply that a lack of conscious *awareness* is crucial to the concept rather than simply a lack of conscious *control* – although subsequent case law, at least in England and Wales, does not seem to bear this requirement out.

[5] Provided, that is, that the offence in question is not one of strict liability – see, eg, *R v Larsonneur* [1933] 24 Cr App R 74 for an example of a case where liability was found despite the lack of deliberate action on the part of the defendant.

[6] That is to say that the defence will fail if the defendant retains *any* control over his or her actions – see, eg, *Broome v Perkins* [1987] 85 Cr App R 321, in which the defence was denied to a diabetic defendant who had fallen into a hypoglycaemic state while driving, on the grounds that, while his awareness was impaired, he retained sufficient conscious control to direct the vehicle out of the path of other drivers at certain points during the journey.

[7] The relationship between insanity and automatism in English and Welsh law is complex, and requires rather more explanation than it is possible to provide here. Briefly – where a defendant acts in a state of general-sense automatism, the law interrogates the cause of the automatous state in order to determine whether automatism or insanity rules should apply. If the cause is held to be *internal* (eg: chemical imbalance, psychological or physiological illness, brain tumour, arteriosclerosis, etc) the

made out on the basis of prior fault.[8] I call this understanding of legal automatism 'the ordinary view', as it is the analysis most frequently encountered within judgments, commentary, and textbooks:[9]

The ordinary view:
Automatism is a special excusing defence that applies where a defendant, at the relevant time, completely and faultlessly lacked conscious control over his bodily movements for reasons not falling within the scope of legal insanity.

In recent years, however, the ordinary view of automatism has increasingly been subject to challenge. According to some commentators, the orthodox understanding of legal automatism as a positive defence is misguided; in reality, the exculpatory function of general-sense automatism can only be understood in terms of act negation.[10] I will call this the alternative view:

The alternative view:
What we call legal 'automatism' amounts to a specific kind of act negation tied to a lack of voluntariness on the part of the defendant.

The alternative view is rooted in an understanding of *voluntariness* as a crucial element of criminal conduct. It is a generally accepted principle that culpability requires a voluntary act; this is sometimes referred to as the 'voluntary act requirement' (VAR), and it is set out within the US Model Penal Code in the following way: 'A person is not guilty of an offence unless his liability is based on conduct which includes a voluntary act or the omission to perform an act of which he is physically capable.'[11] The rationale underlying the VAR is perhaps best expressed

defendant will fall within insanity rules and (subject to fulfilment of the M'Naghten test for insanity) be entitled to a defence on those grounds. If the cause is held to be *external* (eg: physical injury, gas leak, carbon monoxide poisoning, etc) legal automatism applies, and the defendant will be entitled to an unqualified acquittal. Consequently, many paradigmatic cases of general sense-automatism – sleepwalking, for example – do not in practice give rise to a 'defence' of legal automatism, but fall instead under the rules of insanity. For a full discussion of the relationship between automatism and insanity in England and Wales see C Hogg and JJ Child, 'Not Guilty by Reasons Other than Insanity' in AP Simester (ed), *Modern Criminal Law: Essays in Honour of G R Sullivan* (London, Bloomsbury, 2024). For case law, see, eg, *Bratty* (n 2); *R v Kemp* [1957] 1 QB 399; *R v Quick* [1973] 3 WLR 26; *R v Hennessey* [1989] 2 All ER 9; *R v Burgess* [1991] 2 QB 92.

[8] This principle is set out particularly clearly in Scots law, which specifies that for the defence to apply, the automatism cannot be self-induced, nor brought about by a cause which the defendant was 'bound to foresee' (*Ross v HM Advocate* [1991] JC 210). In English and Welsh law, Lawton LJ references the same exclusionary conditions of self-induction and foreseeability in *Quick* (n 7).

[9] Within England and Wales, that is. Notably, there are jurisdictions – Germany and the Netherlands among them – in which the alternative view constitutes the orthodox position.

[10] See, eg, JJ Child and A Reed, 'Automatism Is Never a Defence' [2014] *Northern Ireland Legal Quarterly* 167; Hogg and Child (n 7).

[11] US Model Penal Code s 2.01. Note the inclusion of omissions here – this has led some commentators to prefer 'voluntary conduct principle' over 'voluntary act requirement' (see, eg, J Mason, 'The

by Hart, who states that in cases of involuntary conduct, 'both the ordinary man and the ordinary lawyer might well [say] that […] there is not "really" a human action at all …'.[12] In other words, involuntary movements of the body do not constitute *actions* in the sense required for criminal responsibility; to identify a defendant's conduct as involuntary is not to present an excuse for his actions but to deny that he acted at all. For this reason, it may be natural to think of the voluntary act requirement as being part of – or foundational to – the *actus reus* of the crime; without voluntariness, there is no act, criminal or otherwise. This, then, is the logic of the alternative view: if general-sense automatism refers to behaviour enacted without conscious control, then cases falling within the scope of legal automatism are cases in which the defendant acted involuntarily. If the defendant acted involuntarily, then a key element of criminal conduct is missing. In principle, this ought to be sufficient grounds for exculpation without the need for any positive excusing defence.[13]

A frustrating feature of the discussion around automatism is how much of it sits within a fuzzy middle ground between the ordinary and alternative views. In this in-between space, the prosecution's inability to prove voluntariness is taken to provide the basis for automatism as a positive defence, effectively conceptualising automatism as defence *and* act negation simultaneously. Robert Schopp, for example, describes automatism as a 'failure-of-proof defence regarding the voluntary act requirement',[14] while the Law Commission offers an interpretation that thoroughly blurs the lines between *actus reus* and defences: 'We believe that the correct classification of the defence is as a denial of actus reus. That classification is important in reflecting the true basis of the defence as a denial of voluntary "action"….'[15] My inclination is to regard this kind of conceptual muddying as a mistake – to accept that act negation can serve as grounds for a positive defence is to erode the line between elements of the crime and defences almost to the point of total erasure. If we wish to speak coherently about automatism, then we have to decide, once and for all, whether it is to be conceived as a special defence (the ordinary view) or a subset of act negation (the alternative view). My preference is for the latter;[16] that said, for the purposes of this chapter, I will consider the implications of both models for our subsequent understanding of the role of prior fault in the context of legal automatism. What should become clear in the following discussion is which of these two competing analyses we adopt will necessarily impact our

Willed Trance: Volition, Voluntariness and Hypnotised Defendants' (2021) 85(1) *The Journal of Criminal Law* 26).

[12] HLA Hart, 'Acts of Will and Responsibility' in *Punishment and Responsibility: Essays in the Philosophy of Law* (Oxford, Oxford University Press, 1968) 107. See also Law Commission (n 1): '[A]n act done without voluntary control is not an act at all for the purposes of the criminal law'.

[13] For a comprehensive account of this view see Child and Reed (n 9).

[14] RF Schopp, *Automatism, Insanity, and the Psychology of Criminal Responsibility* (Cambridge, Cambridge University Press, 1991) 132.

[15] Law Commission (n 1) 5.8.

[16] For discussion see Hogg and Child (n 7).

understanding of the function and role of prior fault in this context – and, consequently, our understanding of the role addiction would need to play in order to be capable of undermining or blocking that prior fault mechanism.

III. On Prior Fault

We will begin with a very straightforward example. At time T1, D voluntarily engages in a bout of heavy drinking. A few hours into the evening, D is so intoxicated as to be in a state of (general sense) automatism – technically awake but lacking conscious, deliberative control over his actions. At time T2, while still in this state, D ends up in an altercation with V, which concludes with D punching V in the face. To summarise this simple scenario, then:

T1: D engages in heavy drinking, leading to a state of blackout drunkenness at T2.
T2: While blackout drunk, D punches V in the face, causing injury.

The current legal position is that, even though D acted automatously (that is, without conscious control) at T2, he will not be able to avoid legal liability for his conduct at that time through appeal to legal automatism. The reason for this is that D's voluntary intoxication at T1 engages prior fault rules, which then operate to prevent his automatism at T2 from playing its usual exculpatory role.[17]

How *precisely* we understand the operation of prior fault here depends, however, on which understanding of automatism we adopt. If automatism is an excusing defence, then prior fault can be straightforwardly conceptualised as undermining that excuse; automatism will *only* provide a defendant with an excuse *if* it cannot be attributed to culpable prior conduct.[18] If, however, automatism is understood in terms of act negation, then the role of prior fault requires further examination. In the hope of bringing some clarity to the discussion, I will set out the following competing frameworks for understanding prior fault rules *vis-à-vis* automatism.

Framework 1 (Prior Fault on the Ordinary View)

Definition of Automatism: Automatism is a positive defence in which D has an excuse on the grounds that his action was performed without conscious control.
Prior Fault Condition: That excuse is blocked/does not apply if the defendant brought about the circumstances of that loss of consciousness through his or her own culpable action.

[17] *R v Lipman* [1970] 1 QB 152; *Quick* (n 7); *R v Coley & Ors* [2013] Crim LR 923 CA.

[18] We might identify, here, a parallel to the rule which excludes from the defence of duress defendants who voluntarily involved themselves in situations in which pressure to perform criminal activity might reasonably be expected (*R v Hasan* [2005] 2 AC 467).

On this conceptualisation, the absence of prior fault is a necessary (but not sufficient) condition for the excusing defence of automatism. Automatism provides a defendant with an excuse *only if* that automatism was not brought about by faulty prior conduct. The outstanding question on this framework is, therefore, to determine what makes prior conduct faulty, with reference typically made to self-induction and/or reasonable foreseeability of harm.[19] Of course, this framework only works if we adopt the ordinary view of automatism; that is, if automatism is understood as a positive defence. If the alternative view is preferred, we will need a different analysis of the role of prior fault – one that fits with the conception of automatism as a kind of act negation. To wit:

Framework 2 (Prior Fault on the Alternative View)

Definition of Automatism: What we call legal 'automatism' amounts to a specific kind of act negation tied to a lack of voluntariness on the part of the defendant.
Prior Fault Condition (Option A): Where D's autonomous state at T2 was brought about by an earlier culpable act at T1, overall fault can be imputed despite the involuntariness of the conduct at T2.
OR
Prior Fault Condition (Option B): Where D's automatous state at T2 was brought about by an earlier voluntary act at T1, the voluntariness of this act can be taken to fulfil the VAR at T2.

On this framework, rather than blocking a defence, prior fault plays the same role with regard to absent voluntariness as it has taken to play with regard to absent *mens rea* in the line of cases culminating in *Majewski*.[20] As Hans Crombag et al describe it, in these cases prior fault rules allow us to construct or manufacture liability by looking backwards down the causal chain of events that led to the act to which liability is attached. In their words: 'Although a defendant may lack the requisite *mens rea* when causing harm … the intoxication rules allow us to look back in time to assess whether such mental states or beliefs are attributable to the voluntary ingestion of drugs and/or alcohol.'[21] If so, the law permits the creation of a 'legal fiction: constructing liability essentially by equating the fault for a specific crime with the fault for becoming voluntarily intoxicated'. This can be referred to as 'imputing fault'.[22]

[19] See, eg, Lawton LJ in *Quick* (n 7), discussing the limits to automatism as a defence: 'A self-induced incapacity will not excuse … not will one nor will one which could have been reasonably foreseen as a result of either doing or omitting to do something, as, for example, taking alcohol against medical advice after using certain prescribed drugs or failing to have regular meals while taking insulin.' See also Hughes LJ in *R v Coley & Ors* (n 17), who read Lawton LJ's comments in *Quick* as stating that automatism 'did not amount to a defence if it was voluntarily self-induced or caused by doing, or omitting to do, something which the defendant ought to have foreseen might lead to the condition'.

[20] *DPP v Majewski* [1976] UKHL 2.

[21] HS Crombag, JJ Child and GR Sullivan, 'Drunk, Dangerous and Delusional: How Legal Concept-Creep Risks Overcriminalization' (2020) 115 *Addiction* 2201.

[22] ibid.

Even still, there are different possible ways in which this move can be conceptualised, depending on precisely what we take prior fault to be reconstructing. On one read (Option A), what is reconstructed or imputed is simply the fault, or culpability; while a defendant may not be directly at fault for actions taken while in a state of automatism, we may attribute culpability overall by pointing to *prior* fault in bringing about the automatous state. There is a direct parallel here to the rationale for limiting the degree to which voluntary intoxication can negate *mens rea* to cases of basic intent. Per Lord Elwyn-Jones in *Majewski*:

> If a man of his own volition takes a substance which causes him to cast off the restraints of reason and conscience, no wrong is done to him by holding him answerable criminally for any injury he may do while in that condition. His course of conduct in reducing himself by drugs and drink to that condition in my view supplies the evidence of *mens rea*, of guilty mind certainly sufficient for crimes of basic intent.[23]

In other words, unless the fault element is one of *specific* intent,[24] the law's position is that the fault the defendant bears for taking the intoxicating substance is sufficient to fulfil the overall fault element for the crime, regardless of the defendant's mental state at the actual time of its commission. Applying a similar rationale to voluntariness, then, we might claim that while a lack of voluntariness at T2 would ordinarily negate fault for actions taken at T2, in cases of voluntary intoxication we can impute fault on the basis of culpable drink-taking at T1.

There are, however, a few difficulties with this analysis. First, a consequence of this interpretation is that it does appear to undermine, or at least to dilute, the VAR – contrary to the VAR as set out in the Model Penal Code, it *is* possible for a defendant to be held responsible for conduct that involves no voluntary act, provided there is culpable action somewhere in the causal chain. In order to be consistent with this interpretation of prior fault rules, the VAR must be modified to specify that it is only *faultlessly* involuntary action, and not involuntary action per se, that precludes culpability. Relatedly, there is a kind of asymmetry in the automatism cases that does not apply (or does not necessarily apply) in the context of *mens rea*. The rationale in *Majewski* appeals to the idea of recklessness: so long as drink-taking at T1 can be construed as reckless, then that recklessness is enough to fulfil the missing MR condition at T2. But in cases of automatism, it is not the guilty mind per se that's missing, but more specifically *voluntariness*. In other words, in *Majewski* cases, the missing element at T2 is fulfilled by the presence of that same element at T1;[25] in the automatism cases, meanwhile, the missing act-based element at T2 (voluntary action) is taken to be

[23] *Majewski* (n 20) 474.

[24] In simplest terms, crimes of specific intent are those for which fault requires intention to bring about a *specific* outcome; murder, for example, is a specific intent crime in that its *mens rea* requires *intention to cause* either death or grievous bodily harm.

[25] Although it may not always do so very well; the failure of the fault element at T1 to consistently match up completely with the missing element at T2 has been raised as a potential problem for these cases – see Crombag and others (n 21).

fulfilled by appeal to the presence of a different, mind-based, element at T1 (fault/recklessness).[26]

For those troubled by this asymmetry, an alternative presents itself. In the context of automatism, perhaps it is not overall fault that prior fault operates to reconstruct, but precisely the missing voluntariness (Option B). On this analysis, the crucial fact about D's conduct at T1 is not that it was *culpable*, but that it was *voluntary* – and is, as such, capable of fulfilling the requirement for a voluntary act that was missing at T2. This account allows us to preserve the Voluntary Act Requirement; it does require us to accept, however, that the VAR does *not* require that the voluntary act in question has to constitute the conduct element of the relevant offence, but that the requirement can be met by voluntary conduct at some earlier stage in the causal chain. There is a certain logic to this argument. Suppose I knock over a domino that causes a chain reaction of three miles of dominoes over several hours, with the last domino setting off a bomb. In this case, the explosion would still be clearly traceable to my voluntary act, even though this may be temporally quite distinct from its occurrence. On reflection, however, this example is disanalogous to the voluntary intoxication case in a few important respects. First, the domino example involves one instance of conduct (the pushing of the first domino), while the intoxication example involves (at least) two: first the taking of the drink and then the punching of the victim. In the intoxication case, in other words, we are not looking at an act with a protracted consequence but at two discrete events, one of which fulfils the voluntary act requirement and the other of which fulfils the rest of the conduct element of the relevant offence. For this analysis of prior fault rules to work, then, we must accept that the two discrete events can be combined in such a way as to fulfil all necessary aspects of the *actus reus*. Likely the most natural way to achieve this is to conceptualise the taking of the drink at T1 and the punching of V at T2 not as two discrete *events*, but as two discrete *points* within one single event. Here, however, we run into our second dissimilarity with the domino case. The two events (or event-points) in the intoxication case are not inevitably or intrinsically connected in the same way as the pushing of the first domino is connected to the detonation of the bomb. The domino example is a clear case in which, absent a *novus actus interveniens*, the pushing of the first domino *will* lead to the detonation of the bomb, and it is this feature which makes it plausible to consider the two temporally distinct instances as points in one overarching event. The same cannot be said for the voluntary intoxication example; the taking of a drink at T1 does not inevitably lead to the specific assault at T2 absent an intervention. The most we can say is that D's intoxication at T1 makes it *very likely* that *something like* the assault at T2 will occur. This likelihood may be sufficient to attribute culpability to D's act of drinking at T1, but it does not seem enough to tie the two instances together

[26] A further concern with this interpretation is the possibility of a kind of infinite regress: If determinations of culpability are subject to prior fault rules, and if prior fault rules require prior determinations of culpability to be made, then it would seem to follow that those prior determinations of culpability must themselves be subject to prior fault rules – which would then require prior determinations of culpability to be made. And on and on it goes.

as a single discrete event, consisting of both a voluntary act *and* the additional conduct elements of the relevant offence. If, therefore, we want to adopt an analysis of prior fault as reconstructing voluntariness, it does seem to require us to accept that the voluntariness of D's conduct with respect to event E1 at time T1 can be carried forward to fulfil the voluntary act requirement for a discrete (albeit causally connected) event E2 at later time T2. This naturally leads to questions about when voluntariness can be carried forward in this way and when it cannot – after all, in addition to voluntarily becoming intoxicated, D also voluntarily left the house, and voluntarily ordered a taxi to the club. Why does D's drink-taking at T1 engage prior fault rules while his taxi-ordering at T0 does not, despite both actions being a) voluntary and b) points in a causal chain without which his automatous conduct at T2 could not have come about? To answer this question is beyond the scope of this chapter; I will only observe that it seems to me difficult to envision an answer to this question that does not invoke some kind of culpability condition; there is a sense of *blameworthiness* attached to the drink-taking that does not apply to the taxi-ordering, that makes the former alone a matter of prior fault. The question, in other words, may inevitably come back to the imputation of overall culpability in the end – with all the worries about asymmetry that come with it.

In any case, the purpose of this chapter is not to adjudicate between these competing analyses. Rather, my aim is to bring out some of the less obvious complexities of automatism as a legal concept, and of the relationship between automatism and prior fault. At this point in the discussion, then, our main takeaways should be the following: First, that how one conceptualises automatism naturally changes one's understanding of the role prior fault is playing; one cannot achieve clarity with respect to the latter without having first reached clarity on the former. Second, that it is in some respects easier to conceptualise the role and function of prior fault if automatism is understood as a defence. If automatism is understood as act negation, things get a little more complicated, conceptually. This, to be clear, is not a point against an interpretation of automatism as act negation – merely an observation that adopting this interpretation may necessitate a more complex analysis of prior fault rules in this context.

The final observation to be made at this stage is that which of the competing analyses of automatism, and consequently of prior fault, we adopt will inevitably affect our understanding of the role addiction might play in (potentially) undermining or blocking the operation of prior fault rules in the context of automatism. This is the question to which I now turn.

IV. The Effect of Addiction

Let us return to our original example, in which our defendant (D) takes a drink at T1, only to go on to punch the victim (V) while in a state of (general sense) automatism at T2. The current legal position is that, although D's conduct at T2 would not generally attract culpability, it is possible to reconstruct that culpability by attaching prior fault to his drink-taking at T1. In the preceding discussion, I have attempted to show that there are a number of ways to conceptualise this move, depending on the analysis of automatism we adopt. On one analysis, D's culpable drink-taking at T1 disqualifies him from relying on the defence of automatism; on another, it provides the missing element – either voluntariness or fault – that allows us to attach overall culpability to his conduct at T2. Suppose, then, that we complicate matters by introducing the following element: D is an alcoholic. He is *addicted* to the alcohol he consumes at T1. The question for the remainder of this chapter is the potential impact of this fact on our overall conclusions as to D's culpability. More precisely, the question animating the following discussion is the degree to which addiction might be capable of undermining or negating voluntary intoxication-based prior fault in automatism cases.

First, a clarification as to the scope of my discussion. My aim in this section is not to adjudicate between different accounts of addiction, or to make the case for one analysis over another. To make a declaration as to how addiction works would be well outside the scope of my expertise. What I aim to do is to consider how addiction *might have to work* in order for it to have the effect of blocking or undermining the operation of prior fault[27] – and to illustrate the ways in which the answer to this question changes depending on which of the competing automatism/prior fault frameworks we adopt. I will focus in particular on two alternative possibilities – first, that addiction may undermine the *voluntariness* of D's action at T1, and second, that addiction may undermine our broader conclusions as to D's *culpability* for their voluntary action at T1.

A. First Possibility: Addiction Blocks Prior Fault by Negating Voluntariness

The strongest claim from a prior fault-blocking perspective has to be that addiction is capable of rendering the drink-taking at T1 involuntary. If this case can be made, then addiction looks capable of undermining prior fault on all three of our proposed frameworks: if D's conduct at T1 is involuntary, it cannot be used to construct the missing voluntariness at T2; similarly, if the intoxication is involuntary and not voluntary, the inculpatory prior fault rules simply do not kick in, blocking the attribution of culpability on both the defence-negating and fault-reconstructing analyses. The question, then, is whether this claim can be made.

From a strictly legal perspective, there is at least one context in which the idea has precedent. In the 1989 case of *Tandy*,[28] the Court of Appeal considered whether

[27] I am borrowing this framing device from D Husak, 'Addiction and Criminal Responsibility' (1999) 18(6) *Law and Philosophy* 655, who characterised his approach similarly.

[28] *R v Tandy* [1989] 1 WLR 350, see also later cases *R v Wood* [2008] EWCA Crim 1305; and *R v Stewart* [2009] 1 WLR 2507.

alcohol dependence syndrome could constitute an 'abnormality of the mind' for the purposes of diminished responsibility. Their conclusion was that this *could* be the case – but *only* if the effect of the condition was to render the drinking involuntary in the sense of being the result of an irresistible craving or compulsion.[29] In short, then, there is at least one context in which the courts have appeared to entertain the possibility of addiction rendering ostensibly deliberate drink-taking involuntary. Quite apart from the question of legal precedent, however, there remains the question of whether it is accurate to understand addiction as a disease or disorder of volitional impairment. On the one hand, the idea boasts a certain pedigree; the well-established 'disease model' (or 'brain-disease model') of addiction understands it precisely as 'a neurobiological disease characterised by compulsive drug use despite negative consequences'.[30] As Hanna Pickard explains, the characteristic feature of this 'orthodox'[31] model is its understanding of chemical addiction in terms of a 'hijacking' of the brain's reward mechanisms, the effect of which is that the addicted person's will is overridden by an irresistible compulsion to seek out and take drugs.[32] Orthodoxy of the 'disease model' notwithstanding, however, the relationship between addiction and control has been – and remains – something of a quagmire. Pickard herself argues that there is a growing body of evidence to suggest that behaviour stemming from addiction may not be best understood as compulsive at all; she cites, for example, repeated studies showing the responsiveness of addicted people to incentives, as well as evidence of successful 'cold turkey' cases – neither of which would seem possible if the effect of chemical addiction was to wholly override the subject's will.[33] She observes, in addition, the emergence in recent years of 'learning models' of addiction,[34] according to which changes in the brain associated with chemical addiction are better understood not in terms of

[29] See also *Stewart* (n 28), in which the court held that in order to determine whether a defendant's addiction had this effect, juries should consider factors such as the seriousness of the defendant's alcohol dependency, whether they were capable of abstaining and for how long, their pattern of drinking in general and on the day of the killing, etc.

[30] H Pickard, 'The Puzzle of Addiction' in H Pickard and SH Ahmed (eds), *The Routledge Handbook of Philosophy and Science of Addiction* (Abingdon, Routledge, 2019) 9. For accounts of this kind see, eg, AI Leshner, 'Addiction Is a Brain Disease, and It Matters' (1997) 278(5335) *Science* 45; AI Leshner, 'Science-Based Views of Drug Addiction and Its Treatment' (1999) 282(14) *Journal of the American Medical Association* 1314; SE Hyman, 'Addiction: A Disease of Learning and Memory' (2005) 62(8) *American Journal of Psychiatry* 1414; EJ Nestler, 'Cellular Basis of Memory for Addiction' (2013) 15(4) *Dialogues in Clinical Neuroscience* 431. Also discussed in ch 5 of this collection.

[31] ibid 9.

[32] ibid 10.

[33] For a full rundown of Pickard's evidence against the analysis of addiction in terms of compulsion, see Pickard (n 30) 11; H Pickard, 'Responsibility Without Blame for Addiction' (2017) 10 *Neuroethics* 172.

[34] Along with other alternatives too numerous to address here – choice models, for example, of the kind associated in particular with GM Heyman, *Addiction: A Disorder of Choice* (Cambridge, MA, Harvard University Press, 2009) – and biopsychosocial models that advocate a holistic understanding of addiction in terms of the interplay among biological, psychological, social, cultural, and systemic factors; see, eg, GL Engel, 'The Need for a New Medical Model: A Challenge for Biomedicine' (1977) 196 *Science* 129; GA Marlatt and others, 'Addictive Behaviors: Etiology and Treatment' (1988) 39 *Annual Review of Psychology* 223; F Borrell-Carrio, AL Suchman and RM Epstein, 'The

pathology, but ordinary neuroplasticity – 'a part of the ordinary process of learning and habit formation that occurs when the brain is exposed to reward' – which have sounded a note of scepticism regarding the 'hijack' theory of addiction on which the disease model has tended to rely.[35]

Even supposing we were to accept an analysis of addiction as a disease or disorder of compulsion, however, the move from *compulsion* to *involuntariness* is not necessarily a straightforward one. While there is no unifying concept of involuntariness on which all commentators agree, in the context of discussions on automatism, at least, it does generally seem to mean something beyond impaired control. If we turn our minds to paradigmatic automatism cases – sleepwalking, fugue states, psychomotor epilepsy – they are not ones in which the defendant acts under a very strong, or even an irresistible, compulsion. Rather, what unifies these examples is that they are cases in which the defendant's conscious mind appears to have effectively left the equation; the defendant acts as an *automaton* acts, a physical body propelled by something other than conscious, deliberative thought. And indeed, even within these paradigmatic cases, there is disagreement as to whether a description of the relevant conduct as *involuntary* is always appropriate; while the term is more or less uncontroversially applied to reflex actions, commentators such as Robert Schopp[36] and Stephen Morse[37] have been more reluctant to interpret cases of dissociative action or 'clouded consciousness' in terms of an absence of volition. As Schopp observes, there exist cases of dissociative action – sleepwalking, for example – in which defendants have acted 'in a directed, effective manner to achieve a purpose', in some cases even having 'engaged in preliminary behaviour apparently intended to arrange circumstances in such a manner as to facilitate the offence'.[38] A prime example is the Canadian case of *Parks*[39] in which the defendant, while sleepwalking, drove 23km to the house of his parents-in-law and attacked them both with a kitchen knife, killing one and seriously wounding the other. The dilemma, as Morse frames it, is that actions taken within dissociative states are not instances of 'physically compelled movement' – *some* mental state operates here, 'directing the bodily movements quite effectively'.[40] As he puts it: 'the dissociated defendant has been able successfully to engage in conduct demonstrating accurate understanding of the environment and goal-directedness, suggesting that the bodily movements are intentional actions'.[41] On the other hand, the individual's consciousness 'is not fully integrated', the reason

Biopsychosocial Model 25 Years Later: Principles, Practice, and Scientific Inquiry' (2004) 2 *Annals of Family Medicine* 576.

[35] Pickard (n 30) 172. For learning models of addiction see, eg, M Lewis, 'Addiction and the Brain: Development, Not Disease' (2017) 10(1) *Neuroethics* 7.

[36] RF Schopp, *Automatism, Insanity, and the Psychology of Criminal Responsibility* (Cambridge, Cambridge University Press, 1991) 135.

[37] SJ Morse, 'Culpability and Control' (1994) 142 *University of Pennsylvania Law Review* 1587.

[38] Schopp (n 36) 135.

[39] *Parks* [1992] 2 SCR 871.

[40] Morse (n 37) 1642.

[41] ibid 1641–2.

being (Morse suggests) that 'the normal ability self-consciously to observe oneself, to be aware of and monitor oneself, is missing or severely diminished'.[42] What the dissociating individual lacks, therefore, is not the capacity for *voluntary* action, but 'the self-protective variable of self-awareness', which 'enables us to perceive our conduct and to behave more adaptively by correcting ourselves'.[43] The upshot of this is that, even if the orthodox model of addiction is accepted, a conclusion of involuntariness is not necessarily entailed. The addict's conduct is, surely, even more clearly goal-directed and purposive than the sleepwalker's; if the involuntariness of somnambulistic actions is subject to question, then the case for addicted behaviour as involuntary is shakier still.

To summarise, then, while the strongest case for a PF-blocking function of addiction is that addiction is or may be capable of rendering drink taking at T1 actually involuntary, this is not the easiest argument to make. *If* the disease model of addiction is accepted (which is itself a very large 'if'), then a reading of addiction as negating voluntariness *may* be possible on a 'soft' reading of voluntariness that understands it as essentially synonymous with control. On any harder or stricter read of voluntariness, however, the analysis becomes trickier to run. In order to truly commit to this line of analysis, one might be required to argue that addiction is capable of making an act truly *non-volitional*, in the way of a reflex action – which even on the orthodox model is likely to be a tall order.

B. Second Possibility: Addiction Blocks Prior Fault by Undermining Fault

A more promising line of attack might be to focus on culpability.[44] If addiction is capable of rendering D's voluntary drink-taking at T1 *non-culpable*, then it ought to be capable of blocking prior fault on two out of the three proposed frameworks (the ordinary view, in which prior fault blocks the defence of automatism, and the version of the alternative view which interprets prior fault as imputing fault/culpability). While the relationship between addiction and culpability is a huge topic, with far too much ground to fully cover here, in the interests of finishing off our mapping exercise, there are a few lines we might wish to draw. First, it may be helpful to distinguish between analyses that deny culpability by denying agency, and analyses which attribute agency while denying culpability. In the former camp, we have accounts that appeal either to the absence of *control* on the part of the defendant, or the lack of a specific kind of *cognitive* ability or capacity necessary for culpable action – usually rational capacity of some kind. In the latter camp sit what I would loosely and tentatively describe as 'quality-of-will' accounts – accounts

[42] ibid 1642.
[43] ibid 1642.
[44] Also discussed in ch 6 of this collection.

which acknowledge agency, but exculpate on grounds that D's actions may not reflect or manifest a culpable quality of will, once the effect of the addiction is factored in.

i. Agency-Denying Models of Control and/or Capacity

The complicated relationship between addiction and control was touched on briefly in the previous section; I will not cover the same ground again, except to offer an important caveat to the prior discussion. While Pickard provides reasons to suggest that we should not take impaired control as the defining characteristic of addiction, she tempers this with a concession: just because addiction does not necessarily involve a lack of control, that does not entail that it can never have the effect of impeding control or making an impulse irresistible.[45] This is an important caveat to bear in mind. Addiction does not need to be *defined as* a disorder of control in order for it to undermine culpability on grounds of irresistible impulse; if we think that there exist any cases in which addiction might negate control, then we may have reason for thinking there are at least some cases in which addiction could undermine prior fault on these grounds. With that said, in the absence of a straightforward equivalency between addiction and loss of control, an irresistible impulse exception is likely to prove challenging to apply in the legal context. For such an exception to be workable in practice, we would need to be able to determine with some degree of reliability just which cases of addiction involve genuinely impaired control and which do not. Addiction experts may disagree on the point, but it does not appear to me that we yet have a clear and accepted framework that allows us to confidently disentangle cases of *strong-but-resistible* impulses from cases involving impulses that were genuinely *irresistible*.

Denying control is not the only way to revoke D's agency, however. An alternative might be to appeal to a kind of rational or cognitive incapacity as the potential effect of addiction. A sample argument along these lines might run something like this: 1) culpability for an action at T1 requires that D had decision-making (or rational) capacity with respect to that action; 2) addiction may in certain cases undermine a person's rational or decision-making capacity as it concerns drinking/drug taking; therefore 3) addiction may in certain cases undermine culpability for drinking/drug taking at T1.[46] As far as a more precise formulation goes, there are a number of potential routes we could take depending on exactly how we define the relevant concepts. Here is one possibility: Decision-making involves deciding between reasons for or against acting according to a nexus of desires, beliefs, and values: what we care about, what we want to achieve, what we want to avoid, and so forth. In at least some cases, the effect of addiction may be to tip the

[45] Pickard (n 30) 11.

[46] For an argument along these lines see, eg, SJ Morse, 'Addiction, Genetics and Criminal Responsibility' (2006) 69(1) *Law & Contemporary Problems* 167.

scale so heavily in favour of drinking that it essentially operates to render a person incapable of weighing reasons for or against acting in the way that, *ceteris paribus*, a non-addicted person could. Such an analysis may find support in the work of, for example, Neil Levy, on whose understanding the effect of substance addiction is a loss of cognitive, rather than volitional, control.[47] According to Levy, the effect of addiction on the brain's reward system is not to compel the addict to act against their better overall judgement, but rather to give rise to a 'shift' in those judgements; when presented with cues suggesting drug availability, addicts experience 'a cue-driven oscillation between judgments, transitioning from judging that they ought to abstain from drugs to judging they ought to consume (perhaps just on this occasion)'.[48] What the addict lacks control over, on Levy's analysis, is not their actions but 'the valuational contents of [their] all things considered judgements'.[49] If we agree with Levy, then, that the effect of addiction is to distort one's ability to balance reasons for and against drug-taking when presented with the relevant cues, it is not difficult to imagine how we might proceed to the conclusion that the addict's capacity for decision-making is impaired in such a way as to undermine their status as a rational agent – at least in this specific context.

It is notable, however, that Levy does not regard his observations as providing an argument for a lack of rational capacity on the part of the addicted person. Rather, he takes the view that addicted people 'remain rational agents' despite the dysfunction in the reward system introduced by the addiction, as the fundamental process by which they take decisions is unchanged: 'We all make decisions and form judgements in ways that are guided by the output of subpersonal mechanisms, which dispose us to take some things seriously and dismiss others and may strongly incline us towards a particular judgment. Making decisions in this way is not a limitation on our rationality, but partially constitutive of it.[50] To put it another way, all people make decisions via a system that disposes us toward weighting certain factors in certain ways, and while addiction may change the weighting (which in turn may lead to what Levy describes as a 'maladaptive response'), what it does not do is fundamentally alter the process. As such, while addiction introduces some dysfunction into the system, this should not lead us to the conclusion that the addict ceases to be a rational agent – indeed, it is precisely because they *remain* a rational agent that they will often be inclined to rationalise and make sense of their behaviour through *post-hoc* justifications.[51] On his own analysis, then, if Levy's observations provide grounds for exculpation, this is not due to any

[47] N Levy, 'Addiction as a Disorder of Belief' (2014) 29 *Biology and Philosophy* 337; see also G Ainslie, *Breakdown of Will* (Cambridge, Cambridge University Press, 2001).

[48] Levy (n 47) 352.

[49] E Henden, 'Addiction as a Disorder of Self-Control' in H Pickard and SH Ahmed (eds), *The Routledge Handbook of Philosophy and Science of Addiction* (Abingdon, Routledge, 2019), discussing Levy (n 47).

[50] N Levy, 'Addiction: The Belief Oscillation Hypothesis' in H Pickard and SH Ahmed (eds), *The Routledge Handbook of Philosophy and Science of Addiction* (Abingdon, Routledge, 2019).

[51] ibid.

undermining of rational capacity. Instead, his arguments may be better situated alongside agency-ascribing accounts – that is, accounts which aim to provide an explanation of the impact of addiction on culpability that does *not* rely on a denial of the addict's agency as a rational and/or moral actor. It is to these accounts to which I now turn.

ii. Agency-Ascribing Accounts of Reasonable Expectations and/or Sufficient Concern

Not all accounts of addiction as culpability-mitigating reach their conclusion through denial of volitional or agential control. Both Douglas Husak and Gary Watson, for example, have independently presented duress models of addiction, according to which the intensity of the craving caused by chemical addiction – like more typical sources of duress – may be capable of providing the addict with a legal excuse for substance-seeking behaviour.[52] Along different lines, Timothy Schroeder and Nomy Arpaly argue that addiction may have the effect of reducing (if not entirely eliminating) blameworthiness for certain kinds of conduct, not by undermining the responsibility or agency of the addict, but by altering our overall calculation as to the degree of ill will or moral indifference expressed by the addict through their conduct.[53]

Within these agency-ascribing accounts it is possible to identify a couple of key ideas or 'through-lines', which I will endeavour to bring out here. The first is that the addict, in his drink-taking, may not fall short of *reasonable expectations*, something to which Watson explicitly appeals in setting out his rationale for addiction-as-duress. For Watson (as well as for Husak, who also presents a duress model of addiction), the salient point is not that addiction makes D's drinking involuntary, but rather that it creates conditions in which 'choosing the right thing is too difficult to expect';[54] it imposes, in other words, a cost on resistance that goes beyond that which a person can reasonably be expected to accept in order to avoid wrongdoing. For Watson, then, compulsive desires (including those caused by addiction) are culpability-mitigating not because they undermine control, but because people subject to them 'could not reasonably be expected to hold out'.[55] Applying a model along these lines, then, we might say that addiction undermines the conclusion of culpability at T1 if its effect on D is such that it becomes *unreasonable to expect* them to refrain from drink-taking.

The second reoccurring idea is that the addict, by his drink-taking, may not manifest what Larry Alexander has referred to as *insufficient concern* for the rights

[52] Husak (n 27); G Watson, 'Excusing Addiction' (1999) 18(6) *Law and Philosophy* 589.

[53] T Schroeder and N Arpaly, 'Addiction and Blameworthiness' in N Levy (ed), *Addiction and Self-Control: Perspectives from Philosophy, Psychology, and Neuroscience* (New York, Oxford University Press, 2013).

[54] Watson (n 52) 605.

[55] ibid 606.

and interests of others.[56] For example, suppose D1 takes a drink at T1 in a public place, knowing full well that he has a tendency to become violent when intoxicated and may pose a risk to those around him. In this case, we would likely conclude that D1's drink-taking manifests *insufficient concern*; in drinking to excess, he prioritises his enjoyment of the alcohol and desire to have a good time over the physical safety of those around him. A slight alteration of the facts may change this calculation, however; had D1 always been a cheerful and gentle drunk in the past, and had he underestimated the strength of the alcohol and its likelihood of causing a loss of control, for example, we might conclude that his act of drink-taking did not manifest insufficient concern in the same way. Applying this line of thought in the present context, then, it may be possible to argue that the introduction of addiction may be capable of changing the calculation in a similar way; addiction, to put it simply, makes it *much, much* harder to resist taking drink – hard enough, potentially, to undermine a conclusion that the addict's drink-taking manifests an overall insufficiency of concern for the well-being of others.[57]

While Alexander does not (to my knowledge) apply his analysis in the context of addiction, the work of Schroeder and Arpaly reflects a similar focus on the moral quality of the addict's will. Based on their understanding of culpability in terms of ill will and/or moral indifference, they present an analysis of addiction as capable of re-characterising actions which, in the absence of addiction, would manifest ill will or moral indifference, leading us to regard blameworthiness as mitigated (though not entirely removed). With reference to David Carr's memoir,[58] in which he recounts an incident wherein he abandoned his twin infant daughters in a freezing car to get high, Schroeder and Arpaly present an account whereby the effect of addiction on one's habit-forming and predicative systems provides it with motivational force that goes beyond sheer strength of desire – a move which ultimately allows them to conclude that Carr's conduct need not be interpreted as the manifestation of 'monstrous moral indifference' that, in the absence of addiction and all other things being equal, it almost certainly would.[59]

V. Conclusion

The principal aim of this chapter has been to provide a mapping exercise of sorts. I have attempted, through the preceding discussion, to disentangle some of the complex threads connecting automatism, intoxication, addiction, and criminal

[56] L Alexander, 'Insufficient Concern: A Unified Conception of Criminal Culpability' (2002) 88 *California Law Review* 931.

[57] This kind of calculation is reflected in Husak's duress model, where he focuses on the pain of withdrawal as a driving factor in undermining conclusions as to the addict's overall culpability for drink-taking.

[58] D Carr, *The Night of the Gun: A Reporter Investigates the Darkest Story of His Life – His Own* (New York, Simon and Schuster, 2008).

[59] Schroeder and Arpaly (n 53).

responsibility, and to illustrate how a tug on one such thread can lead to an unravelling down the line. As a consequence – and in deference to the limitations of my own understanding of the science of addiction – my approach has tended more towards the exploratory than the polemical. I will conclude, however, with two firm statements. The first is that, if these discussions are to proceed in a useful way, it is imperative that we reach a robust analysis of automatism as *either* defence *or* act negation. The present ambivalence of English courts and commentators on this point – characterised by descriptions of automatism as something like a 'defence of act negation' – is not conducive to any sensible analysis. The second is this: if our aim is to develop a framework for understanding the relationship between addiction and culpability, and for adjudicating the impact of the former on the latter in specific cases, analyses which appeal to something like quality-of-will, as opposed to impaired or absent volitional or agential control, are more promising. I have a few reasons for taking this line; first, these accounts allow us to reach intuitive conclusions about the relationship of addiction to culpability without miring us in an intractable debate as to the impact of addiction on control. On these accounts, we need not be committed to the idea that addiction removes or even undermines control in order to argue that it may have the effect of reducing culpability – all we need to show is that, once the effect of the addiction is factored in, the relevant actions can no longer be taken to manifest an inadequate quality of will – whether that concept is explicated in terms of insufficient concern, moral indifference, or reasonable expectations of conduct. Naturally, one way to argue that ill will was not manifested would be to demonstrate that the addict's control was absent or impaired; crucially, however, this is not the only way, making absence of volitional or agential control a sufficient but not necessary condition of non-culpability.

This brings us to the second benefit of the agency-ascribing approaches, which is that they allow for greater flexibility with respect to the precise way and extent to which addiction is exculpatory. Rather than committing us to the view that addiction is an *inherently* or *necessarily* exculpatory factor, they allow that it can depend on the defendant, the circumstances, and the illness in question, with overall culpability a holistic determination that requires one to take all factors and circumstances into account to determine if (for example) sufficient concern was manifested or reasonable expectations were met. This flexibility enables us to counteract Walter Sinnott-Armstrong's salient objection to attempts to analyse the responsibility of addicts: given the sheer variety of addiction in terms of its chemical, emotional and psychological effect on sufferers, of their motivations for using, and of their attitudes towards their addiction and the degree to which they regard their impulses towards drug use as integrated, he asks, '[h]ow can anyone say anything intelligent about responsibility that will cover all addicts?'[60] Quality of will accounts effectively frees us from the obligation to do so; rather than

[60] W Sinnott-Armstrong, 'Are Addicts Responsible?' in N Levy (ed), *Addiction and Self-Control: Perspectives from Philosophy, Psychology, and Neuroscience* (New York, Oxford University Press, 2013) 126.

attempting to define addiction in terms of a particular agency-removing feature, they provide a flexible framework that is capable of sensitivity to the idiosyncratic features of a particular defendant's experience of addiction.

A final point in favour of agency-ascribing analyses is a more pragmatic one: there may be a therapeutic benefit to models of addiction which allow the addict to retain agency, even while their culpability may be mitigated. Hanna Pickard's work is particularly influential in advancing this argument, advocating as it does for an approach she characterises as 'responsibility without blame'.[61] Discussing clinical work in a therapeutic setting, Pickard observes that recovery oftentimes requires patients to proactively engage in actions and omissions: 'service-users with borderline personality disorder must stop self-harming; addicts need to quit using drugs and alcohol; anorexics must eat'.[62] Given this, emphasising a lack of agential control is frequently antithetical to the process of recovery – it is, simply, *not helpful* for people to be denied a sense of themselves as agents who act for reasons, even when this is ostensibly done for what appears to be their benefit (denying culpability). Given this, we may be subject to an ethical incentive to – at least where possible – prefer analyses of addiction that allow the addict to maintain a conception of themselves as a rational agent capable of exercising choice. *Ceteris paribus*, then, accounts which allow us to attribute agency will be preferable.

[61] Pickard (n 33).
[62] ibid 174.

9

A Primrose Path Theory of Substance Use Disorder and Prior Fault

GIDEON YAFFE

I. Introduction

Moral intuition testifies that those who engage in wrongdoing in service of their substance use disorders are diminished in responsibility in comparison to people whose identical wrongful behaviour is explicable in other ways. The cocaine addict[1] who yanks a wallet from the hand of an unsuspecting victim in order to feed their habit might be appropriately blamed or even legally punished for the act. Still, intuitively they are morally deserving of lesser blame and lesser liability than the unaddicted person who does the same thing for fun, to impress their friends, or even to purchase cocaine. Exactly why this is true, assuming moral intuition about the matter is veridical, is itself a subject of empirically-entwined philosophical study.[2]

In many ordinary contexts, however, people hold that the intuition either fades or should not guide moral or legal judgement when the history of the illness's causal aetiology is examined. People often justify holding addicts just as responsible as non-addicts for the harms their behaviour inflicts, that is, by appeal to a prior fault. 'It's their own fault they're addicted' is sometimes said to rebut an effort to shield the addict from full responsibility for wrongful behaviour by citing the addiction. They might even say, as Ophelia says in *Hamlet*, '[A] puffed and reckless

[1] I will refer to people suffering from substance use disorders as 'addicts' merely for grammatical ease.

[2] See, for instance: R Holton, *Willing, Wanting, Waiting* (Oxford, Oxford University Press, 2009) ch 5; D Husak, 'Addiction and Criminal Liability' (1999) 18 *Law and Philosophy* 655; S Morse, 'Hooked on Hype: Addiction and Responsibility' (2000) 19 *Law and Philosophy* 3; G Watson, 'Excusing Addiction' (1999) 18 *Law and Philosophy* 589; G Watson, 'Disordered Appetites' in *Agency and Answerability* (Oxford, Oxford University Press, 2004); RJ Wallace, 'Addiction as Defect of the Will: Some Philosophical Reflections' (1999) 18(6) *Law and Philosophy* 621; G Yaffe, 'Lowering the Bar for Addicts' in J Poland and G Graham (eds), *Addiction and Responsibility* (Cambridge, MA, MIT Press, 2013); G Yaffe, 'Compromised Addicts' in DJ Coates and NE Tognazzini (eds), *Oxford Studies in Agency and Responsibility: Themes from the Philosophy of Gary Watson* (Oxford, Oxford University Press, 2019).

libertine, Himself the primrose path of dalliance treads'. Each step along the flowery route is taken voluntarily until the addict finds themselves too far along to stop themselves from inflicting harm.

Two things are being claimed by such an appeal to prior fault. First, it is being claimed that the agent came to possess the features definitive of addiction through a process that warrants attributing the illness to their culpable agency. Something about the way addicts typically come to be addicted, namely through voluntary consumption of substances of abuse, indicates that it is something they often culpably inflict on themselves. While there are cases of people who are born addicted, as when they are exposed to an addictive substance prenatally, such cases are rare. Second, it is claimed that a person would have to be faultless in the acquisition of addiction if they are to shield themselves from blame or liability for their problematic behaviour by appealing to the illness's role in generating it.

The move here is of a familiar sort. It is the same move that is made in response to the sailor who points to a sprained ankle to shield themself from the whip for failing to climb the mast: 'It's your own fault that you sprained your ankle!' says the captain as they lash the sailor.[3] Conceptually speaking, there are two possible reasons why we might think that the captain acts unjustly in admonishing or punishing the sailor for failing to climb the mast; there are two possible rejoinders to the captain's appeal to the sailor's prior fault for the injury. Perhaps the sailor was not at fault for the sprained ankle; perhaps they tripped even while being careful. Or perhaps a disabling condition, like a sprained ankle, shields from blame for otherwise obligatory conduct that it prevents or impedes, *even if* the agent is culpably responsible for the fact that they are in the condition.

In many moods, I am strongly attracted to this second line, which can be developed further by identifying the quite narrow conditions under which faulty action leading to a circumstance undermines the ordinary shield from blame or liability that such a circumstance provides. Plausibly, for instance, if the faulty action was performed *in order to* produce a shield to blame or liability, as when the sailor sprains the ankle *so as* to disable themselves from later following the order to climb the mast, then the shield loses its force. But such a circumstance is not the default. More often than not, people do not become disabled so as to use their disability as a shield to blame or liability. So, I'm attracted to the thought that, at least often, if you can't do it, you can't be expected to do it, even if it is your own fault that you can't. But I will set this line of thought aside here. Let's assume that an act performed because the agent is suffering from addiction is, on those grounds, reduced in blameworthiness or mitigated in liability *only if* the agent is not at fault for having the illness.[4] Our question, then, is this: Are agents at fault for being addicted?

[3] For closely related ideas, see PH Robinson, 'Causing the Conditions of One's Own Defense: A Study in the Limits of Theory in Criminal Law Doctrine' (1985) 71 *Virginia Law Review* 1; M Vargas, 'The Trouble with Tracing' (2005) 29 *Midwest Studies in Philosophy* 269.

[4] So while we are assuming that someone who becomes addicted so as to be shieled from liability undermines their shield, we are also allowing that lesser degrees of culpability for the illness (eg, knowingly becoming addicted) also suffice to undermine its excusing force.

This question is best addressed from within a particular theory of addiction – an account of what addiction is and how one comes to be in that state through voluntary consumption of substances of abuse. It is because we have an idea of what leukaemia is and how one comes to have it that we know it is absurd to, on the grounds of prior fault, persist with an attitude of unmitigated blame towards the leukaemia patient for harms they cause because of their illness (eg, harms that are caused by leukaemia-induced fatigue). It is, to be sure, conceptually possible to acquire leukaemia faultfully; one could knowingly ingest leukaemia-causing chemicals. But given what the illness is and how it is acquired, this is, at best, very rare; there is next to no room at all for acquiring leukaemia in this way. We should expect, for similar reasons, for accounts of addiction to have implications for our question. Given a particular theory of addiction, is there meaningful room for its faulty acquisition? The goal here is to explore the question under one important and neglected economic theory of addiction, namely that offered by Richard Herrnstein and Drazen Prelec.[5]

This chapter offers an account of what would have to happen for an agent to be at fault for the fact that they are addicted under the Herrnstein-Prelec theory. There are, as we will see, broadly two different ways that one can undermine a condition's blame- or liability-shielding force by culpably causing oneself to be in the condition. An action that causes one to be in a condition might be performed with *awareness* (that is, conscious, occurrent knowledge) that it will or might cause the condition, or without such awareness, *where one's obliviousness derives from one's failure to take steps that one should have taken* to become aware.[6] One might put the needle in one's arm *knowing* that one might thereby become addicted or oblivious to that possibility, *thanks to failing to take steps to inform oneself of the risks*.[7] For

[5] R Herrnstein and D Prelec, 'A Theory of Addiction' in G Loewenstein and J Elster (eds), *Choice Over Time* (New York, Russell Sage Publications, 1992). For a brief overview of the empirical support for economic models of addiction, including Herrnstein and Prelec's model, see W Bickel and others, 'The Behavioral Economics of Substance Use Disorders: Reinforcement Pathologies and Their Repair' (2014) 10 *Annual Review of Clinical Psychology* 641.

[6] The distinction drawn here cuts across the Model Penal Code's mens rea categories. See MPC 2.02(2). Knowledge and recklessness are both included in the first group involving awareness. Whether all of the purpose cases are also included there depends on one's view about the possibility of intending to do something that one is certain one will fail at doing; if that's possible, then such cases are in neither category. I set aside the question here. In addition, for those who hold that it is possible to be negligent without there having been some prior act one failed to take that would have cured one of one's obliviousness with respect to one or more of the conditions of which the reckless actor is aware, the second category of cases is only a proper subset of the cases involving negligence. For those who deny this, the second category is identical to negligence. I do not weigh in here on this question, either. The discussion here, therefore, does not reach the question of whether there is prior fault of a sort that undermines addiction's shield to blame or liability when either (1) the agent uses drugs of abuse with the aim of becoming addicted, but with certainty that they will fail, or (2) the agent uses drugs of abuse oblivious to some aspect of the risk of becoming addicted, but where their obliviousness (a) could not have been avoided by the agent, and (b) reflects badly enough on them to constitute culpability for addiction.

[7] The case of drug use performed with the unexercised disposition to be consciously aware of the risk, or the certainty, that addiction will follow – purely dispositional knowledge of the risks – is discussed in section II.

reasons to be explained, the second route is not possible under the Herrnstein and Prelec theory – acts of voluntary use of substances of abuse are, themselves, efforts to know what the effect of such use on the agent will be – and the first is, at best, extremely rare. The result: if Herrnstein and Prelec are right about what addiction is, there is as little justice in the prior fault assertion when directed at the person suffering from addiction as there is when it is directed at the leukaemia patient.

II. Prior Fault, Generally

I am here assuming the following, where D performs wrongful act W because D is in condition A: The fact that D is in A provides D with a shield from unmitigated blame or liability for W *only if* D is not at fault for the fact that they are in A.[8]

While it is perfectly possible, consistent with this principle, that D's blame/liability is never mitigated thanks to the fact that D W'd because they are in A, the more interesting cases involve conditions that would mitigate in the absence of prior fault, such as disability or, arguably, addiction. What is being granted is that such a condition would not have this mitigating effect when there is prior fault. The goal of this section is to identify necessary and sufficient conditions for being at fault for being in a condition that is supportive of this assumed principle. Say you believe that it is true that being at fault for a condition undermines using that condition as a shield from unmitigated blame or liability. There are several ordinary senses of the term 'at fault'. Under what sense of the term is it plausibly true that a condition's shield to blame/liability is weakened or eliminated when the agent is at fault for the condition?

I propose the following:

D is at fault for being in condition A *if and only if*:

(1) D's action, U, (non-deviantly) caused D to be in A &
(2) D knew or should have taken steps to know that U would or might cause D to be in A.
(3) The fact that U would or might cause D to be in A provided D with a sufficient reason not to U.

Let's say that if these conditions are satisfied, U is 'the locus of fault' for D's being in A. If we understand 'A' to be the state of addiction to a drug of abuse and 'U' to

[8] This formulation is intended to be neutral on the question of whether prior fault weakens or undermines a condition's shielding force only if the agent causally contributes to the condition. I am therefore neutral in two respects on the question of whether the excusing force of addiction is weakened or undermined when the addict asks the friend to inject them rather than injecting them themselves: I am neutral both on the question of whether the addict thereby causes their addiction in a sense that matters to culpability for harms inflicted in service of the illness (perhaps the fact that the causal chain passes through another's agency undermines the addict's culpability for their addiction), and also on the question of whether causal contribution of any sort is necessary for the condition's excusing or mitigating force to be weakened or removed.

be the act of using that drug, then, according to the theory, what the prior fault accusation amounts to – the accusation that 'it is your own fault you are addicted' – is the following: You knew, or wrongfully failed to take steps to know, that using might cause you to be addicted; that fact about the act of using was a sufficient reason to do something else; you used anyway; and your use did in fact cause you to become addicted.[9]

Why should we think that being at fault for being addicted, in this sense, might serve to undermine addiction's excusing or mitigating force? It is worth talking through an example. Imagine someone who performs U for the purpose of putting themselves in condition A; addiction is what they are aiming at in smoking crack. If U does not cause them to be in A (or cause them to be in A through some roundabout, deviant route), then they are not on those grounds at fault for being in the condition. It's just bad luck that they ended up in A. To be at fault, the condition must be *attributable* to the agent of the act. A necessary condition of attributability for a state or event is the causation of that state or event of a sort that allows the description of the act by reference to the event caused – as in 'you broke your ankle' or, awkwardly, 'you addicted yourself'. Only non-deviant causation meets this criterion. This is the intuitive idea behind condition (1).

Condition (2) is similarly motivated. To be at fault for a state or event thanks to the performance of an action is not just for it to be appropriate or fitting to describe the action with reference to the state or event but also, in so doing, to be attributing the state or event to the agent of the act. To use Donald Davidson's classic example, the agent moves his finger, flips the switch, turns on the light, and alerts the burglar.[10] While flipping the switch and alerting the burglar are both things the agent does – the action can be described both with reference to the one thing it causes as well as to the other since both are caused non-deviantly by the agent – the former act is more attributable to the agent than the latter. It is a product of their agency in a way that the latter is not, even though something that they do causes both of the relevant events; they are more of a switch-flipper than a burglar-alerter.

What is necessary for there to be this greater form of attributability? At least, the agent must have performed the act in some mental state thanks to which various features of the agent are manifested by the act. For instance, if the agent performed the act knowing that it would cause a particular event, then he would not reconsider the action in light of the fact that it would have that effect, and so was not to that degree averse to the effect's occurrence. Similarly, if the agent failed to take steps they should have taken to inform themselves of what the act might

[9] Some who think that prior fault can undermine addiction's shielding force will take being 'at fault' in this sense to be insufficient. They will require, quite plausibly, some kind of culpability at the time of use with respect to the crimes that follow use. Note, however, that if the addict is not at fault for becoming addicted, then whether additional conditions that are needed to support the claim at issue are met is not our concern here.

[10] D Davidson, 'Agency' in *Essays on Action and Events* (Oxford, Clarendon Press, 2001) 43.

cause, then it is true that the possibility that it would cause the event was insufficiently salient to the agent to prompt taking such steps. That is, for the fact that they are in condition A to be something that has its source in their agency, their role in making it the case that they are in that condition must tell us something important about the way their agency operates, about what they value, care about, or take to be reason-giving.

To clarify condition (2), consider someone who has a purely dispositional belief that their use of cocaine will risk causing them to become addicted and uses while having this disposition, although it is not triggered. They never consciously think, 'This is risky!', but they are disposed to have that thought under certain narrow triggering conditions that they never encountered. The set of mental events – occurrences in the head, as it were – that we would appeal to to causally explain this person's behaviour are identical to those of the agent who lacks this disposition and is motivated and behaves the same way. The disposed agent and the undisposed agent are equally oblivious; we do not find in either of their heads a representation of the risk. About each of these agents, we can ask whether they should have taken steps to be consciously aware of the risks. This question, however, has a slightly different form in the two cases: Should the disposed agent have taken steps to place themselves in the conditions that would have triggered the disposition, or taken steps to acquire a disposition that would have been triggered by conditions they did face? Or, alternatively, should the undisposed agent have taken steps to acquire the disposition and then take steps to place themselves in a condition that would have triggered it? If the answer in either case is 'yes', then condition (2) is met; the agent 'should have taken steps to know'.

What if the answer about both agents is 'no'? That is, what if both lack conscious awareness that U risks addiction, and neither failed to take steps they should have taken to remedy this? Is the addiction that results more properly attributable to the disposed agent than the undisposed? No. For one's agency to extend to an event is for the actual causal chain leading to the event to include events that are themselves intrinsically entwined with the features of a person thanks to which they are an agent.[11] Where we have the same chain of events, we have the same degree of attributability.[12]

The satisfaction of conditions (1) and (2), then, supports the thought that the fact that the agent is in the condition is attributable to them in a richer way than

[11] For an argument that this was John Locke's position, see G Yaffe, *Liberty Worth the Name: Locke on Free Agency* (Princeton, NJ, Princeton University Press, 2000) ch 2.

[12] What is the case is that it is much more likely, as an evidential matter, that the answer to the question is 'yes' in the case of the disposed agent than in the case of the undisposed. This is, quite simply, because it is easier to place oneself in circumstances that would trigger a disposition than it is to acquire a disposition. The disposed agent might merely need to bring a sober friend to the party in order to prompt their awareness that their use might lead to addiction, while the undisposed agent might need substantial experience or education to even be disposed to know of the risks, and would then also need to bring the sober friend to the party. Since the former steps are easier to take than the latter, the fact that the disposed agent has the disposition demonstrates that it is more likely that they failed to take steps they should have taken than the undisposed.

the way in which the burglar being alerted is attributable to the switch-flipper. But to be at *fault*, there must be something criticisable about the act. Further, the fact that the act would or might cause the event must be (at least part of) the source of its critisability. The agent is not at fault for spraining their ankle simply because they tripped while defying the superior officer's order to clean the deck. Such a sailor had a sufficient reason not to defy the order (assuming there's sufficient reason to follow orders in the circumstances), but the reason did not derive even in part from the fact that defying the order might cause them to sprain their ankle. Under condition (3), an agent is not at fault for everything that happens thanks to their norm-violating act. They are at fault only when a central part of *why* there is sufficient reason to refrain from the act is that acts of the requisite sort might cause events of the kind the agent is at fault for.

Notice that people do know, and sometimes consciously and occurrently at the time of use, that substances of abuse are addictive; they know, that is, that people who always abstain do not become addicted, and so they know that use places one at a non-zero risk of suffering the illness. Does such conscious awareness make an addict at fault for their illness? No. To see this, consider an analogous example. Imagine that you have a mosquito bite on your arm. You know that people who scratch bites of this sort sometimes end up with open sores on their arms. But you also know that a single act of scratching will cause this only when coupled with many other similar acts; you only end up with an open sore if you scratch repeatedly. Do you, then, have sufficient reason not to scratch once? Scratching once will provide momentary relief. Still, that reason to do it is outweighed by the reason to avoid an open sore; if the choice were between the temporary relief of scratching and having an open sore, reason would favour resisting the urge to scratch. But the momentary relief likely rationally outweighs having an open sore *corrected for the probability that you will scratch repeatedly* (given what you know about your tendency to succumb to the urge). The choice is not between momentary relief and an open sore; the choice is between momentary relief and *a chance of repeatedly continuing to scratch and thereby causing an open sore*. What you do have sufficient reason not to do is *to scratch repeatedly*. Do you perform *that* act – which consists of many small acts of scratching – with the occurrent knowledge that you are thereby risking giving yourself an open sore? It is possible – and were you to do so, you would be at fault for the open sore – but such cases are rare. Typically, one's attention is at least sometimes drawn to the itch and the relief that a single act of scratching provides, so the knowledge of the risks that accompany at least some acts of scratching that are parts of the series that causes the open sore is purely dispositional. If one is at fault in the face of such dispositional knowledge, it is because one failed to do what it took to trigger the relevant disposition. In the mosquito bite case, that is common: the scratcher should have paid attention to what they were doing to themselves. That is, what is common is for the act of repeated scratching to be the locus of fault for the open sore not because that temporally extended complex act consisting of many smaller component acts of scratching was accompanied with conscious, occurrent knowledge, but because it was accompanied by purely dispositional knowledge that one should have taken steps to make occurrent. Similarly, repeated use of a substance of abuse is rarely accompanied by occurrent knowledge of the risks of thereby becoming addicted; it is accompanied more often by dispositional knowledge. Therefore, such repeated usage can be the locus of fault only if the addict should have taken steps to make their dispositional knowledge occurrent. We will return to the mosquito bite example, for it illustrates the point of central importance to the explanation to be offered as to why addicts are rarely at fault for suffering the illness.

What we are still lacking is an explanation for why the excusing or mitigating force of a condition is weakened or undermined when one is at fault, in this sense, for being in the condition. To successfully shield yourself by appealing to a condition is, at least sometimes, to point out that, in light of the condition, the act does not manifest the problematic fact about yourself that it would have appropriately been taken to manifest in the condition's absence. If you point out that you struck someone because you did not see that they were there, what you are implying is that the fact that you struck them does not indicate that you granted insufficient weight to their well-being.[13] Striking them would have manifested that you had seen them there, but in the absence of seeing them, it does not. If, however, the fact that you are in the condition manifests exactly the problematic feature that the act fails to manifest, given the condition, then, by citing the condition, you are granting that your conduct, taken as a whole, does, in fact, manifest precisely the problematic feature of yourself that you correctly claimed not to be manifested by the act alone. If the reason why I didn't see you there is that I grant insufficient weight to your interests, then in appealing to the fact that I didn't see you there to explain why I struck you, I am confessing, rather than denying, that the relevant feature of me, namely insufficient regard for your interests, is manifested in my conduct taken as a whole.

What was just offered is closely related to the 'equal culpability thesis' under discussion in connection to wilful ignorance.[14] According to the thesis, the person who knowingly does something wrongful is exactly as culpable as the person who does so unknowingly, but where their ignorance is their own fault. What has just been suggested is that if there is to be equal culpability between the person lacking the potentially mitigating condition and the person who engages in conduct of relevance before entering the condition, then the person must be at fault for being in the condition in light of the conduct, in the sense of 'at fault'

[13] For an account of criminal culpability that fits snugly with this idea, see G Yaffe, *The Age of Culpability: Children and the Nature of Criminal Responsibility* (Oxford, Oxford University Press, 2018) ch 3.

[14] See, for instance: D Luban, 'Contrived Ignorance' [1999] *Georgetown Law Review* 957; A Sarch, 'Willful Ignorance, Culpability, and the Criminal Law' [2014] *St John's Law Review* 1023; G Yaffe, 'The Point of Mens Rea: The Case of Willful Ignorance' (2018) 12 *Criminal Law and Philosophy* 19.

just offered.[15] If the non-addicted recreational user who steals for drugs, and the addict who steals for drugs, are equally culpable, it must be because the addict's voluntary use – the locus of fault for their addiction – manifests the same disregard for the rights of others to use their property as is manifested by the theft committed by the non-addicted thief. How else would the locus of fault manifest the problematic facts about the agent that the act would manifest in the absence of the condition?

III. Two Types of Theory of Addiction

People suffering from substance use disorders decide repeatedly, over and over, to use the substance of abuse. These decisions issue in often quite complicated steps taken as means to use and, if all goes as planned, use itself. Perhaps the most striking feature of these decision-making and linked behavioural patterns is that they are far from optimal. Moreover, it is not just that they are bad for the agent engaging in them by objective standards, but also that they are bad for the agent under *their own* settled preferences and values about how their life should go. People suffering from substance use disorder themselves grant that a life of frequent abstention is better than a life of frequent use. Yet, they decide to use, and use, over and over, all the time.

Furthermore, the problematic repeating pattern of decisions to use is the product of a particular disposition that the agent possesses, and which explains the pattern.[16] Put more carefully, a general conditional of the following form is true: 'If the agent recognises such-and-such reasons for action, they decide, and form the intention to perform, such-and-such actions.' The conditional is true thanks to some settled features, or mental structures, of the agent. The conditional may be true *for the most part* rather than without exception. It may happen

[15] What has just been offered is at best an explanation for why an excusing, or culpability-diminishing condition, rather than a justificatory condition, might lose its shielding power thanks to prior fault. The locus of fault might manifest exactly the problematic quality that the excuse is supposed to show not to be manifested. But justifications do not work by demonstrating the act to manifest lesser culpability than one might have thought. They demonstrate, instead, that the act is not actually wrongful in the way that it appears. However, since addiction seems to undermine not the wrongfulness of things done in its service, but the culpability of the actor who engages in wrongful conduct, this complexity need not concern us here.

[16] The talk to follow of 'dispositions' is easily misunderstood. The proper object of legal and moral evaluation is, in the first instance, not a disposition, but an action. However, the illness of addiction consists not just in an action, or a series of actions, but also in various dispositions: most notably, dispositions to crave drugs of abuse and dispositions to decide to use them. To blame the addict for wrongful or illegal acts done in service of the illness on the grounds of prior fault is not to blame the addict for the addiction, or for the dispositions that the illness includes, but to blame the addict *for the wrongful or illegal actions* in part on the grounds that the addiction, including the dispositions that it includes, were faultfully acquired.

that, sometimes, the agent recognises the relevant reasons but chooses otherwise, perhaps siding with other reasons or, perhaps, deciding irrationally.

Theories of addiction vary in two broad respects. First, they vary in their account of what the disposition is that is repeatedly triggered in a destructive pattern of decisions to use. They vary, that is, in how they fill in the blanks in the relevant conditional. Second, they vary in their account of how that disposition is acquired; they vary, that is, in their accounts of how it came to pass that addicts come to have the features or structures thanks to which the conditional is true of them. Consider a pair of toy theories to illustrate these two points, which will, in turn, illustrate a distinction between two types of theories of addiction. According to the first toy theory, the addict at time t0 is possessed of a disposition to decide to pursue that which they most prefer at the time of the decision. Thanks to the fact that they prefer cocaine to everything else on the menu at time t1, this disposition is triggered, and they decide to snort cocaine at t1 and do so. (Or, say, they steal cash from their parents at t1, buy cocaine at t2 and snort it at t3.) The consumption of cocaine, however, causes them (because of its effect on their brains) to acquire a new disposition: a disposition to choose cocaine if it is on the menu, *even when it is not maximally preferred*. So, when cocaine is available, but the agent prefers to stay sober for work or family or something else, or even prefers another drug, they still choose to use cocaine after this second disposition has been acquired. The result: the agent finds themselves in a pattern of frequent decisions to use, despite the fact that they often prefer to abstain.

The following diagram illustrates the first toy theory, where D1 is the disposition to choose that which is most preferred, and D2 is the disposition to choose cocaine, even when something else is preferred more. The arrows here roughly indicate 'followed by in a normal way' or, perhaps, 'leads to'. The arrow that loops back indicates the problematic pattern of decisions: use leads to more decisions to use, thanks to the triggering of the second disposition.

Figure 1 A decision-making disposition is triggered resulting in use, which causes the acquisition of a second disposition which is repeatedly triggered resulting in repeated use

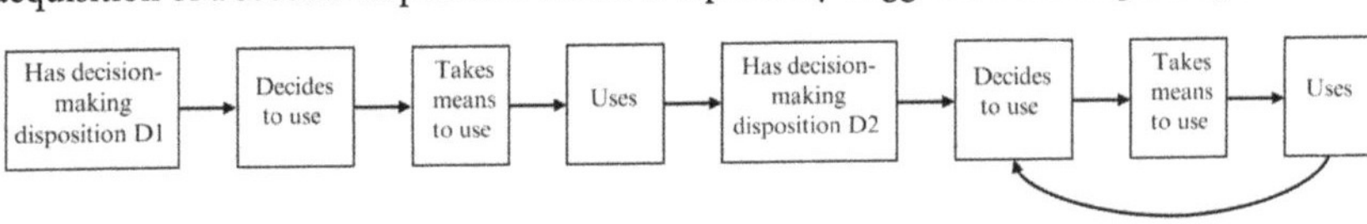

Thus, in the first toy theory, a different decision-making disposition is triggered in prompting initial consumption than in prompting the destructive counter-preferential pattern of decisions. Consumption of a substance of abuse causes the acquisition of the problematic disposition, namely D2.

Under this first type of theory, while the problematic pattern of repeated decisions to use derives from a settled disposition of the agent, that disposition is acquired through use. A second type of theory of addiction, however, posits only one disposition, which prompts initial use and also prompts the actions in the problematic pattern. A diagram of such a theory looks like this:

Figure 2 A single decision-making disposition is triggered resulting in use which triggers it again, resulting in repeated use

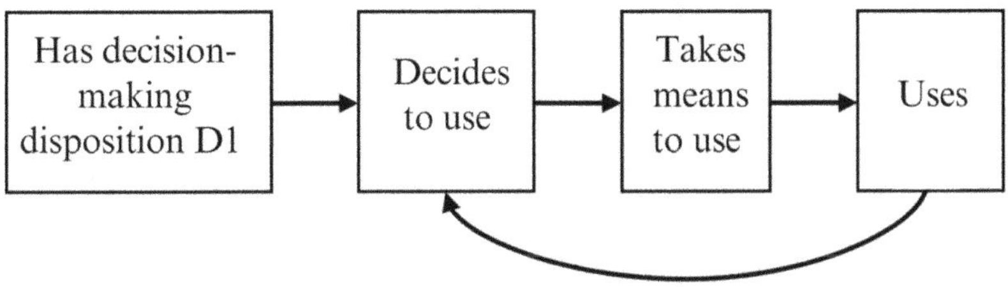

To illustrate, consider a second toy theory, which is of this second sort: According to this theory, as before, at t0, the agent is disposed to choose that which is most preferred at the time of choice. But, unlike under the first theory, the use of substances of abuse does not alter the agent's relevant dispositions at all. Rather, what it alters is the agent's *preferences*. The first time, the agent prefers use to abstention because it is pleasant to get high, more pleasant than the alternative. But the cocaine causes the agent to *prefer* use to abstention even when it promises less pleasure than abstention, or even when it eliminates the possibility of other things of value, such as sober time at work, or with family. Under this second toy theory, then, there is just one decision-making disposition of relevance: the disposition to choose that which is most preferred. Substances of abuse alter the inputs, as it were, rather than the machine itself.[17]

We might say that under the first type of theory, substances of abuse cause unhealthy dispositions that give rise to problematic patterns of use, while in the second type of theory, substances of abuse do not alter the fundamental way in which the user makes decisions, but hijack, as it were, the user's 'normal' decision-making mechanisms.

Actions triggered by a decision-making disposition are possible loci of prior fault. It is perfectly possible, that is, for a decision that is triggered by a decision-making disposition to be opposed by reasons (typically reasons that are not of the sort that appear in the antecedent of the relevant conditional), and to satisfy the

[17] Notice that under the first toy theory, it is easy to explain the sense in which the pattern of repeated decisions to use is problematic: it is counter-preferential. The agent engages in it despite this fact because the substance of abuse has caused them to be guided counter-preferentially. It is less easy to see what is problematic about the pattern under the second toy theory. After all, under that toy theory, the agent has come, thanks to using the substance, to prefer repeated use to abstention. To explain what is non-optimal about a pattern of decisions to use under the second theory, the theorist must appeal to some standard other than the agent's preference. The theorist can appeal to objective value: repeated use is worse than repeated abstention even if the agent does not think so. Or the theorist can take the agent's standards to be set by something other than their preferences: while repeated use is preferred, for instance, it is not valued by the agent.

other conditions of fault specified in section II. On either type of theory, then, there are two possible loci of fault: actions that cause the acquisition of a problematic decision-making disposition or actions that are performed thanks to such a disposition being triggered. In the first toy theory, for instance, the loci of fault might be acts of use that result in the agent having D2, the disposition to choose the substance of abuse even when things preferred to it are on the menu; alternatively, the loci of fault under the first toy theory might be acts of use that are performed when disposition D2 is triggered.

In theory, acts that cause the agent to have the disposition that, when triggered, produces the first decision to use at t1 – the disposition to choose that which you most prefer on both toy theories – could be a locus of fault. But, in fact, theories of addiction, without exception, take the first decision to use to be the product of a decision-making disposition that is not acquired through voluntary action by the agent at all. In both toy theories, for instance, the agent is not disposed to choose that which they most prefer because they did something to acquire that disposition; rather, it's how they are built. What this implies is that for theories of the second sort – where the t1 decision to use is produced by the same disposition as the decision to use repeatedly later in the destructive pattern – there is only one meaningfully possible type of locus of fault: acts of use that play no role in the agent's acquisition of any relevant disposition, but are parts of the destructive pattern of use. To say 'It's your own fault you're addicted!' on the second type of theory is to say, more completely, 'While it's not your fault that you are disposed to make decisions as you are, it is your fault that you decided to use knowing full well that you thereby contributed to a pattern of destructive use, or, if you didn't know that, you should have taken steps to find out.' Herrnstein and Prelec's economic theory, to be described in detail in section V, is an example of this second type of theory (although very different from the toy theory rehearsed here). So our goal will be to assess whether, under it, addicts are at fault for their condition in the sense just identified.

IV. Economic Theories of Addiction

According to 'economic' theories of addiction, destructive patterns of consumption of a substance result from the operation of the very same decision-making disposition that guides typical consumption decisions operating in the distinctive, untypical situation brought on by the consumption of the substances of abuse. They are, therefore, theories of the second type, described in the previous section. The distinctive and destructive behaviours of addicts are guided by decision-making dispositions that are entrenched features of not just addicts' but of everyone's psychological lives, driving many, and perhaps all, even entirely healthy, consumption decisions.

What makes these theories *economic* is that they involve the identification of a formally-specifiable algorithm that is thought to describe voluntary decision-making concerning consumption and acquisition of goods (broadly construed) in many contexts. The disposition of relevance, then, is a disposition to conform one's decisions to the algorithm the theorist identifies. What the economic theorist demonstrates, then, is how conforming to the algorithm can lead to problematic patterns of consumption of substances of abuse. Economic theories differ in the algorithm that they identify and in the accompanying explanation of how decision-making in accordance with the algorithm leads to problematic patterns of consumption.

Economic theorists are committed to the view that agents are never responsible for the fact that they are disposed to act in accordance with the algorithm the theorist identifies. Perhaps we are born with such dispositions; if not, it is still not the case that human beings are ever at fault for them in the sense of 'at fault' identified in section II. The result is that economic theorists are committed to thinking no addict is at fault for possessing the dispositions that give rise to the patterns of destructive consumption involved in addiction. Sometimes, as economic theorists – of course – realise, we have dispositions for which we are responsible, as when, through repeated practice, we acquire certain tastes or reflexes or abilities. But the disposition to conform to the algorithm, whatever algorithm the theorist takes to guide consumption decisions, is not of this sort. Acquiring the disposition that guides our consumption decisions is just a matter of being human, something for which no human being is at fault.

It is worth walking through an example. Imagine the second of the two toy theories discussed in section III – according to which substances of abuse change our preferences and so prompt repeated decisions to use by triggering the disposition to choose that which you most prefer – being developed into an economic theory. In one version, for instance, people have an ordinal preferential ranking of all goods: for every x and y, x is preferred to y (xPy) or vice versa (yPx). The algorithm of relevance is the following: $\forall xt(\forall y(xP_t y) \rightarrow C_t x)$. Or, put in English: anything that is preferred to all its alternatives at any particular time is chosen at that time. Further: $\forall xti(C_t cocaine \rightarrow (\forall y(cocaineP_{t+i} y))$. In other words, if the agent uses cocaine at any particular time, then they come to prefer cocaine to all alternatives at all later times. To claim that someone is at fault for being addicted under this toy theory is not to claim that they are at fault for being disposed to choose what they most prefer but rather that they are at fault for choosing to use when using is most preferred, but is also part of a pattern of use that is ranked preferentially below another pattern of use, and when the agent knows, or should have taken steps to know, that use is part of such a pattern.

V. Herrnstein and Prelec

Herrnstein and Prelec's economic theory of addiction arises directly out of their view that when making ordinary consumption decisions, people often follow a strategy they call 'melioration', which involves conforming to a particular formally specifiable algorithm. To adopt the strategy of melioration is to choose at any particular time the token act of one's options with the highest quantity of a particular type of value, which I will call 'generic value', which is defined relative to some implicitly assumed prior temporal interval. At a particular time, call it t3, the generic value of a token act of type U that one might be considering (such as the token act of using heroin) over a specified prior temporal interval [t1, t2] is a ratio:

$$\frac{\left(\textit{The reward rate of tokens of U occurring in}\left[t1,t2\right]\right)}{\left(\textit{The number of times U is tokened in}\left[t1,t2\right]\right)}$$

In the ordinary case, t3 immediately follows t2; that is, we are assessing the generic value of tokening a type of act next, immediately after the end of the temporal interval relevant for calculating the token's generic value. As will become clear, however, the generic value is a function entirely of prior events; the generic value of tokening an act now does not depend, at all, on what that token act might cause (in fact, or relative to the agent's beliefs), or what its intrinsic qualities might be.

The reward rate is the quantity of reward that prior tokens of U yield, on average, during [t1, t2]. For instance, say that U was frequently tokened during the temporal interval and 1/3 of the time the tokens yielded a reward of 3, 2/3 of the time they yielded 0. Then, the reward rate is $(1/3*3)+(2/3*0)=1$. That same reward rate could be yielded by a different type of act; imagine one that yields, without exception, a single reward each time it is tokened in [t1, t2]. We can think of reward rate (the numerator of the ratio involved in generic value), then, as a measure of the track record of tokening a type of act over a temporal interval; higher reward rate, better track record.

Two acts of different types could have equivalently good track records over a temporal interval only because one of them is rarely tokened but generates a small reward when it is, and the other is frequently tokened and generates a large quantity of reward rarely, perhaps only once, and very little the rest of the time. Imagine that one type of act, U1, generated a reward of 1 the one time it was tokened, and, over the same temporal interval, U2 was tokened 10 times and generated a reward of 10 once and 0 the other 9 times it was tokened. Both acts have a reward rate of 1, but intuitively, they are not equally choice-worthy.[18] Notice, however, that they do not have the same generic value. U1 has a generic value of $(1/1)/1=1$, while U2 has a generic value of $(10/10)/10=1/10$. So, in this example, meliorators will choose to token U1 rather than U2. This is the algorithm at the heart of Herrnstein and Prelec's economic theory.[19]

[18] Exactly how people should, normatively speaking, choose between tokening types of act with the same reward rate in cases like this is a hard question, intertwined with issues about the rationality of different degrees of risk aversion and, often, of temporal discounting. Whether you should token U1 or U2 at t3, in this example will turn, in part, on how risk averse you should be. If you should be very risk tolerant, then you should token U2. If not, then U1. But how risk tolerant should you be? Even if there is an appropriate degree of risk tolerance – perhaps the 'reasonable person' is exactly this tolerant of risk – the question arises of what role one's degree of risk aversion ought to play in guiding one's actions.

[19] Whether it is therefore correct to say that meliorators are risk-averse, is a hard question. The meliorator does choose the same way as the risk-averse agent in this example, but not because the meliorator explicitly weighs risks in the calculation of expected reward.

It is worth pausing to reflect further on the concept of generic value. We have some inkling of what is meant by a numerical measure of the reward generated by a particular act; it's a numerical measure, plausibly, of the advance in the agent's interests by the agent's lights produced by the act. Perhaps the child is made better off by eating the detested spinach, but improvements in the child's health do not contribute to the reward of the act. Eating the spinach provides only the reward, if the child achieves any, found in doing the parent's bidding, offset by the misery of the experience. It is true that a bit of darkness surrounds the meaning of a number placed on that, but we have an inkling of what is meant. And we consequently have some inkling, also, of what is meant by a numerical measure of the *average* reward generated by a set of tokens of a particular type of act. Add up the numerical measures of the rewards from each of the 10 helpings of spinach the child consumed over the last year and divide it by 10. But, still, darkness surrounds the idea of generic value. Darkness surrounds the meaning of the number produced by dividing the numerical average reward generated by a set of token acts by the number of token acts in the set. Can we provide an intuitive gloss on what that is?

Although this goes beyond anything that Herrnstein and Prelec say (or anything that Herrnstein, who has written extensively about closely related ideas, has said in other work), I suggest the following way of understanding generic value, which also explains what is attractive about melioration. Imagine that we have a pair of data sets, W1 and W2, consisting of a set of measurements of samples taken from populations P1 and P2, respectively. Both W1 and W2, for instance, represent the weights in ounces of not all, but some apples from two different groups. Perhaps W1 is the weight of a group of apples taken from one orchard, and W2 is the weight of a separate group of apples taken from a rival orchard. We can calculate the averages of W1 and W2, the average weight of the apples in the two samples. But let's assume that the populations from which the samples are taken are very large, and much larger than either sample; we can't even estimate how many apples are in either orchard. The sample average – the average, for instance, of all the members of W1 – is an estimate of the respective population average. It gives us some information about how heavy, on average, the entirety of apples in the first orchard are. But how good an estimate is it? Ceteris paribus, the bigger the sample, the more information about the population average is contained in the sample average; the average weight of 10 apples tells us more about the average weight of the very large population from which those 10 came than the average weight of only five apples from that same population. The reciprocal of that number (1/10, if the sample size is 10) is an estimate of the uncertainty that attends the inference from sample average to population average: the higher that number, the greater the uncertainty.

Now imagine that you can take one apple a day from one orchard or the other, and at some future day, who knows how long from now, maybe tomorrow, maybe not for a year, a buyer will appear and (over-)pay you $10 per ounce for the collection of all the apples you have collected from both orchards. Which orchard should you next visit? The larger the sample *average*, the more pro tanto reason you have to visit the orchard from which that sample came. The sample average gives you some information about the population average, and you should choose from the orchard with the greatest average weight. But the smaller the sample *size*, the more pro tanto reason you have to visit the orchard *from which that sample came*. The reason is that visiting an orchard is the best way, possibly the only way, to get more information about the weight of the apples there. Such information will, in turn, inform your future decisions about which orchard to visit. Since you have a reason to eliminate your ignorance, you have a reason to collect more information, and so you have a pro tanto reason to visit the orchard that you have visited less.

Multiplying, then, the sample average and the reciprocal of the sample size (that is, dividing the sample average by the sample size) gives you a numerical measure of the strength of the combined reason to visit the orchard from which the sample was taken. This is the generic value of the act of taking from a particular orchard. Put in the terms developed so far, the generic value of an option gives you a numerical measure of the combined reason to take that option. The meliorator, then, acts on this reason.[20]

In this example, the matter about which taking from an orchard gives you useful information is the weight of the apples in the orchard. But of particular interest to us in connection with addiction is information gained about the reward to be gained from consuming something *given your history of consumption of it*. To illustrate, let's adapt one of Herrnstein and Prelec's examples.[21] Say that every day for lunch at work you choose between pizza and a sandwich. Because of contingent facts about your tastes, how rewarding each is is a function of how your last ten lunches have been distributed between pizza and sandwiches; you are fickle. If you have had no sandwiches for lunch in the last ten days, then a sandwich will yield 20 rewards.[22] The reward is reduced by two for every day of the last ten that you've had a sandwich; that is the speed at which you get tired of sandwiches. If you've had nothing but sandwiches for ten days in a row, then you will receive a reward of 0 (that is, no reward) from the next sandwich. By contrast, pizza starts lower – a reward of 16 if you have had none in the last ten days[23] – but you get tired of pizza

[20] Notice that if you have no history of tokening a type of act, or have not tokened it over the relevant temporal interval, then its generic value is not defined; you have a division by zero problem. Herrnstein and Prelec do not tell us how agents choose which act to token when the generic value of one of their options is undefined. They seem to be operating with the view that people have what we might call 'prior generic value' views about an act that has not been tokened in the relevant temporal interval. Perhaps the prior generic value is learned from repeated tokening of the act before the relevant temporal interval begins or perhaps from the testimony of the experienced; a middle-aged teetotaller may have a view derived from drinking whisky repeatedly during adolescent binge-drinking experiences, for instance, or from the reports of friends who are seasoned scotch drinkers and have gotten 'a taste' for it. For simplicity, let's assume that prior generic value judgments are accurate predictions of the reward from tokening a type of act given no prior history of tokening that act. The prior generic value that one assigns to an act untokened in the relevant temporal interval is the reward one will, in fact, receive the first time one tokens an act.

[21] R Herrnstein and D Prelec, 'Melioration: A Theory of Distributed Choice' (1991) 5 *Journal of Economic Perspectives* 137.

[22] That is also your prior generic value from a sandwich in the sense identified in Yaffe (n 11).

[23] n 16 is also pizza's prior generic value.

less quickly. The reward from pizza reduces by 1 unit per day for each of the last ten days that you've had it for lunch.

If you have eaten nothing but sandwiches for the last ten days, then the reward rate of sandwiches, over that time, depends on the reward earned from a sandwich in the first of the last ten lunches, which is itself a function of how many times you had sandwiches in the 10 days before that. So, the generic value of a sandwich is a function of both the number of times you had sandwiches in the last ten days[24] and the reward gained from the first sandwich lunch of that prior ten-day period.

Now, say that after a long bout of having some third thing for lunch (perhaps you were on vacation for several weeks), you expect to face the same sandwich-pizza binary choice. But the pizza place is closed, so you have five sandwiches in a row. Right when the pizza place reopens, in time for the sixth post-vacation lunch, the sandwich place closes, so you return to pizza for five days. So, your rewards from lunches since vacation are, first, five sandwich rewards (20, 18, 16, 14, 12) followed by five days of pizza rewards (16, 15, 14, 13, 12). In time for your 11th lunch, both lunch places open again, leaving you with a choice.

So, the generic value of having a sandwich relative to days 1–10, which is relevant to your decision about what to have for lunch on your 11th day, is:

$$\frac{\frac{(20+18+16+14+12)}{5}}{5} = \frac{80}{25} = 3.2$$

The generic value of pizza relative to that same temporal interval is:

$$\frac{\frac{(16+15+14+13+12)}{5}}{5} = \frac{70}{25} = 2.8$$

Since 3.2 > 2.8, a meliorator will choose to have a sandwich for the 11th lunch, rather than pizza. Notice that pizza promises a reward of 11 on the 11th day, and a sandwich promises a reward of 10. But by having a sandwich, you will also learn more about the way in which your reward from sandwiches is affected by prior sandwich consumption. You might not know, for instance, that the rate of your boredom has not diminished after five days off, and learning this is one of the advantages of having a sandwich on the 11th day. All things considered, then, you have greater reason to have a sandwich than pizza. The additional evidence gained by having a sandwich provides a stronger reason to go that way than the additional reward gained by having pizza instead. We might say that the superior *exploration* value of the sandwich outweighs the superior *exploitation* value of pizza.[25]

[24] Or the prior generic value if you had none. See Herrnstein and Prelec (n 21).

[25] There is uncertainty about when the terms 'exploitation' and 'exploration' were first introduced. The distinction, however, has been recognised at least since JA Schumpeter, *The Theory of Economic Development* (Cambridge, MA, Harvard University Press, 1934).

After the 11th day's lunch, then, the meliorator's previous ten choices, over days two through 11, are (where 's' is sandwich and 'p' pizza): s, s, s, s, p, p, p, p, p, s. The sequence is still evenly divided between pizza and sandwiches. However, since the first sandwich reward in this sequence is lower – it is, after all, the reward gained from a sandwich on the second day, not the first, after vacation – the rewards have changed. The sequence of rewards are: four sandwich rewards (18, 16, 14, 12) and then five pizza rewards (20, 18, 16, 14, 12), followed by a reward of 10 for the final sandwich in the sequence. This implies that the generic value of pizza is still 2.8, while the generic value of a sandwich has changed. It is:

$$\frac{\frac{(18+16+14+12+10)}{5}}{5} = \frac{70}{25} = 2.8$$

At this point, then, the strategy of melioration does not determine what the agent will choose next; after all, the two options have the same generic value.

Herrnstein and Prelec say that the options the agent is choosing among are at 'equilibrium' if the generic value of the options are all equal; the relevant quantity of generic value is the 'point of equilibrium'. Consider, for instance, the situation faced by a meliorator in the example just given. They return from vacation and must choose each day between pizza and a sandwich, and each day they elect the option with the highest generic value.

Figure 3 The generic value of the meliorator's lunch choices reaching a point of equilibrium on day 15

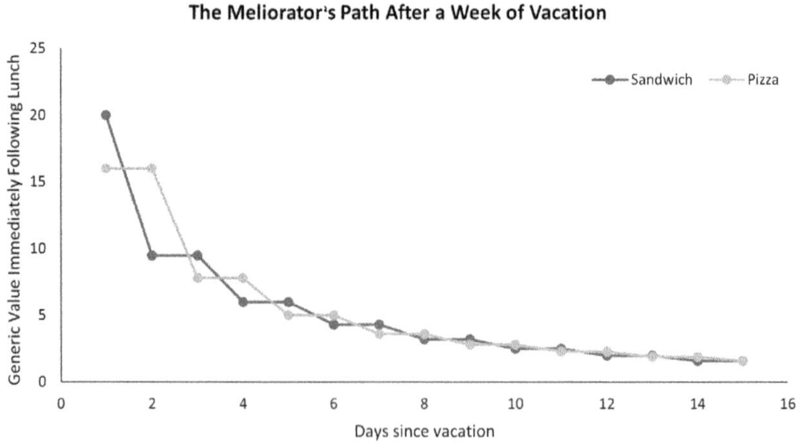

Before making their first choice, the numerical values associated with the options of relevance to the meliorator's decision are 20 for a sandwich and 16

for pizza.[26] They have a sandwich. After their first lunch, the generic value of a sandwich is (20 / 1) / 1 = 20, as indicated in the figure above. By contrast, since the number of pizza lunches in the last 10 is still 0, the number associated with pizza has not changed; it is 16. Since 20 > 16, the meliorator elects a sandwich again for their second post-vacation lunch. Now, as indicated in the figure, the generic value of a sandwich is ((20 + 18) / 2) / 2 = 9.5, while the number associated with pizza is unchanged at 16. Since 16 > 9.5, they opt for pizza for the third lunch. And so on. After 15 days, a meliorator has reached a state of equilibrium. After lunch that day, both of the options have a generic value of 1.6, which is the point of equilibrium. The strategy of melioration does not, at that point, dictate what the agent should choose.[27]

A point of equilibrium is 'stable' if it has the feature that the strategy of melioration will lead back to it. In this case, if, on the 16th and 17th days, the agent were to choose a sandwich (for some reason or another, perhaps as a result of a pair of coinflips), then the generic value of a sandwich would be slightly lower than the generic value of pizza, pushing the meliorator to choose pizza on the 18th day. A choice of pizza at that point pushes in the opposite direction. Such a choice will result in the generic value of pizza decreasing a bit. Choices of sandwiches tend to drive down the percentage of lunches of the last ten that were of pizza, and so tend to drive up the generic value of pizza while tending to drive down the generic value of sandwiches. Choices of pizza have the opposite effect. The result is that the meliorator will find themselves stably looking at options of around the generic value of 1.6; sometimes pizza is slightly higher than that and sandwiches slightly lower, prompting choices of pizza, and sometimes the two options swap, prompting choices of sandwiches.

Now imagine that the meliorator's choice is between using a drug of abuse or abstaining. The meliorator chooses each evening between having shots of tequila or staying sober before spending the rest of the evening with friends. There are upsides to having shots by the agent's lights: it feels nice to be a little drunk, and the tequila makes the agent more talkative and outgoing, thereby boosting the reward from the time with friends. There are also downsides: there's a painful hangover, and tequila increases the likelihood that the agent will embarrass themselves by slurring words, drooling, or vomiting, or in some less dramatic way, breaching social norms, which, in turn, diminishes the reward from time with friends. Thanks to tolerance, the upsides diminish with time; the more tequila a person has had, the more they need to get sufficiently drunk for it to feel nice and for them to become disinhibited, and so the less improvement they have, by their own lights, from a single shot. The downsides remain stable, however. The agent

[26] More carefully, these are the prior generic values of the options in the sense defined in Herrnstein and Prelec (n 21).

[27] In other words, neither Herrnstein nor Prelec specifies what determines the agent's choice when the generic value of the alternatives is equal. The tools that they might appeal to here are all of those that might be used to explain why Buridan's ass does not starve.

still suffers hangovers and embarrasses themselves. We might associate the reward from use with the net total of upsides and downsides. In addition, each time the agent has shots, they learn more about how their history of consumption affects the net rewards from having shots.

Abstention, too, has upsides and downsides, which are added together in the reward of abstention. There's nothing particularly fun about being sober, but it makes for a pleasant morning tomorrow. The impact of sobriety tonight on one's state of bodily pleasure tonight or tomorrow morning does not change with one's history of consumption. By contrast, one's history of consumption does affect other aspects of the reward of sobriety. How rewarding time with friends is a function of the impact of being sober one evening, given a particular history of use. If one is always sober, then that is stable. But if one is ordinarily a bit drunk but is then sober one night in contrast to one's friends' expectations, the reward from time with friends is, we can imagine, a bit lower than it would have been if one were ordinarily sober. The drunker one ordinarily is in the recent past, the lower the reward from being sober, let's assume. Furthermore, there is exploration value in abstention: by abstaining, one learns something about how a particular history of consumption affects the reward of abstention. One might learn, for instance, that one will suffer withdrawal after abstaining, given a pattern of heavy use.

In this first simple example, we imagine that the generic value of use and abstention both decline, but at different rates, as a function of the amount of time spent using, as follows:

Figure 4 The generic value of use and abstention as a function of time spent using. The stable point of equilibrium is at 50% use

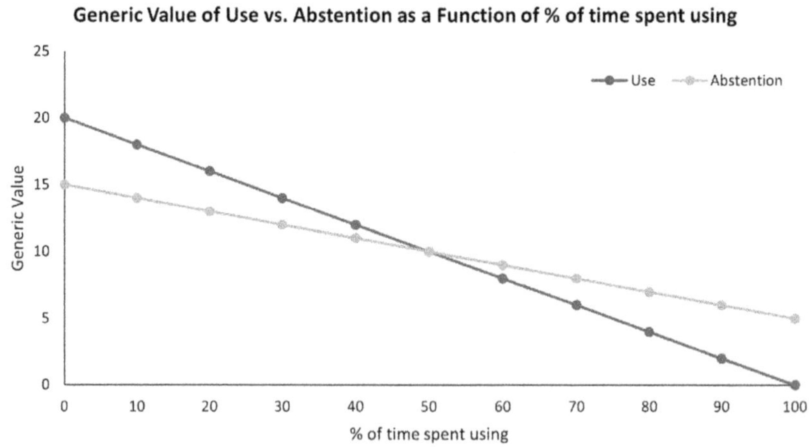

The curves here are linear just for simplicity. What is important is, first, that both the generic value of use and of abstention decline with a greater percentage of time spent using; more use means that both using and abstaining are less valuable in

the sense of generic value. And, also, use declines more rapidly in this respect than abstention.

In this example, a generic value of 10 is the point of equilibrium. A meliorator who has spent exactly half their time using and uses again will move to the right of the point at which these two lines cross. The strategy of melioration will then dictate abstention, pushing them to the left until they regain a generic value of 10. A meliorator who has used half the time and then abstains (for whatever reason) will then have used slightly less than half the time and so will be to the left of the point of intersection. At that point, melioration dictates rightward movement, and so on. They will vacillate between using slightly more and slightly less than half the time.

Being at a stable equilibrium point between use and abstention is the central feature of addiction under the Herrnstein and Prelec position. It is because there are such stable points that triggering the disposition to meliorate – the disposition to choose the option with the greatest generic value – leads to repeated decisions to use. Crucially, the pattern of behaviour around a stable point of equilibrium might be substantially below an optimally rewarding one that the agent would enjoy if they consumed much less. In the example just given, the agent receives a far greater reward from simply never using. If one never uses, abstention always has a generic value of 15.[28] Of course, use is ordinarily more rewarding than abstention, and so the teetotaller misses out on the pleasures of having a drink. The challenge for the teetotaller is to resist their meliorating nature. A person can enjoy the rewards of a drink so long as they do not lapse into a habit of melioration, for down that road, the primrose path leads to a point of equilibrium that is far below optimal.

In the example just given, to travel down the primrose path is simply to be guided by one's disposition to meliorate. Avoiding the stable but non-optimal equilibrium point requires resisting melioration at some point, as both the teetotaller and the occasional drinker manage to do.

Now imagine that use and abstention bear a more complicated relationship than that just described. Imagine the following: Drinking tequila increases in generic value until you're consuming four out of every 10 nights. Given no change in hangovers and increased tolerance, the pleasure diminishes from its height, and, at that point, your pace of learning about the effect of tequila on you, given a history of consumption, also decreases; you keep learning, but you learn less each time you use. So, at greater levels of consumption than four out of every 10 nights, the generic value of use decreases. Further, thanks to bonding with your friends when you're drunk, you get closer, and this, in turn, drives up the fun that you have together when you skip a night and stay sober. Abstention, that is, becomes more

[28] What the implications are for the reward from abstention, from its stable generic value, depends on the size of the relevant temporal interval. If the temporal interval simply grows as time passes, then the reward from abstention would also grow for generic value to remain stable. If the temporal interval remains of a single fixed size, as in the pizza-sandwich example, then the reward from abstention would remain stable also.

and more rewarding as you increase to having shots three out of every 10 nights. The reward of abstention increases at a sufficient rate to drive up the generic reward of abstention. More than three nights out of every 10, however, and your friends start to wonder if you have a problem, and this doubt interferes with your friendship at a sufficient rate to start to drive down the reward of dry nights from its heights. There are similar changes in how much you learn about the effects of abstention on your body and friendships as abstention frequency increases. So, the two generic value curves – the *generic value of use*-to-*use frequency* curve (where use frequency is on the x-axis and generic value of use is on the y-) and the *abstention*-to-*use-frequency* curve (where use frequency, the complement of abstention frequency, is on the x-axis and generic value of abstention is on the y-) – cross. Further, the curves cross again at high levels of consumption. When you are drinking eight out of every 10 nights, nights off give your friends a glimmer of hope, and your time spent with them is not completely unrewarding. Not great, but not 0. By contrast, when you increase beyond eight nights out of every 10, the highs, such as they are, are outweighed entirely by the hangovers, and the misery of the hangover outweighs what little you learn from having another drink. And we can imagine there are comparable changes in what you learn from use and abstention. Having a drink is, at that point, entirely without generic value.

Here is a graphical presentation of this suggestive story:

Figure 5 The generic value of use and abstention as a function of time spent using. The equilibrium point at 30% use is a knife's edge. The equilibrium point at 80% use is stable

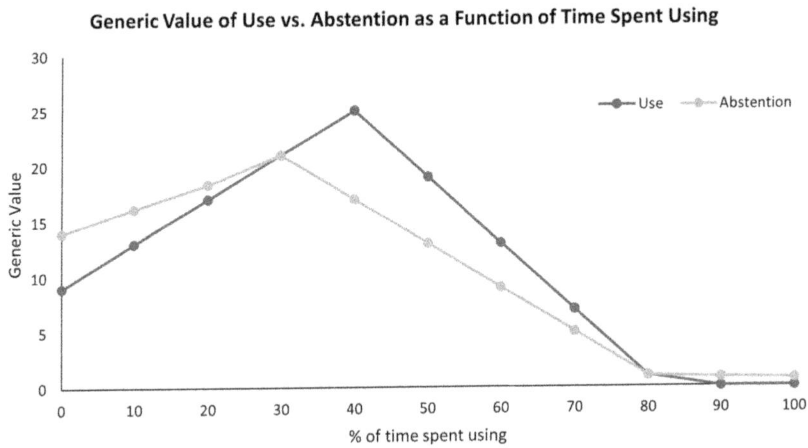

There are, then, two equilibria, only one of which, the lower one, is stable. The first equilibrium point here, encountered at a generic value of 21, when you have spent 30 per cent of your time using, is unstable. (It is what Herrnstein and Prelec call 'a knife's edge'.) Greater consumption increases the generic value of use, but decreases the generic value of abstention. When you consume, for instance, 35 per cent of the time, the generic value of use is higher than the generic value of abstention. So the strategy of melioration dictates increasing consumption to higher rates, and so moving farther to the right, away from the point of intersection. A meliorator, then, will continue to increase consumption until finding themselves at the second equilibrium point, at 80 per cent of the time spent using. This second equilibrium point is stable. With increased consumption, abstaining has higher generic value than use. By abstaining so that use drops below 80 per cent frequency, this reverses, encouraging the meliorator to increase consumption back towards the point of equilibrium. Since this stable equilibrium is far below an optimal point, the agent has reached the behavioural pattern involved in addiction.

In this second example, there are, in a sense, two stages to the primrose path. In order to reach the first unstable equilibrium point, the knife's edge, the agent's choices must be contrary to those dictated by the strategy of melioration. The agent must choose to use, even though using has less generic value than abstaining. After this point of equilibrium, however, someone who adopts the strategy of melioration is led down the primrose path to the second equilibrium point, which is the behavioural pattern involved in addiction.

For the vast majority of consumable goods, two things are true. First, the rewards of consumption are a function of how frequently one has consumed it, and other goods, previously. And second, one's knowledge of how reward is affected by one's consumption history is gained by further consumption. So, for any two goods, G1 and G2, we can plot the frequency of consuming G1 on the x-axis, and the generic value of consuming G2 on the y-axis. And there is no saying, prior to empirical study, what the shape of this curve will be. Now imagine choosing one thing to place on the y-axis; the frequency of consuming tequila, for instance. And generate one curve for each thing on the menu, including tequila, where we place that choice's generic value on the y-axis. These curves will intersect, and every point at which they intersect, every equilibrium point, will either be a stable equilibrium or a knife-edge. Under the Herrnstein and Prelec position, a stable equilibrium point that is far from being optimal marks the addict's problematic pattern of use.

VI. Prior Fault and the Primrose Path

Herrnstein and Prelec's position is a theory of the second sort identified in section III. There is only one decision-making disposition that needs to be appealed to in order to explain the agent's problematic cycle of decisions to use: the disposition to meliorate. Addicts are not at fault for the fact that they suffer from the disease because of anything they did to acquire this disposition; it is just how consumers like us are built. However, as we've seen, different substances of abuse have, under the Herrnstein and Prelec theory, different *generic value of use*-to-*use frequency* curves, as well as different *generic value of abstention*-to-*use frequency* curves. What this implies is that prior fault is a bit more complicated under their theory than under simpler economic theories.

To see this, start by noting that one possible locus of fault under their theory is decisions to use surrounding a stable point of equilibrium. These are acts that are not causes but constitutive parts of the problematic pattern of behaviour. You might say to the unflinching meliorator who is caught in a cycle of use, 'Why don't you just stop meliorating? Stop and stick to it, and you'll find yourself using at a superior, lower level!' Whether this is a just accusation depends on whether the meliorator, stuck at a stable and low equilibrium, knows or should have taken steps to know that their decisions to use are part of this problematic pattern. Note that under Herrnstein and Prelec's view, acts of use are themselves performed in part *because* of the fact that they provide the agent with information about how use affects them, given their history of consumption. Insofar as acts of use are efforts to gain such knowledge, it is entirely unfair to say to the meliorator who claims not to know that using was part of a problematic pattern, 'Well, you should have taken steps to learn that!' Since the meliorator's act of use was exactly such a step, they should reply to this rejoinder, 'But I just did!'

What this implies is that the only acts of use surrounding a stable equilibrium that are loci of fault are those that are performed with *awareness* that they are part of a repeating problematic pattern. Such conscious occurrent knowledge, it seems to me, is very rare for the reasons rehearsed earlier through consideration of the mosquito bite example. The rewards of single acts of use typically outweigh the harms of addiction, corrected by the probability of a cycle of acts of use. What one has sufficient reason not to do is to engage in the act of *repeated use* – the complex act that consists of the conjunction of many single acts of use. But that conjunctive act is very rarely performed in conscious awareness of the fact that one is thereby involved in the behavioural pattern involved in addiction. One is typically distracted by the rewards of use. Therefore, if the conjunctive act is a locus of fault for the illness, it is because the agent should have taken steps to become consciously aware of the potential consequences. But that, under Herrnstein and Prelec's theory, is precisely what one did by using; using, after all, is a way of informing oneself about its effects, given one's history of consumption.

Notice that not every act of use, under the Herrnstein and Prelec theory, is performed thanks to activation of the disposition to meliorate. This is particularly clear in acts of use performed at a point of equilibrium, where melioration gives no advice about what to choose, or to the left of a knife's edge, where melioration counsels against use. Both kinds of acts do yield information about the effect of use, given a history of consumption, but they may not have been performed, even in part, for the reason that they supply such information. But consider the perspective of somebody who used for other reasons (to impress their friends, for instance) while oblivious of the fact that they thereby participated in the problematic cycle of use, and is accused of having used in circumstances in which they should have taken steps to inform themselves about use's effect. Indeed, this person did not use *in order to* provide themselves with such information. But they did perform an act that provided them with such information. And so, given this, the accusation is without merit.

An analogy might make the point more clearly. Imagine that D drives their car across the border, not knowing that the trunk contains illegal drugs. D responds to the accusation of wrongdoing by saying, 'I had no idea there were drugs in the trunk!' The accuser replies, 'Well, you should have looked!' D then points out that they did look; they opened the trunk looking for a coat they thought they brought, and the drugs were concealed from view. This undermines the accuser's rejoinder that D should have looked, despite the fact that D did not look in order to answer the question about whether they were carrying drugs but in search of the coat. Similarly, the agent who uses thereby gains information about the effect of use, given their history of consumption. So, even if they didn't use in order to gain such information, it is inappropriate to fault them for failing to take steps that would provide such information; they took steps.

The result: under the Herrnstein and Prelec position, there is as much justice in the claim that it's the addict's own fault they are addicted as there is in the claim that it is the leukaemia patient's own fault they have leukaemia. Given what these illnesses are, while it is possible to acquire them faultfully, to do so is exceedingly rare.

VII. Conclusion

There are two important forms of scepticism to the claim that addicts enjoy a moral shield from unmitigated blame and ought to enjoy a legal shield from unmitigated liability for harms that they sometimes cause when performing acts in service of their illness. One kind of sceptic asserts that there is, at best, a metaphorical similarity, and not a substantive similarity, between addiction and other undeniably excusing conditions. While many addicts report that they simply cannot refrain from use and that they lack the ability to abstain, the sceptic claims that this is only a metaphor. No mystical force put the needle in the addict's arm; they did it themselves. Similarly, this first type of sceptic insists that using in order to avoid withdrawal is only superficially similar to handing over money to a gun-wielding assailant. We all face tough choices and ought to take steps to avoid harming others, even when it is painful. No steps have been taken here to answer this first type of sceptic. Our concern here has, instead, been with a second type of sceptic who holds that even if addiction's place in the aetiology of harmful acts does diminish responsibility for those harms *ceteris paribus*, all else is not normally equal. In particular, as addiction is typically the product of voluntary behaviour by the person who suffers from it, addicts are typically at fault for the fact that they are addicted. This, the sceptic insists, implies that, in the typical case, addiction's excusing force is undermined.

The response to the second sceptic offered here is that when we combine a plausible account of what it is to be at fault for a condition with a plausible theory of how addiction is ordinarily acquired, we find that people suffering from addiction are not at fault for the fact that they are in the condition. The main obstacle to their responsibility for being at fault for the fact that they are ill is that they are experimenters, just as we all are. There is always more to learn about how anything we consume will affect us, given our always-changing history of consumption. We are always, to some degree, in the dark and have normative reasons to shed light on the matter. If we find ourselves in a condition because we failed to take steps to learn that we should have taken, then we are at fault for being in the condition. But the step the addict takes to learn is to consume, a step which is either on the road to a problematic pattern of consumption or part of such a pattern. But since the addict took the step to learn, they are not at fault for the condition in which they find themselves. The sceptic makes an unsound inference – an inference from the observation that voluntary consumption of drugs of abuse is ordinarily among the causes of the addiction to the conclusion that the addict is at fault for being addicted. Voluntary steps taken to cure us of ignorance cannot be loci of fault.

When coupled with an answer to the first sceptic, we learn that actions springing from addiction are at least often diminished in responsibility. There is moral reason, it seems to me, for the law to follow the contours of morality as much as possible. This brings us to our conclusion: addicts should be shielded from unmitigated legal liability for the harm they cause.[29]

[29] Thanks to Anna Goldberg for comments on an earlier version, and to Anna and Paloma Manguele for the invitation to write this piece. Thanks also to Jeesoo Nam, Conor Mayo-Wilson and Alwin Van Dijk for comments on an earlier draft, to Scott Shapiro, for helpful discussion of the issues, and to Peter Ferretto for a helpful discussion of the paper's methodology.

INDEX

www.ingramcontent.com/pod-product-compliance
Ingram Content Group UK Ltd.
Pitfield, Milton Keynes, MK11 3LW, UK
UKHW020810290926
15470UKWH00003B/1066